CW01511100

REACHING NIRVANA

Andrew Bamber

Raider Publishing International

New York   London   Cape Town

First Printing

The views, content and descriptions in this book do not represent the views of Raider Publishing International. Some of the content may be offensive to some readers and they are to be advised. Objections to the content in this book should be directed towards the author and owner of the intellectual property rights as registered with their local government.

Cover images courtesy of istockphoto.com

ISBN: 978-1-61667-162-4

Published By Raider Publishing International
www.RaiderPublishing.com
New York London Cape Town
Printed in the United States of America and the United Kingdom

Many thanks to Alison and Maria, without whose help I would not have completed this work.

REACHING NIRVANA

Andrew Bamber

Nirvana (n): spiritual enlightenment

The attainment of enlightenment and freeing of the spiritual self from attachment to worldly things, ending the cycle of birth and rebirth.

A transcendent state free from suffering and individual phenomenal existence...

Nirvana derived from a verb (Sanskrit), meaning 'to become cool', or 'to blow out', as in the extinguishing of a candle. The connotation is that only in nirvana are the flames of lust, hatred, greed, and ignorance extinguished. With the attainment of nirvana, the otherwise endless cycle of transmigration is broken. Its nature has been much debated in Western scholarship, some scholars maintaining that it involves total annihilation and others interpreting it as eternal bliss. Both views are problematic, for nirvana is ultimately indescribable and can only be known directly.

ENCARTA ENCYCLOPAEDIA: ENGLISH (U.K.)

Regaining a Conscious State of Mind

Am I awake or is this still a dream? I'm struggling to open my eyes. My head is spinning. It is difficult to focus, to concentrate, to remember, but, for some reason, I am experiencing a sense of euphoria like never before.

I'm bathed in a sea of bright, white light, but my vision is blurred. My body feels numb, although there is a sharp pain at the base of my skull. I squint with one eye, which lessens the intensity. As if to comply with my wishes the light is dimmed. That's better...

I try to comprehend my situation. I cannot move my head, but I look around to examine my surroundings. The compartment is familiar. Glossy, white, panelled walls stretch out on either side. Two solid slabs of light make up the floor and ceiling. Before me is a simple, tall, white narrow plinth. Inexplicably, I seem to know that it hides a complex technology within. Tubes emanate from both sides and spiral towards me. There is liquid moving within. The constant, muted humming behind me is regularly interrupted by the sound of my own breathing, which seems strangely amplified. I force my eyeballs to extremes of movement in every direction to discern more detail. I look beyond the plinth. My vision is still hazy, but I can see a human form in the far corner of the chamber. She is motionless. It prompts me to look down at myself. Now I understand. All at once, memories come flooding back.

I

The End and the Beginning

1

Jodie had survived ten summers, although, now more than ever, there was little to differentiate the passing of the seasons. Her skin was tanned, but it was no darker in tone than the rocks that surrounded the encampment. She had fine, sandy locks and large crystal-blue eyes. Her cheekbones were high and her petite nose had survived without damage. Together, these features made her unique amongst her people. Indeed, Jodie's beauty transcended race and time but for the grime encrusted on her body and clothes. However, the loose-fitting cream cotton wraps that she wore were neatly made; her father was proud of his skills. Food was relatively plentiful at certain times of the year, but there had been a drought of late. Consequently, Jodie was just a little too thin, but she knew that her parents cared for her as best they could and that she was loved.

Jodie's mother, Anya, was sitting beside her on the ground facing the glowing embers of a small fire contained within the boundary of a shallow pit. Appreciating the need to sustain the heat and light that it yielded, Anya leant forward to pile on a few more of the logs that were stacked next to her. Moments later, the fire began to smoke and crackle. It had rained earlier that week and the outer bark had retained some of the precious moisture. They had hoped that the first downpour would mark the end of the dry season. Unfortunately, not a drop had fallen since.

With few trees and shrubs nearby, it made the job of wood collecting ever more difficult. This brought the future of their settlement into question, but it did give the arid landscape, with its orange sand and red stone, a natural beauty all of its own. They all took turns to scavenge for firewood and although her people appreciated their current proximity to a small stream running down the rocky river valley, Jodie knew that it would soon be time to move to a new location.

The weather no longer seemed to follow a predictable pattern and just a short time after sundown it was now turning cooler than of late. Jodie did not mind though, as it encouraged people to sit together by the fire and enjoy the dramatic vista above. The sun had set and a deepening violet sky was now being populated with an ever-increasing number of sparkling celestial bodies.

Anya looked on whilst her friend and companion, Jadine prepared the food. There were twenty-two in all who shared the encampment; behind them stood their semi-permanent homes. Each was constructed of stone and tree branches; many used recycled materials from a more distant past. Most were lighted by lamps fuelled by animal fat. A variety of materials was used to furnish their homes. Interspersed with more naturally occurring substances were plastic crates and glass bottles collected from nearby sites that had once been heavily populated. Larger pieces of wood were prized, being in such short supply. Cottons traded with people from the north and animal skins covered a variety of stone furniture.

Jadine placed meat across the iron grill that straddled one end of the fire pit. Jodie suspected it was probably from one of the large rodents that foraged the scrubland nearby. She salivated at the thought of the delicately seasoned fillets that she would soon be enjoying. Jodie was fond of Jadine. When her mother and father were otherwise occupied,

Jadine would be charged with looking after Jodie. She would invent games to pass the time and Jodie was already intelligent enough to understand Jadine adapted the games as she developed. Today, they been counting and distinguishing between the numerous bird species that surrounded their encampment. Jodie counted twelve different types in all and was rewarded with her favourite fruit. It resembled a very sweet-tasting tomato.

Jadine seemed old to Jodie, as all adults do to children, but she recognised that Jadine was still younger than both of her parents. Jadine's complexion was slightly darker than that of most of the others. She was tall and thin although she had a well-proportioned figure, perhaps this was her reward for doing more than her fair share of work around the settlement. Her thin brown wrap, moistened by beads of perspiration, defined her small, pert breasts in the glow of the fire.

Jodie wondered when she would develop a fuller, more adult figure. She knew it would be soon. Jadine had told her so not long ago when Jodie had asked about them whilst they were bathing. Jadine had wrapped her thick, straight, dark hair back into a ball to prevent it from falling into the fire. Her fringe had stuck to her forehead, but it did not detract from her well-defined cheekbones and hazel-almond eyes.

Jadine continued to tend the meat whilst she listened to the others talking about the 'Fartherland.' They often talked about a great Journey to find people living now as their ancestors had in the past. Jadine was dismissive of their existence, sure that if these people did exist, they would be have been seen in the machines of the past. To Jodie, it was conceivable that they could be out there, in a better place, perhaps living halfway between what Man was then and is now. The wood crackled and the meat was ready. Other dishes containing breads and pickled fruits were brought out and placed on the matting. The aromas were enticing. They had waited two days to share this feast.

Jodie was quick to react and hurried to her place. She knew she would have to wait for the others to be seated before she could begin. The dining table was made of stone, one that had been fixed within the same locality for many thousands of years. The people had learnt to make the best of what they could find. Smaller stone blocks had been used to fashion seating. Each had an individual pad for comfort made from the pelts of a variety of small animals. She looked around and was disappointed to see that her parents were the last to make their way over. Jodie knew that they had been arguing again earlier. She had an idea of what it was about, although as yet, she did not fully understand the reasons why. A jug was passed around to enable everyone to wash their hands. When the last person had completed this ritual – it was her mother – the meal began. The gathering was supposed to be informal and comfortable, but not everyone seemed relaxed.

Jadine could see that Jodie looked troubled, so she seated herself to Jodie's left and attempted to cheer her young friend. "Don't worry, Jodie, I'm sure that things will be better tomorrow. This feast is bound to put your father in a better mood. Good food always does!"

"Jadine, will we be moving on soon? I think that we all need a change of scenery. Perhaps that would make everyone seem a little happier."

"No one has said as much, but I suspect that a move can't be far from everyone's mind. I'm sure Francis would have wanted it. After all, things aren't as plentiful here as they used to be. Anyway, I think that your father may have a surprise for you tomorrow."

"And what would that be, Jadine?"

"Now if I told you, it would no longer be a surprise, and

Keon would be mad at me for telling you."

"Does it involve a new outfit? I know that he has been making something with the skins he's collected."

"Jodie, stop trying to guess! I wish I hadn't mentioned it now. Anyhow, it's much better than that. Get a good night's sleep and we'll see what the morning brings."

"Perhaps I should ask my father now?" Jodie was not altogether serious about her suggestion.

"No, Jodie, I do not think that would be a wise idea. Let him eat and relax. Besides, if you said anything to him now, he would think that I told you about his plans."

"What plans?"

"Oh, me and my big mouth! Please, Jodie, wait until tomorrow!" Jadine's voice had gone far beyond a whisper, causing Keon to glance over. "Now finish your food and I'll take you to bed. I'm sure that your mother would appreciate a little time on her own with your father."

Jodie just shrugged, but her concerns seemed to ease with every mouthful of food.

Keon was a well-built, broad-shouldered and muscular man, with an olive complexion similar to the rest of the people and dark, short-cropped hair.

To Jodie, he seemed like a giant of a man. When he stood by her, he towered over her, but, in reality, he was little taller than Jadine. It was his bulk that gave him presence. He sipped a drink from a curved, grooved and fluted glass bottle. If Keon had been able to read, he would have been able to decipher the flowing script of Coca-Cola, but, for him, it was a bottle that he liked and was able to use over again. He had had four, but had dropped and smashed one recently. He hoped to find another.

The other people gathered around the table continued with their conversations about the day's events and their successful hunting trip. The odd compliment was thrown in Jadine's direction, praising the fare that she had helped to prepare. When all the food had been consumed, along with several jugs of an alcoholic beverage made from the fermentation of palm leaves, Jadine scooped Jodie up and carried her to bed. Jodie soon fell asleep. When Jadine returned a short time later to cover her up with an animal-skin patchwork blanket she was careful not to wake her. Jadine extinguished the lamp and returned to the others, most of whom were enjoying staring up at the stars. She sat next to Anya.

Keon took a fleeting look at Jadine before returning his gaze to the dying embers of the fire.

Jadine whispered, "Anya, this has to stop now. There shouldn't be a problem between you and Keon. Everyone knows that Remy is a fool and that you would never leave Keon for a lesser man. Even Remy realises the truth of the matter. I'm sure that most of the time his flirtation is in jest."

"Everyone knows; except Keon, that is! I have tried to tell him on several occasions, but he either doesn't listen or doesn't believe me. I'm worried that sooner or later it will come to blows."

"I'm sure that deep down, Keon knows that you only have eyes for him. Since Francis passed, there has been no clear leader within our community. This has undoubtedly led to tension inside the settlement. Can you not convince Keon to take charge? I know that he feels that it is not his place, but the others would respect him and I'm certain that it would make him feel more secure."

"I'll see what I can do. It doesn't pay to pressure a man like Keon, but I will try to talk to him over the next few days." Anya looked towards her partner. Keon was still fixated on the fire. "But, for Jodie's sake, I'll convince him tonight that everything is fine between us."

Jadine smiled. "And how do you plan to do that, then?"

Anya responded with a giggle, and then stood to face

Keon. She spoke slightly louder then she needed to so those nearby could also hear. "Keon, take me to bed."

Keon hardly responded.

Anya was unsure if he had tried to force a smile or suppress one.

"All right," replied Keon in muted response.

Anya briefly visited the far partition. Jodie was asleep. After making sure that the insect net completely covered the entrance to their compartments, Anya joined Keon on the bed. There was little light inside now, but Anya could tell that Keon's eyes were wide open, staring up at the reeds inside the roof of their dwelling. Anya leant over and gently put her lips to his, pressing her body gently against him.

"Keon, please," she whispered.

After a few moments, he responded.

* * *

Jodie neither feared nor welcomed her dreams, merely accepting them as they were. They came to her most nights. She rarely talked about them, occasionally confiding in Jadine, whom she sensed did not really take much notice.

She was flying. She knew she was heading south again. She was not aware of her body, just the ground not far below. A small canyon in the middle of the rift plate flashed below her and she recognised the river up ahead from previous dreams. She was moving through the air at considerable speed, but felt no chill. She crossed a patch of lush vegetation and enjoyed the fragrance of jasmine in her nostrils. Vast tracts of desert passed below. To her left, near the horizon, there was a large, ruined stone building. The land was dry and dusty now, away from the river. Reddish rock strata and flowing desert continued to mark her journey.

Her dreams were often punctuated or incomplete. Tonight, however, she journeyed on.

Finally, up ahead there was a bright light on the horizon that she had only seen once before. She had never gone beyond this point. As the light neared, it revealed itself as a large bright dome, perhaps a glowing orb, buried in the sand. It radiated a pure white light, the likes of which she had never seen. She circled it and felt safe in its presence. Through the dome she thought she could make out structures and ...wait, people, no, not people, but she sensed there was life within the dome. Then came the voices within her head – or were they calling from below? This was not the language that she knew, but she understood that they were calling her.

* * *

Keon was already up and about when Anya awoke. Anya too had been dreaming; normal, pleasant dreams. She felt a warm glow. It had been some time since Keon had made her so happy. She recalled that after their lovemaking, she had finally managed to convince Keon that Remy was not a threat. Smiling, Anya reflected upon how easily men could be persuaded. She recognised voices outside.

Keon and Jodie were returning. They entered the dwelling carrying a slate tray topped with several portions of flat bread and steaming jugs of red-topped tea. Jodie was excited. "Anya, Anya, Keon has brought breakfast for you, and then we're going to go and explore." Jodie clearly sensed that any divide between her parents had been healed. "Will you and Jadine come, too?"

"Now that depends where you're planning to go." Anya tucked into her bread and sipped her tea. "Well, Keon, just what are we going to do today?"

"I thought we could take a trip south towards the great

river. We could camp overnight in the caves."

Jodie was about to burst with excitement. "Yes, yes, please, can we go to the caves? I've never been. Please!"

Anya pretended to consider the matter. "Well, I'm not sure. It's a long way for a little girl to go and how do we know that you'll be safe?"

"'Cos Daddy will be there!"

"I suppose he needs a break from the usual chores," Anya replied whilst smiling up at Keon. "All right then, let's go and explore."

"Yes, yes, yes!" Jodie ran to her compartment, her excitement heightened still further.

Keon mouthed a thank you to Anya. Anya hurriedly pulled out some clean garments and then dressed. As usual, it would be hot by day, so a brown, linen thigh-length wrap would suffice. She packed some warmer skins for the cold night that would follow.

Breakfast finished, Keon gathered some things of his own. In his rucksack he packed some spare clothes for himself, some hand-woven netting to provide protection from the insects, matting to sleep on and several lightweight blankets. He tied string around a rectangular box containing some cooked meat left over from the night before, and in a similar box was more flat bread. He was accustomed to finding other sources of food once away from the settlement. He placed the food boxes on top of the pack and then, as an afterthought, packed the glass lens that he had traded for last season. He knew that this would be useful for making a fire. Flints were getting harder to come by and he had little patience for rubbing wooden sticks together. On either side of the sack were two large water carriers. He hoped that these could be refilled en route. As Keon raised his tall, muscular body, he tied his belt, which was equipped with a utility hammer on one side and a hunting knife on the other. The knife was designed for multiple purposes. It was well balanced and could be thrown accurately to bring down prey and it had a serrated edge to skin the carcass and trim the meat. The hammer could be put to a variety of uses. It was balanced with an axe-like blade, so was included wherever he went. Finally, he placed his wide-brimmed hat over his thick, dark locks and walked over to meet the girls.

Jadine had no family of her own, so was happy to go wherever Keon and Anya went. They had been good to her, treating her like a daughter of their own. Survival without them would have been far more difficult. She did not have a partner although she was clearly old enough. Most of the men at the encampment were either spoken for, too old or in her opinion, lacking in one or more essential qualities... often a good sense of humour! She knew that Keon was a handsome man, but there was no real attraction there, either. Anya would have sensed it if there was and Jadine would not be with them now.

No, Jadine was happy for the time being. She knew that one day she would find the right person, and until that day, she would be content to be part of Anya's family.

"Anya, are you sure that you would like me to come? I just thought that it might be better if you and Keon spent a little time together on your own."

"What, with Jodie accompanying us?" Anya laughed, at the same time as shaking her head. "No, please join us. I might get closer to Keon if you help me to entertain Jodie."

Jadine knew that if she stayed behind, Remy would devote his efforts into convincing her that there was a better place many miles away. He would offer to take her there, expecting companionship on the way. He was harmless enough, but his conversation became tiresome after a few hours and she knew that several days alone with him at the encampment would be unbearable.

Jodie could not understand why the group had not

journeyed south-east to find the 'promised land', the 'Fartherland.' She was, however, old enough to understand that many people within their community would prefer to talk about or even dream about such a place, rather than to journey there, only to be disappointed.

Jadine was packed and ready, but still seemed a little uncertain. "Keon, are you sure that you want me to come?

Keon was now smiling. "Fine, stay here for a few days. Keep Remy company... Of course I want you to come, Jadine!"

"Lead the way, then!"

"Okay, Jadine?" enquired Anya rather tentatively.

"Fine, let's go."

"Go, go, go, go, go!" shrieked Jodie rather childishly as she ran ahead towards the edge of the encampment.

The three adults, packs loaded, strolled purposefully after her

2

Recent history was not readily debated by the people of the desert regions. Nobody was really sure what had happened to their world, few even cared. Communities were now content just to survive. Written descriptions were scarce, confined to a handful of centres across the globe. It was clear that the world had experienced vast fluctuations in population density.

In 2022, near the Egyptian town of Akhmim, the discovery of an underground crypt led to the greatest archaeological find of the millennium. Although no human remains were found, buried within were a series of clay pots containing scrolls inscribed over two thousand years previously. They were in pristine condition and easily deciphered. Their authenticity was independently verified by three scientific institutes before their contents were released to the general public and leaders of world religions. The author of the texts was identified as Maria of Magdala, otherwise known as Mary Magdalene. Her writings expanded upon many of the controversial revelations arising out of the existing, incomplete Gospel. They confirmed her relationship as the wife of Jesus of Nazareth and affirmed her role as his most senior disciple. The 'Magdala Scrolls' went on to describe how Mary and Jesus practiced procreation, without the inconvenience of conception and raised key issues about the role of women within the church.

Soon after Pope Paul the Ninth took office in 2028, the Catholic Church finally conceded to their critics. On a historic day in 2029, the head of this mighty religion finally accepted the need for contraception and decreed that the purpose of sex within marriage was not only for procreation. Whilst specifically avoiding mention of the Magdala chronicles and revisiting traditional scriptures, Pope Paul declared that 'God acknowledged the desire for pleasure'.

'The husband should fulfil his marital duty to his wife, and likewise the wife to her husband. The wife's body does not belong to her alone, but also to her husband. In the same way, the husband's body does not belong to him alone but also to his wife. Do not deprive each other except by mutual consent and for a time, so that you may devote yourselves to prayer.' [1 Corinthians 7:3-5] Reinterpretation of The Bible had legitimised their decision and they saved face.

Forms of contraception that actually killed or caused the expulsion of a fertilised egg were still categorised as abortion and condemned. However, the many forms of contraception that simply prevented fertilisation, such as pre-emptive sexual practices, condoms or diaphragms and hormone injections that the Bible did not expressly prohibit, were allowed, even encouraged. Physical sterilisation continued to be debated for some time. It was another two decades before such methods were approved. A new, safer birth control injection was given to men the world over on an annual basis. Thanks to MIMCOM Netscape, populations all over the world were educated, just as the planet was on the brink of exhaustion. Population growth was finally reversed when world leaders and non-Christian individuals alike finally realised that they needed to limit the size of their families. Taxation succeeded in many countries where religion had failed.

Birth control was needed as nature's own population control measures were being reversed. In 2025, the HIV vaccine was licensed for the first time. The World Health Organisation persuaded Western governments to sponsor a worldwide vaccination program and within two decades it was virtually eradicated. Other biological challenges came and went with some effect, but lessons had been learnt. Many governments realised that in the longer term it did not make sense to buy expensive treatments from profiteering pharmaceutical companies. The Western Alliance countries set up their own heavily funded research programs to develop, test and produce new antibiotics, cancer therapies and vaccines. There were reciprocal agreements that enabled each country to benefit from the others' developments. Crucially, the money diverted away from drug companies was used for excess production of therapies that would be donated to developing countries

By the middle of the 21st century Man had made other great scientific and technological advancements. Humanoid robots quickly gave way to more process-centred 'hidden' automation. Less became more. Many families in the east took on the ways of the West during the second electronics revolution. The world prospered. Against the odds Mankind managed to avoid the nuclear holocaust that everyone feared. Well, almost! In most parts of the world there was no radiation poisoning, no more congenital abnormalities than we see in populations today. Despite a small tactical detonation, a third world war was avoided when the USA finally brokered a peace treaty between China, Japan and the Indian alliance. Developing Asian countries were only too willing to gain advanced technological expertise from the Japanese and Americans.

The effects of global warming were, shall we say, 'contained'. The Maldives and a number of other important ecological destinations disappeared, together with coastal regions the world over. This was a gradual process, as was the prohibition of the internal combustion engine. Crucially, transport manufacturers and the super-rich oil companies finally yielded the much needed investment in the development of alternative power sources. Deforestation of the Americas was finally halted and they became the new tourist Mecca.

Against all odds, world peace reigned. Jews and Arabs, Catholics and Protestants, French and English all learnt to live in relative harmony. For many people, religion became a less important part of their lives, but several minor belief systems gained many more followers. The most notable growth in faith was seen when the prominent head of the world's leading robotic corporation combined the teachings of the Church of Scientology with his own radical business principles. Backed by an ever increasing number of celebrity followers, he encouraged all employees and customers alike to follow the teachings of the late Ron L Hubbard. What was once seen as a radical cult was now accepted as a mainstream religion.

Even the Islamic nations finally conceded a degree of tolerance. Over several decades, Western leaders and those from the Far East collaborated with rulers of the Middle Arabic States countries to eliminate radicalism. Aid was given to African nations, and following the peoples' expulsions of corrupt regimes, most finally entered the developed world.

Those who did debate the past spoke of the machines that had finally brought an end to Man's old civilisation. Computers had led to supercomputers, which, in turn, advanced technology still further. It was the subject of much controversy, as to why, simultaneously, a vast array of machinery had almost brought about the mass destruction of the planet, bringing a sudden halt to any further technological advancement. It was not in their interest to do so. Clearly, they had developed intelligence and evolved far quicker than any living species on the planet, so why would they destroy themselves? Almost spontaneously, every computer, every vehicle, every machine in the world with a computer controlled processor destroyed those around them in a vast electrical storm and in doing so they destroyed themselves. Vast fires raged the world over. Those who weren't electrocuted were burnt alive or suffocated by the thick smoke that choked the planet. Man was able to disable or destroy most of the missiles before they reached their targets, but some nuclear strikes were made. Chinese, American, Arab and European governments had, however, secretly feared just such an event and placed the final launch controls in the hands of a person. So, on that day, it was the launch controls themselves that were destroyed. However, very soon, world communications were a thing of the past. Ironically, it was not the service robots but the transportation vehicles, food processors and other networked household appliances controlled by networked master systems that did most of the damage. Disease and starvation then took hold of those that survived. The world's climate cooled for almost a decade. The world came in close proximity to another ice age.

Other factors in the story of the catastrophic fall of the human race were more questionable. Why did the safety devices in the systems that man had built fail their intended purpose, and where did all the power come from to fuel such a cataclysmic event? Surely power grids the world over did not contain enough energy to simultaneously produce the vast electrical storm that ensued. However, fact was undeniable. The world had almost perished and now the survivors who maintained the species were content to live without the old technologies that had almost brought about the mass extinction of the human race.

3

They had walked now for most of the day, stopping to eat next to the freshwater spring that flowed down from their encampment and fed into the great river. There were more springs in the surrounding hills now. Perhaps it had rained more heavily in this region. The lower reaches of the desert were greener than they could remember. Some of Keon's community had wanted to join the people in the north beyond the great sea, but stories of harsh winters and violent tribes had dissuaded the others from moving in that direction. To the east was a great desert and to the west was a smaller expanse of barren desert wasteland bordered by another great tract of ocean. However, Keon thought that their prospects might improve if they tracked south along the river. The flood plain was lush and the vegetation would cater for all their needs.

Keon was used to walking to collect building materials, but the others in his family were less accustomed. Jodie was doing well though. Everybody paced themselves with Jodie stopping as she did to smell the fragrance of a new flower whenever one appeared, or to gaze up at a bird soaring overhead. After all, part of the purpose of this trip was to give Jodie a boost, to widen her experience of life and to give her and everybody else a break from the encampment. Keon though, wanted to explore even further south. He had not ventured beyond the caves. An ancient desire to explore had been awakened by his rivalry with

Remy. He did not plan to venture much further than the caves on this trip, but he sought knowledge of what was beyond them. Could a 'Fartherland' really exist where people lived in harmony with advances of the past?

As the hills and valleys of red rock neared, Keon declared, "Not far now; we'll reach the caves in time to start a fire for the night."

"I'm tired," declared Jodie.

Keon laughed and scooped her up in one simple movement with his powerful arms.

"Perhaps you would like to ride on my shoulders for a while?"

"Hey, I can see much further from up here!"

Anya and Jadine trudged on, chatting as they went, but clearly fatigue was affecting them too.

Keon had collected some twigs and branches along the way, and as they reached the cave entrance he immediately set about building a fire. He allowed Jodie to help. Keon used his lens to focus the sun's rays on some dried grass. As it began to ignite, Jodie placed some more on top, and then some dried leaves and twigs. In no time, flames leapt up high into the air. It was not cold yet, but had they waited any longer, the sun would have started to set and Keon's lens would have not worked. Jodie stepped back into the cave, away from the heat for now.

The main cave vault spanned the height of three people, tapering towards the rear. Once everyone was settled just inside, Keon set about finding more food. Jodie followed, taking in the ancient symbols that adorned the walls. Jadine and Anya had collected berries from a thicket they had passed around midday and they still had a number of flat bread loaves between them. They had consumed the leftover meat. Gripping a burning torch for illumination, Keon ventured soundlessly towards the back of the cave. Likewise, Jodie took cushioned steps walking behind her father before walking past him to take the lead. Keon was just about to draw her back when Jodie let out a shriek. In a hollow between two rocks, a large snake was coiled. Black and brown stripes on its thick head warned of danger, as did the hissing noise as it raised its head. Jodie began to back away as the snake lunged forward, mouth gaping, in an attempt to eliminate any potential threat. The snake missed its quarry, but was about to recoil for a second strike when a single blow from Keon's hammer crushed its skull, rendering it lifeless. Keon was experienced enough to wait a few moments to ensure that it was indeed dead before approaching and examining his kill.

"Would a bite from that snake have harmed me?" asked Jodie in a tone that suggested she already knew the answer.

"This snake delivers a nasty bite that brings on fever and makes limbs wither away. You find them all around here in amongst the rocks. Never go poking under stones and always check a cave such as this before settling down to sleep."

"So might there be more?"

"Perhaps. I'd better check, and this time Jodie, please stay behind me."

Keon completed a search of the cave before lifting the snake from its resting place and carrying it to the front of the cave. He then set about preparing it with his knife. Although they still had sufficient water with them, the blood was not wasted. The flesh was cut and arranged on a large stone placed in the centre of the fire that Jadine had started.

"What are those symbols on the walls?" asked Jodie.

"There are words carved by those that have been here before."

"What do they say?"

"I'm not sure," replied Keon. "If you look around, though, some are repeated. I think, perhaps, they are names."

"There are some pictures over there." Jodie was pointing and smiling. "A man with a big thingy!"

Keon chuckled. "Yes, I've seen it."

Jadine enjoyed the simple food that Keon had prepared. It was a welcome change for her not to have to cook.

Jodie always enjoyed food!

Anya and Keon were chatting in subdued voices about their day's events. Jadine remained silent, but did not feel excluded. She looked upon her two friends and companions in the glow of a crackling wood fire. Life had indeed improved simply because they had journeyed out. Anya caught Jadine looking at her and smiled back. Jadine, almost embarrassed, glanced over at Jodie who had fallen asleep unnoticed.

"With the day's exertions, it's to be expected," offered Jadine. "Look at her eyes moving!" Jadine was smiling now. "She's dreaming."

* * *

Once again, Jodie was flying. She did not have quite as far to go this time. She was already a small part of the way there. As the desert and canyons gave way to the river valley, Jodie noticed that the river had flooded and that the landscape was a lush green for several miles on either side. The ruins soon passed by and she was nearing the glowing orb. If she went inside she knew she would be welcomed, but she chose not to. Tonight was not the time. She would fly around and try to gain a better view of those inside. Perhaps a part of the dome would be translucent. The voices called to her again, but now there were other voices, in her own tongue.

"Leave here, leave now, get away," they called.

They were not coming from the dome. She could not

accurately sense their direction. Why did they contradict the other voices? Who was calling to her now? Were they jealous of her being there? Or might they be sounding a warning?

* * *

Anya, too, was beginning to feel the effects of the long day. As she placed a blanket over her daughter, Anya stroked Jodie's head so as to soothe her dreams. Anya snuggled down beside her and drew her into her bosom. Jodie awoke briefly, opened her eyes and kissed her mother on the cheek. Keon placed the last of the wood on the fire. He made one last check, to secure the camp and ensure that no more snakes were moving in the immediate vicinity, before joining them. Jadine slept where she had sat, wrapped in the warmth of an animal skin, and having been helped on by a flask of palm wine.

The next morning, when everyone was awake, Keon discussed the plans for the rest of the trip.

"It will take us a further day to reach the great river at a relaxed pace. We can enjoy some time there, collect reeds to take back with us and, if you are all agreeable, camp there overnight before returning tomorrow."

"Is it that way?" asked Anya, pointing south-west.

"Yes, down the valley and across the rift," offered Jodie.

"That's right," replied Keon, somewhat bemused. "How did you guess that?"

"Oh, I didn't guess; I saw it in my dreams."

The others chuckled. Jodie's face reddened and she fell silent.

"Come, let's move on," ordered Keon.

The sun was noticeably hotter than the previous day. The lightweight long-sleeved clothes and hats that they had brought with them protected them from the sun's rays. The land was flat now, but they had seen from the hills at the far side of the rift the rich, fertile plains bordering the great river that they were about to meet. Almost without warning the desert fell away and they were surrounded by lush greenery. There was a great diversity of plant species, the predominant trees being palms. With the plants came flowers, and with the flowers came intoxicating fragrances to perfume the air.

Jodie recognised the heady smell of jasmine.

"It's wonderful; why do we not come to live here?" Jodie was the first to speak, but everyone was thinking the same.

Keon felt obliged to defend their current residence. "The river is prone to flooding. Our homes would be washed away at least once a year – we would spend most of our time rebuilding them."

Anya thought that this was a poor excuse and retorted, "We could simply find some higher ground, or build them back away from where the river floods. We could even build them on stilts! I've heard from the northern traders about whole villages built on stilts over water."

Keon did not have an answer for this. "Let's find some food," he said instead.

After gathering food, they ate in a shaded area adjacent to a clearing. There was evidence of old campfires and human footprints were mixed in with animal tracks.

"The river is not far now," stated Keon

"Yes, yes, yes," screeched an excited Jodie, childlike once again.

Jadine smiled. "She is so adorable when she sees 'the good'."

"The good?" asked Anya.

"When she knows that good things are coming."

"Yes, ever the optimist, even at her age. She hasn't been

spoilt yet by the responsibilities of age. Oh, to be young again...."

"You're old?" Keon chuckled.

"Ha-ha – you, old man."

"I'm not old at all," said Keon, now rather more seriously. "I'm approaching my prime!"

"I hope so," added Anya with a knowing smirk. "But Jodie does seem to have an awareness way beyond her years."

"She's special," stated Jadine matter-of-factly.

"I know," responded Anya.

"I'm not sure that you do."

"What do you mean?"

"Oh nothing...."

"I am here, you know!" Jodie's statement was rather dramatic.

Everyone laughed as they prepared to move on in unison.

* * *

Jodie's short legs again dictated a slower pace. It was late afternoon when another change in vegetation marked the approach of the great river. The party walked on silently as they contemplated the sight of a vast expanse of water. None of them had ever crossed it and were not intending to do so this day. No, exploration of this side of the bank was the only thing on their minds. Jodie thought of nothing else and began to run as they approached the river. Its broad banks were now in sight.

"Don't stray too far," warned Anya.

Keon began sprinting, overtook Jodie and arrived at the riverbank ahead of the others. He did not alter his stride before diving in head first. The girls stopped on the bank to hastily remove most of their clothes. They edged their way in, splashing water at each other as they went. Anya stayed with Jodie in the shallows leaving Jadine to swim off and join Keon.

"This is so refreshing. Our people should move here, even if we have to build our homes in the trees!"

"This is not our land, though. Other people claim it," said Keon, once again serious. "They would not take kindly to our people coming."

"And what if they find us here now? What would they do then?"

"I'm sure they would be tolerant of a visit," said Keon, his relaxed mood soon returning.

"Come on, I'll race you back!"

Keon won comfortably. Within moments of hauling himself out of the water, Keon fell to his knees clutching his head.

Anya ran over. "What's the matter, Keon?"

Keon was taking short and rapid shallow breaths. He managed to let go of his right temple with one hand to signal with the flat of his hand that he would be all right. Anya grabbed his large, rough and weathered hand and stroked the back with her smaller, but equally worn, fingertips.

Keon straightened his back and looked towards Anya. Jadine knelt by her side displaying a look of obvious concern. "I'm okay now. I just had a sudden pain in my head. I've had a few lately, but they soon pass...."

"Perhaps you should lie back and rest a little."

Keon got to his feet. "I'll be fine! I just feel a little dizzy."

* * *

Jodie was more interested in moulding the sand on the shore of the bank than actually playing in the water. Anya was content to allow her daughter to do whatever she wanted provided she did not wander too far. Keon, Anya and Jadine lay on the soft green grass to rest after their exertions. Keon seemed to have recovered. In time, Jodie joined them and had a nap.

* * *

Jodie had crossed the river again. She must have flown as usual, but she could not recall the journey this time. She was walking in the warm soft sand. The giant orb loomed up before her. It had a reflective metallic sheen, but it was not made of any material that she had ever seen. Was there movement inside? Was there any detail? Although she was less than half a mile away, she could not discern any internal structures. There were no voices of warning this time so she had no fear. She was being drawn nearer and nearer. Yards away now. Movement inside, but no detail. Were they figures? People? No, surely not people, their movement was slower.

* * *

"It's late now," stated Keon. Although they had no accurate means of time keeping, the sun told its own story. "We'll camp over there, where it's drier. We will journey home tomorrow."

Anya did not look too happy. "Could we not make it back to the cave before darkness if I carried Jodie? There is no cover here, and there may be strange beasts and who knows what else in these parts."

Keon tightened his lips and shook his head. "Nothing would be more dangerous than moving after dark."

Anya and Jadine knew that look and knew better than to argue. Jadine wondered why Anya was so keen to return. Parental concern for Jodie, she concluded. "Let's gather firewood then. Can you catch our supper?"

Keon was not looking, but knew the last remark was directed at him. He nodded, then added, "I will get you ladies a wild boar, or even a young ground-herder."

"Yes, well do so then," replied Anya. "Come on, girls, let's gather some wood and make a shelter for Jodie."

Jodie smiled. This meant another night would be added to her adventure. She did not celebrate birthdays as such, but this would be what she would have chosen to do had she had one. Jodie skipped off whilst singing to herself to help the older women in their quest for materials.

4

The next morning they began their return journey. They were not at all downbeat, contented with their time at the river. Keon had been successful in his hunt and they had eaten well. There was even some meat left over to take back to the camp, perhaps to be salted and preserved for the coming weeks. Keon carried the meat along with the rest of his pack. Jadine and Anya shared the responsibility of carrying Jodie when she tired, in addition to the rolled up skins and blankets that they now carried on their backs. They reached the cave in good time and decided to walk on in order to reach their home settlement by nightfall.

Now every tree, bush and rock was familiar. They were nearing the camp. Dusk was approaching, heralded by the chorus of a thousand insects. Jodie had been bitten on the ankles by one of them and began to scratch with some regularity. Once Anya recognised the plant she had been looking for, she grabbed one of its green and yellow leaves and crushed it in the palm of her hand before applying it to the site of Jodie's irritation.

The acrid smell of wood smoke filled the air. Something was wrong. The others sensed it too. There was too much smoke! Keon's pace quickened as he surveyed the canyon entrance.

Concern was etched on every face except Jodie's, but moments later she too was in tune with the concern of the adults. It was almost as if she had been able to zoom out

27

and focus on the events that had taken place. Keon was running ahead now. He rounded the corner into their camp, halting abruptly. He surveyed the carnage around him. Once again his head felt fuzzy, but, this time, he attributed it to the scene that was playing out before him. Every shelter was torn down. Fires seemed to burn randomly around the site. Clothing, tools, pottery and human remains were scattered everywhere. The bodies of friends and family littered the camp. The stone and sand was stained crimson. Keon was a stranger to brutality. He had not seen such mutilation and could never have imagined such an event in his worst nightmares. He fell to his knees as the full horror of the situation dawned. Tears ran down his dusty cheeks. He let out a murmur, but it was barely audible. Anya, Jadine and Jodie! He turned to go back, to stop them and spare them from this scene of horror.

It was too late. Anya and Jadine stood at the canyon entrance. Jodie's head was buried in Anya's hair. Tears had not yet appeared in their once innocent eyes. Jadine came forward. Her chest rising visibly as her heart pounded. To the left she caught sight of a familiar tunic. She did not want to look, but her momentum took her on. The tears come now as she stood over the body of Remy. His throat cut, and the side of his face still sticking to the broken end of a spiked club that was responsible for his downfall. Jadine levered it away and tossed it aside. She grimaced at the shattered remains of her close friends that now littered the encampment.

Keon, having now regained his senses and some degree of composure, ran over. Instinct had kicked in. Whoever, whatever had done this could not be far away. His people had been massacred a short time ago. The fires told him that much and the scavengers that were certain to feast had not arrived yet. He dragged Jadine away from Remy's corpse. She was reluctant to move at first, but, moments later, her legs turned to jelly and gave way beneath her. Keon caught her fall and carried her towards Anya who now cradled Jodie at the edge of the clearing. Keon remember the old shelter above. Words were not exchanged. He led the others up to the left of the canyon's rock face. It was dark now. Demons seemed to flicker on the rock faces, guided by the many nearby fires. Quickly, they reached the spot overlooking the burning camp. Although Keon wanted to flee as far away as possible, he knew that it might be foolhardy to move at night with the aggressors still in the vicinity. With one arm around each of the women and Jodie secured in his lap, Keon reflected on the scene of devastation below. Who had done this? What should he do now? Where should they go? Were they essentially all alone in the world now?

Mentally, Jodie had screamed hysterically at the sight that had greeted them on their return. Outwardly, she had kept silent. She had not sensed this beforehand and she found it difficult to comprehend just what had happened. She did not need an adult's voice to tell her of their predicament, but the naivety of her age spared her from worrying too much about the future. She had become numb, her eyelids gradually shutting on her tear-streaked face.

Sleep came quickly and covered her like a black cloak thrown from above. The dream was soon to follow.

* * *

She was instantly transported to the orb. The dome stood majestically before her. Tonight she could see movement within. Wait, what was that? An opening above? Yes, about one third of the way up the dome there was an opening. How would she get there? Did she even want to go inside? Yes, she did. Jodie concentrated on the detail of the entrance. Slowly but surely, a ramp emerged, building a metallic platform for itself as it drew down. It looked too steep to climb, but, as it neared, Jodie noticed that a silver stairway rose inside. Without thinking, she stepped forward. Her consciousness outside the dream was, however, more troubled by the situation. Previous warnings echoed in her mind. Should she resist and return? She stepped forward and climbed up towards the opening. She battled with her dream to turn back and flee, but this did nothing to halt her progress into the great orb.

She was inside now. All around her, shadows shifted. What looked like grey stone monoliths appeared to move. There was terror deep within her. She was grabbed from behind, an arm across her face, preventing her from screaming. She became enrobed in a veil of darkness.

5

Daylight was approaching. Jodie awoke, disturbed by her dream. Moments later, she realised it for what it was, just a dream. Part of a sequence, a nightly ritual, but it was not real. Then came the horror of her true reality. The night before, that was actual. Her friends and all of her people had all been slain. She was old enough to realise the brutality of the situation. What now? She surveyed the area. Her father was awake and gazing down at the scene below, his eyes glazed over by troubled thoughts. Anya and Jadine were snuggled close to her, just beginning to wake. At least she still had them. She still had hope. But would there be salvation?

They had survived the night. No one had returned to finish them off. That was Keon's first thought, but it was clear that they could not stay any longer than was necessary.

"Anya, we have to get away from here! We need to plan for our survival, to keep our family alive!"

"And do you have a plan?"

Keon could not answer.

"They did not come back." It was Jadine who stated the obvious.

"I kept watch most of the night. You slept out of sheer exhaustion." Keon's words were cold.

Anya began to sob. "They're all gone. All of them. Oh Jodie!" Anya was trembling as she took Jodie in her arms

31

and started to rock her to and fro.

Fresh tears ran down the cheeks of mother and child. Jadine remained composed and came across to comfort them, but words would have seemed inadequate in view of the horrors they had witnessed the previous day.

Keon's voice was cold and collected. "We must do what we can for the dead, and then leave this place."

Jadine brushed aside a lock of Anya's thick, dark hair and stared deep into her hazel eyes. "We have our lives, but we have to move on soon."

"I know, I understand… But the others?"

* * *

Keon had climbed down to survey the camp. His first self-imposed task was to gather up all of the bodies. Several scavenging animals had to be warded off. One by one, he laid his friends to rest in a great pile. It was not done with any degree of dignity. Keon simply wanted to spare them from the hungry animals.

Once he had finished, Keon placed some torn linen and rugs around the remains of his people. These materials would serve to ignite the funeral pyre when they were ready to leave.

"Jadine, Anya, we must collect as much as we can carry with us without compromising our progress too much. We must only take what we need. There will be no room for sentiment. Search what remains and take what you want. The others cannot use them now. We must accept that what's left is now ours."

"We cannot take what we do not own," replied Anya harshly.

"We must; we have to survive. For Jodie's sake, we must do what we have to!"

Anya glanced back at her companion, but did not offer

up any further challenges to his authority. Instead, she reluctantly began collecting items from around the encampment.

Jadine walked past the end of the human pile. She looked down one final time at the shattered face of Remy. Across his waist lay the form of his brother, one arm partially severed, his tunic soaked in dried blood. She wondered what would have happened to her if she had stayed with them. It was Remy's persistence that caused her to go and perversely saved her life.

The stench was now overwhelming and the flies were drawn from all around. Jadine took a gold chain from around the neck of Remy, feeling the clasp with her fingers to avoid having to see what she was doing. She turned away, paused, and held it close to her heart before slipping it around her own neck whilst walking away in search of the articles essential for their journey.

Between them, they had gathered everything that they considered might be necessary. Jodie was even allowed to take a carved wooden doll, a concession that the adults were forced to make. Now all they needed to do was to decide upon their destination.

After adding unwanted clothing and animal skins, Keon covered the pyre with vegetable fat, then used flints and dried reed fibres to start the fire. It was slow to take hold at first and Keon was concerned about the amount of smoke, but the flames gradually took hold of his friends and family. The four remaining survivors gazed at the man-made inferno for a few brief moments then, without words, they turned in unison to depart from the place that they had known as home.

With them, they carried dried foods, spare clothes and a limited supply of water carriers that they were able to recover from the camp. They brought with them several small gold artefacts and other valuables, which they planned to trade if the need arose. Strangely, the aggressors had neglected to take all such items. Keon had gathered resources such as rope, twine and animal glue, knowing that such things would come in handy to begin their brave new world. His flint kit was brought along by necessity, but any other heavy items were discarded. He also carried hunting knives, spears and a bow. These were never intended for aggression, or even defence, but he now realised their potential.

Keon decided that they should retrace their steps towards the great river. He knew, however, that this would not be without its risks. He wondered if the aggressors came from the river area. Generations had co-existed without such brutality so he concluded that this was unlikely. With the exception of the people who guarded the passage to the far north-east, people from the adjacent communities were generally very friendly even though they did not all speak the same tongue. From time to time, they would meet. They might assist each other in times of adversity and it was not unknown for relationships to develop between younger men and women from visiting tribes. However, he was not sure how they would take to his family relocating. Perhaps he should seek out the neighbouring elders and talk to them. He was no longer part of a community, just a family. Could they integrate with another one? Would they be welcomed or rejected? Although it was clear that they had to leave, Keon decided that he must convince everyone, including himself, of what was best before they wandered too far.

As they hiked out of the canyon nobody even ventured to ask where they were heading, automatically following Keon's lead, everyone reflecting upon the burning mass that they left behind. The stomach-churning stench of burning flesh and animal skins filled the air. It would follow them for some time to come. It would stay with them forever.

* * *

They spent that night back in the caves they had so recently visited. There was little conversation that night. Their world had been turned on its head. Even Jodie realised that things would never be the same again.

They had agreed that their options were limited. They would not feel safe in their old encampment and returning would prolong and intensify the emotional scarring. To the north-west lay a vast desert mountain region where resources were limited and the nights were cold. Beyond that was the northern extremity of the river that fed out into the great sea. There was a land bridge to the north-east, but they knew that the people of that region who lived in and around the ruins of a once-great city were extremely hostile, and best avoided. They had little choice but to journey further south, perhaps with the possibility of settling in the river plain and living along side its local inhabitants. Time would decide their ultimate fate.

Dawn had broken. Outside the cave, the morning seemed too beautiful in the context of the previous day's events. Birds were calling and the vista of the rock face was framed by a deep blue sky. The temperature was already rising, but there was sufficient breeze to gently sway the surrounding foliage.

"Are we going back to the river?" asked Jodie, somewhat cheerfully. "Can we go there? Can we stay? Can we build a home? Oh please…."

"It makes sense for now," replied Keon.

The adults knew how resilient children could be, but they were not prepared for how quickly Jodie had bounced back to near her normal self. Anya was concerned that the enormity of their situation may hit Jodie later or that her mind's eye image of the horrors that she had witnessed would soon begin to disturb her. "Are you okay?" she asked.

"Yes, things are better now, aren't they?"

"I hope so," replied Anya. "Anyway, now that we have decided to go back to the river, at least we have a plan. We will have to see what happens once we get there."

"We'll get by," exclaimed Jadine in a very positive tone as she swept Jodie off the floor and lifted her into the air.

"Keon will return to the camp today to salvage anything else he can." Anya's comments were directed at both the girls.

This time, Jodie knew better than to ask if she could accompany her father.

"He hopes to return by nightfall carrying as much as he can. In the panic of the day before, he left some tools that might come in very useful if we are going to have to build somewhere to live. He also wants to gather some of the preserved foods from the back of the old cave. They will see us through for a while."

"Will it be a single trip?" enquired Jadine, in a worried tone.

"Yes, of course."

"Good! If anything happened to Keon, we would all be doomed. All I want is to erase that place from my mind forever."

"So do I, but any hostiles will be long gone," stated Anya in a tone that suggested she was herself unsure. "And it makes sense to better prepare ourselves for what lies ahead. Days ago, we only entered the upper part of the river region. Keon wants to travel further south. He thinks it will be safer there. We are more likely to encounter the local people, but he is confident that they will be friendly, or at least tolerant."

"I hope so!"

"We cannot predict what we will encounter, but Keon is sure that journeying further down the river will improve our chances of survival."

"Is that what it's all about now? Survival?" Jadine paused and lifted her hand in a gesture to prevent Anya from responding. "You're right. I know, I know."

Keon returned with berries he had gathered not far from the cave. "After we have eaten these, I will head off back to the settlement."

Jodie wriggled free from Jadine's grasp and ran over to hug her father. "I'll miss you," she whispered in a tone more mature than her years. "Hurry back!"

"I will; you just take care of your mother and Jadine. We will trek down the river tomorrow."

"Of course I will." Excitement was beginning to return to her voice one again.

Keon gathered his things together methodically. He strapped the hunting knife in its scabbard to his belt and secured a small axe on his right hand side. He placed another smaller knife in his boot. He packed some water and berries in a small shoulder bag made out of animal skin. Keon could not afford to carry much more in anticipation of his return trip. The only other addition was his empty back pack. He adjusted the fit of everything he carried once again before kissing Jodie gently on the cheek. His eyes met Anya's and there was a brief exchange of understanding, then he left the encampment without a further word to anyone.

* * *

Knowing that Keon would be gone for most of the day, the women busied themselves. They spent much of the morning collecting fruits and berries for their journey. They interrupted this task on a regular basis to play and frolic as only the female of the species knows how. It wasn't that the events of the previous day were forgotten or that they felt totally safe in their environment, but driven along by

Jodie's youthful enthusiasm they allowed themselves a few moments of enjoyment.

Keon was the main provider for the family, so was an experienced hunter. However, Jadine often accompanied him. Whilst stretching over a stubby, thorny bush to pluck a bunch of ripe purple berries, she spotted movement out of the corner of her eye. She used a single finger to warn the others to be silent. Somewhat alarmed, Jodie and Anya suddenly ceased all movement simultaneously, as if frozen to the spot. Jadine pointed towards the thin clearing not far to the right of where she was standing. Anya and Jodie followed her gaze. Whilst remaining motionless Anya began to grin. A large, light brown rodent was too busy foraging to notice them. Fortunately, they were downwind of the animal. It scampered around the clearing with jerky movements. Suddenly, it became aware of a threat in its close vicinity and bolted, but it was too late. Jadine used her spear with lightning precision. The rodent was impaled. The spear had punctured a lung and torn through major internal organs, including its heart. Blood trickled from its mouth as it lay motionless on the ground. Jadine sprang forward and lifted it aloft. She left the spear in situ as she knew it would stem the blood loss and then proceeded to sling it over her shoulder using the shaft as a carrying handle.

"Well done," applauded Anya. She was unsure if Jadine was just lucky or, indeed, a skilled hunter. "We can feast later when Keon returns."

Jodie was unmoved by the experience. To her, this was not barbarity, but simply a way to catch a meal. "Yes, good shot, Jadine. Can I see it? Will you skin it later?"

"I can show you how if you like, Jodie."

"You, skin it?" exclaimed Anya.

All three were chuckling as they made their way back to the cave.

* * *

That afternoon, they prepared their supper then went about the business of repacking and securing all the goods that they had collected from the camp the day they had hastily departed. The plan was to incorporate everything else that Keon would manage to retrieve, before eating and spending one last night at the cave. They would depart at first light before it got too hot.

The sun began its daily ritual of swooping down towards the horizon. The sky morphed into a vivid display of orange, red and purple hues, reflecting brilliantly off the underside of a solitary cloud. The day had passed quickly. Anya had prepared a fire, but was awaiting Keon's return to light it and roast the meat. She had not been overly concerned about his mission to recover items from their old camp, but, as night would soon be upon them, her concern grew. She did not want to worry Jodie, but Jadine's eyes told the same story.

As dusk descended, it was Jadine who broke the silence. "He cannot return tonight. Darkness is upon us. He would realise that it would be unsafe to move after sundown, and he must have made camp elsewhere. I'm sure he will join us at first light."

"Yes, you are right. He probably took more than he could comfortably carry, slowing his progress. He may even have moved some of the heavier things to a secure area and stashed them some distance away. I knew he would be greedy and overdo it, but I guess he was just thinking of the coming days. I hope he doesn't expect us all to carry too much, though," said Anya, as much to herself as the others.

"I'm hungry," interrupted Jodie. She was used to her father being away, but simply could not tolerate an empty stomach for too long.

"Come on, let's eat," suggested Anya.

Jadine lighted the fire. Once again, a blanket of silence had descended over them.

* * *

Jodie descended into a troubled sleep. Once again the dreams returned to fill her sleep with activity as she journeyed to the dome....

* * *

Jadine covered her body with an animal hide and stared into the fire whilst Anya paced the ground, stopping ever so often to stare out into the darkness. Each had a slightly different perspective, but both were very concerned about Keon's whereabouts. Deep down, they knew that he was capable of sustaining a pace that would have comfortably facilitated his return by nightfall. Though consciously they were reluctant to contemplate his fate, both replayed many terrifying scenarios in their mind. Eventually, Jadine fell asleep out of sheer exhaustion. Anya stayed up well into the night.

Despite her lack of sleep, it was Anya who awoke just seconds before Jadine. Jodie was still sleeping. Anya turned to face Jadine and their eyes met. Anya looked around the cave as if to emphasise her fears and simply shook her head. Jadine rushed over to comfort her. Anya began sobbing, her tanned face, streaked with dust and tears, was now buried deep within Jadine's chest.

Jodie awoke. "Is Keon here?"

"No, he's not back yet," stated Jadine, trying to sound comforting.

"I thought he would be back by now."

"So did we, so did we," said Anya, trying to compose herself.

"Must we wait now?" asked Jodie.

"Yes, I am sure that your father will return very soon."

"What if he doesn't?" Jodie's question was almost aggressive.

"If he does not return this morning, one of us may have to go and look for him." Jadine's tone was soothing.

Anya knelt before Jodie and looked into her eyes.

"My dear, something bad might have, indeed, happened to your father, but, for now, we do not know. Maybe that is the worst of it, the not knowing, but it would be wrong of us to make false assumptions. Let's wait and see."

* * *

Hours passed and all three came to realise that things were far from well. Anya continued to pace the cave whilst Jadine repeatedly adjusted their packs. It was mid-morning now.

Anya finally acknowledged that her companion had disappeared. "I'm going to go back to the camp. I have to know. Maybe Keon tripped and injured himself along the way, particularly with all that he was carrying. You stay here and mind Jodie. I hope to return by nightfall." Anya paused for a moment.

Jadine understood that she had not finished and did not interject.

"If I do not return, do not come after me. One way or another, I will be with Keon... You must promise me that you will care for Jodie as your own."

"Anya, don't talk like that! You know I would, but it is I who must go. Jodie needs her mother."

Jodie stared at the only two people now in her life. Once again, tears trickled down her face. She did not want to choose. She wanted her father back. She looked up at her mother. "Please stay with me. Please both of you stay.

Keon will return."

"Jodie, your father may be hurt. I need to go and find him. Anya was already contemplating just what hurt meant. She grabbed a water bottle as Jadine went to comfort Jodie.

"No, let me go," pleaded Jadine, but Anya had already left the cave.

6

Anya returned as the sun disappeared below the horizon. She looked tired and was covered in dirt and perspiration. Her thick hair had been tied back using a vine to form a makeshift ponytail. Her eyes were glassy and her eyelids reddened.

"I think that Keon must have reached the camp. The things he went to collect were gone."

"Perhaps someone else took them," ventured Jadine, concern now clearly evident on her face.

"Maybe so, but then Keon would have turned around and come straight back to us."

"Did you check… Check around?"

"Yes, I checked the camp and zigzagged on my return as well as I could. I called out from time to time, but I was too afraid to raise my voice in case of hostiles. There was no sign of him anywhere."

"What now?" Jadine's question was an obvious one, but Anya was not immediately forthcoming with the answer.

"Keon might have had to divert from his path for some reason. We will stay here until he returns."

Jodie began to sob. She cried herself to sleep.

* * *

Jodie was inside the dome again. This time she was high up near the translucent roof.

All around below were the grey, stone monoliths. Each was moving very slowly, but, after a few minutes' observation, she saw that their progress was relentless. Each had direction, but she was unsure of their destination. Once again, there was shadowy movement in her peripheral vision. This time she was able to focus. Was it a person in a dark hooded cloak? An arm was waving and it seemed to be beckoning her to approach...

7

Days passed, then weeks. Deep down, all three had given up any hope of Keon's return, but nobody dare say it out loud, as if doing this would be an act of disloyalty or confirm the finality of his fate. Anya had even made one more return trip to survey the route to the old encampment. They survived relatively comfortably at the cave, but both the elder women were now thinking about a more plentiful supply of fresh water. It still had not rained, the springs were dry and the nearby stream that drained the hillside was little more than a muddy swath.

It was Jodie who finally made the suggestion. "Why don't we head on to the river now? It would be much better there." She made no reference to her father.

It was clear that Anya had already thought this through before she needed to reply. "Yes, you are correct, and so knowledgeable for one so young. We will leave tomorrow. Jadine?"

"I had been thinking... but I didn't want to say..." Jadine's voice trailed off.

"No need. We have been close for long enough.... Nevertheless, I know that you were waiting for me. Keon was my partner, so it was my decision."

Jadine seemed somewhat relieved. "Then we can repack again this evening and make a fresh start?"

"Yes, we can. We need to move on." After pausing for a few moments, Anya added, "There, I have said it now!"

Relief was seeping into her expression. "We cannot deny the truth any longer. Keon is not coming back. He is lost forever."

Jodie seemed energised by the thought of returning to the river levee. Although still grieving within, this suggestion helped put aside her heartfelt sadness about the loss of her father. "I am sure that it won't be our final destination, but I do think it will be a move in the right direction."

Jadine added a poignant conclusion. "Last time I took a trip, it saved my life."

The hike to the exact location on the riverbank that they had visited weeks before was mostly uneventful and was completed by late afternoon. Jadine and Anya talked relatively little, both still contemplating Keon's fate. Jodie though, babbled away, stopping regularly to pick a flower, eat a berry or some fruit before running to catch up or charging on ahead. From time to time, Jadine or Anya would call out to either hurry Jodie along or stop her from disappearing off into the distance.

* * *

Jadine gathered fire wood around a small clearing set back from the river bank. It was backed by palm trees, with a line of large bushes sporting huge violet flowers providing ground cover. Anya unpacked all that they had brought with them. Nearby reeds were harvested, which would later be combined with palm leaves and branches to produce a shelter and hammocks. That night though, they would sleep out under the stars on the animal skins they had carried with them.

It was noticeably warmer and humid; all three women perspired with the slightest effort. They now had a plentiful supply of water; they had filled one of the large vessels with water from the river. This enabled them to drink whenever they pleased without concern or the need for rationing. Even at their old encampment, water had to be drawn from underground springs. Excavations would collapse and have to be re-dug regularly. All this required a considerable effort, therefore Jodie viewed their move in a very positive light.

"Anya, can you get our fire going whilst I try my luck with the fishing line at the river?" asked Jadine. "I will use some of those large hemp seeds as bait." She smiled. "If I am successful, we can enjoy fresh fish for our supper. If not, it's just fruit!"

Anya was now smiling too. With a degree of sarcasm, she declared, "I am sure that the brilliant hunter, Jadine, will be able to catch us a fish or two."

"Maybe three," added Jodie. "Can I go fishing, too?"

"Wouldn't you rather help your mother?"

Jodie shook her head.

"Well, you'll have to be very quiet then, or you will frighten all the fish away."

"I will, I will, if I can have a go, too," said Jodie excitedly. "Come on, Jadine, let's get ready to go now!"

"Just a minute," replied Jadine as she threaded a large pod-like seed onto a bone hook. "I will take five more with me. If I lose all of them, I will give up!"

"Unless you are overwhelmed by fish that should last you way past dark."

"Okay, come on, Jodie."

The river was not far away. The bank was covered in long grasses and small bushes with tiny silvery-green leaves. Reeds filled large areas adjacent to their location, but here they had easy access via a small clearing. Indeed, it was why they had chosen this stretch of the river to camp by. Its width at this point also offered a degree of protection; the opposite bank was some way off and Jadine assumed it was relatively deep.

Jadine tied one end of her line to a long reed. At the other she attached her hook and bait. With a flick of her wrist she was able to cast the bait near the bulrush thickets. The bait pod floated on the surface supporting the weight of the hook. Jadine grabbed a handful of smaller grass seeds and scattered then near to her bait to attract the fish. She encouraged Jodie to do the same although her efforts had neither the required distance nor direction. On her second attempt, a light gust of wind blew them back into her face.

"That's it, I've had enough!" Jodie was cross.

"But we've only just got started."

Jodie quickly interrupted, "Look, look!"

The lips of a large fish had taken the bait. Jadine struck back and up with the reed to ensure that the hook retained itself in the mouth of the fish. The fish began to run. Any free line was quickly taken up and, soon, the reed was bending and changing direction. "Stay back, Jodie," advised Jadine. "I think this fish is going to be too big to land."

"You can do it! Keep a tight hold," shrieked Jodie.

As the fish briefly turned and swam towards them, Jadine seized an opportunity to grab the end of the reed where the line was tied. She wrapped more line around the end of the rod, consolidating her position. She now had what was effectively a hand line. She dared not hold the line on its own as she feared that it would sever her hand, with so much load being applied.

"Go and get Anya," cried Jadine. Exactly for what, she was not sure.

Jodie hastily complied and ran down the bank towards her mother who had already heard the commotion and was now running in their direction.

"A big fish! Jadine has hooked a really big one!"

Anya had in her hand a long spear. "Let me see!"

Moments later, she was by Jadine who had held on to

her quarry with dogged determination. Her knuckles were white and the line had made a small laceration on the inside of her middle finger. "I don't know how the line has survived this far without breaking, although I sense the fish is beginning to tire."

The fish made one final bid for freedom and headed towards the reeds. Jadine resisted its movement, but ran with it a little to lessen the strain.

Anya addressed the fish as she caught sight of it surfacing near the bank. "Hold still, you beauty." She let out a shrill cry as she released the spear. She jumped up in the air, kicking her heels backwards and shaking her hand over her head. "Yes, yes, yes!"

"You got it!" Jodie tried her best to copy her.

The fish was now motionless and had rolled over on its side. Jadine used her line to haul it to the bank. Anya grabbed the spear to haul it out.

"Wow!" said Jodie.

The fish stretched out over half the length of Jodie and perhaps weighed nearly as much. The circumference around its girth approximated its length. Its deep body was covered in large scales that graduated from a deep bronze along its dorsal line through dark brown down to lighter shades on its stomach. Its tail and fins were an orangey brown, their small size relative to its body, suggesting it was not adapted for rapid movement. The large mouth that had two large barbels on both its upper and lower lips was clearly evolved for taking seeds, fruit or insects that landed on the surface of the water. Grass seeds had already begun to stick to its body. Anya inserted a hand inside its gill flap and tried to lift the fish. This action seemed to emphasise its dimensions. It was indeed larger than Jodie and was too heavy for Anya to lift cleanly on her own. Jadine helped her to carry it back to the camp.

"I still have five bait pods left," declared Jadine,

somewhat triumphantly.

"Better save them for another time," retorted Anya unnecessarily. "But we have so much food from just one catch. We will eat well tonight, and then save some for the coming days. It's so easy. I don't know why we didn't think to move to the river a long time ago." Anya beamed widely.

Jadine suddenly looked serious. "You know why. This is not our land. Other people lay claim to these parts. I hope they will tolerate our presence, but, if all of our people had come here to live, I am certain that there would have been trouble."

"We are our people!" Anya interjected.

Jadine looked hurt and did not reply.

"Forgive me; that was uncalled for. If the local people come, our only problem will be that we are three women alone."

Anya skilfully filleted the fish using one of the ancient knives that they had brought with them. She then skewered the fish using long thin twigs that she had sharpened to a point. They could allow themselves a generous portion, but all the fish had to be preserved in some way so as to keep it edible for as long as possible. The smell had already started to attract flies and other insects. Some of the fillets were placed side down on a pile of stones in the centre of the fire, whilst Anya secured others in an upside down pot, which she hung from a branch way above the fire in an attempt to slowly cook and smoke the fish.

Anya decided to dispose of the fish carcass as soon as she had finished her dissection and offered it back to the river from whence it came. She had no sooner disposed of it when there was a huge commotion at the spot where it hit the water. Several large scavenging birds were swooping down from the sky and fish from below were instantly attracted.

Anya decided that she needed to clean herself up. She did not want to attract half the wildlife in the area. She walked a short distance up the bank, not wishing to bathe near the carcass. She found a shallow inlet where the bank had been eroded. It provided a safe way into the river to bathe.

Anya shouted over to Jadine, "I am going to wash now. Please turn the fish; don't burn it. It won't take long. Oh, and don't let Jodie do it!"

"Okay!" Jadine's reply was distant, but audible.

Anya's feet sank into the mixture of sand and clay at the water's edge. She had already removed all her clothes, and laid them on some dry grass before wading in. Her elbows were raised out to the side as she used her arms for balance. Anya still had an admirable figure. In spite of her age and the fact that she had carried Jodie and given birth to her, she was still quite proud of her looks. The challenge of her daily activities meant that all the muscles in her body were well toned, although not overly developed.

Inexplicably, after giving birth to Jodie, Anya had never conceived again. On many occasions, she had tried to increase the size of their family, or at least enjoyed trying, but without success. Both Anya and Keon loved Jodie though, and they were not overly concerned by their lack of further progeny.

Anya was now in knee-deep water. She bent over and splashed her body. Droplets of water settled on her dark olive skin. As she resumed an upright posture, they traced a line down over her flattened stomach returning to the river via the dense glossy mat below. She waded in until her hips were covered, and then launched her body under the water. She surfaced a considerable distance away, tossing her head back, once her torso was clear of the water. Her long black hair arced over the water sending a fountain of glistening beads up and back down again. She waded back into the shallows, squeezing the water out of her silky locks with one hand whilst holding tightly onto her clothes with the other. Anya looked up to see Jadine on the bank.

"Anya, the fish is cooked. I have put it up high above the fire to ensure it is kept warm. The heat should keep scavengers away, but Jodie is standing guard."

As Anya stooped to wash through her clothes, Jadine paused to admire her friend's body. Jadine had seen Anya naked many times before so her gaze did not make Anya feel uncomfortable. When Anya lent forwards, using both hands to wring the water out from her clothes, Jadine allowed herself one final glance.

The sun was setting on the day. Anya had dressed. It was still incredibly hot and humid. The fire still crackled away, but all three were sitting far enough away not to feel any additional warmth. It had served its primary purpose to cook the fish, but was now providing a flickering light source, enabling them to see each other whilst they ate and chatted.

"We did really well today catching this big fish," offered Jodie, munching on a portion. "Food is so easy to catch here; I think that we should stay."

"We haven't got any other plans; at least, for the time being," said Anya, without much thought.

"But what are we going to do in the longer term?" asked Jadine. "At the encampment, we had our family, we kept some animals and hunted others. Most importantly, we were a community. Is this it now? Are we going to build shelters and settle here? Just the three of us?"

"We still do not know what happened when we were away from the encampment. In some ways, I hope that we never will; nor do we know Keon's fate. I think that we should stay put for the time being."

"I think that we should travel much further south and go in search of the utopia that our people used to describe," ventured Jodie with astonishing maturity.

"You are so much like your father," stated Jadine. "But I do not believe in such a place. The machines ended it all and now we must make a more honest existence."

Anya looked thoughtful as if genuinely contemplating her daughter's suggestion.

"Maybe one day we will travel further down the river, and find whatever lies at the end. All I know is that, either side of the great river, lays a vast desert wilderness. For now, we will stay put and see what fate brings...."

A branch snapped somewhere behind them. They all heard it, but their response was silence. They strained to listen for further evidence of something or someone in the palm forest behind them. They did not have long to wait. There was another crack, slightly to the left of them this time. Jadine grabbed her knife. Anya plumped for two spears. Jadine brought a finger up to her lips to silence the others, but there was no need. Fear was etched across their faces. Jodie began to tremble. Jadine held up a hand to Anya directing her to stay motionless before she took off into the palms behind her.

8

Jadine heard more twigs breaking in the direction that she was now running. Suddenly, a human form broke cover and sprinted away to her right. Seconds later, there was blackness. Jadine had failed to spot the low-level stump before her. One foot was stopped. Her momentum threw her over at speed sending her head crashing into the solid trunk of a large palm. She lay unconscious on the ground.

Anya had led Jodie away from the glow of the fire. They were hiding in a thicket of bushes when they heard a collection of sounds emanating from the trees. Anya was too afraid to call out to Jadine and she did not want to give their position away. She tightened her grasp on Jodie who continued to tremble.

There had been silence for some time now. Jadine had not returned and Anya feared the worst.

"What's happening…?" Jodie attempted to whisper, but Anya used her hand to muffle the sound.

Anya's heart was pounding now, to such an extent that she thought it might be audible to anyone standing nearby. She looked up to fix the position of the moon crescent against the branches. She decided to let it track across the sky before breaking cover. It had moved a considerable distance before she heard rustling at the far side of their camp. Jodie closed her eyes as tight as she could.

Jadine staggered from the tree line, blood dripping from the deep gash on her head. Anya recognised the outline of her friend, illuminated by the orange glow of the fire. She peered into the blackness beyond to see if anyone else was present.

Jadine slumped down near the water urn. She slurped the first handful, threw several more over her face, then used her arm to wipe away the mixture of water and blood.

Anya whispered to Jodie, "Stay put. Do not move for anything." Then she broke cover to tend to Jadine.

Jadine began to re-orientate herself.

"What happened?" asked Anya.

"There was somebody in the trees, so I gave chase. Unfortunately, I tripped on a tree stump and went flying through the air before banging my head on another. I think I lost consciousness for a while. Was I gone long?"

"It seemed like forever, but I guess you weren't out too long. Was there any sign of anyone when you came to your senses?"

"No, everything was quiet and still. Where's Jodie?" enquired Jadine.

"She's over there." Anya gestured.

Jodie still had not moved.

"Who was it? What did they want?"

"I don't know. One thing's for certain. We are all still alive. If they wanted to slay us, they could have started with me. I would have been an easy target."

"Do you think that there was more than one out there?"

"I only saw one, but I cannot be sure. A little earlier, I heard sounds coming from different directions."

"Me too! Maybe whoever was watching us means us no harm…. Maybe we should try to make contact."

"Or perhaps they were just observing us, to gauge whether or not we are a threat, assessing our strengths and weaknesses until next time…."

"What threat?" Anya was indignant. "There won't be a next time! We are leaving in the morning."

Jodie broke cover. "Are you okay, Jadine?"

"I'll be fine, Jodie."

"Jodie, I told you to stay put!" Anya's tone was harsh. Jodie was indignant. "The danger's passed now."

"Come on, Jadine, let me tend to your head," said Anya.

* * *

That night, Anya and Jadine agreed to take turns to keep a watch over the camp, anticipating that their visitor might return. It was Anya who took the final watch before daybreak. Jadine was sleeping soundly, but Jodie tossed and turned on her makeshift reed bed. Anya was exhausted. She battled hard with the onset of sleep.

* * *

Jodie was dreaming. Her dream was different from usual and somewhat confused. She was transported to the orb once again, climbing the silver stairway to gain access. The grey stone monoliths were still all around, but, this time, they were motionless. Once again, there was shadowy movement and it was the person in a hooded cloak. The individual removed his hood to reveal an old face with weathered, wrinkled skin and white hair. Around his neck were masses of glistening golden beads. In his hand, he held a weathered old staff. He approached Jodie. A wicked grin spread across his face like a fungus invading the cracks in his skin. Jodie knew that he did not belong, that he was not part of this world. She awoke in a cold sweat.

9

"Hello, we did not mean to startle you," said the visitor. "Are you hurt?"

Anya woke up suddenly. Immediately, she admitted to herself that she must have finally lost her battle with fatigue. A tall, slim man with very dark ebony skin and jet-black hair was standing over Jadine. He wore loose fitting, brown animal skins draped over his right shoulder, exposing the left side of his chest. A chain of different coloured beads interspersed with the skulls of small animals hung around his neck. His feet were bare and very dusty, but the rest of his body was relatively clean. A second man approached from the edge of the tree line. He was similar in appearance to the first man, if a little smaller. A spear was supported across the back of his neck and shoulders by both arms. He looked calm and relaxed. As he drew nearer, he offered a warm smile. He suddenly became conscious of the threat posed by his weapon and thrust the spear into the ground, leaving it three or four paces behind.

The other man spoke again. "I saw you fall last night, and, er, well, I was frightened that you might attack me."

Jadine approached the man. "Me attack you? You might have thought about that before sneaking up and watching us. What would you expect us to do?"

"I am sorry. My people are wary of strangers visiting our region. We have lost whole families to marauding tribes, so we have to be careful. We were sent to observe you. To check you out… so to speak. We see now that you are not a threat. Indeed, you might need our help. Once again, our apologies."

By this time, the first visitor had also embedded his spear in the ground. Jadine's demeanour suggested that she now felt less threatened, but Anya continued to stand in front of Jodie in a protective manner, holding onto both of her shoulders to keep her hidden. Jodie tilted her head to see what was going on.

"We don't need any help. We just want to be left in peace," stated Anya.

"As you wish," stated the taller man. "But there are things we can offer you. Food, perhaps, or even shelter or protection. We would not ask for anything in return."

The second man remained silent and continued to grin. "Why are you alone? Where are your men?"

"Our villagers were slain whilst we were away. My man, as you put it…" Tears filled Anya's eyes. "He is missing."

"I am genuinely sorry. Really, I am."

Anya glared at the second man, who continued to grin.

"Don't mind him. He is my brother. He is not as sharp as an eagle's claw, but he is a good companion and a loyal family member. He hunts well, too! We were going to offer you some food, but clearly your fishing skills provide all that is needed."

"That may be so. Perhaps we were lucky. Were you watching us, then?"

The man looked uncomfortable again. "As I said, it's been our duty."

"And will you continue?"

The man collected his spear, and his brother followed suit. Both were headed in the direction of the river.

"You take good care of the little one. We'll be seeing you."

Anya and Jadine gazed at the two men as they departed. Jodie broke free and ran around in front of her mother. She pulled a face of sheer annoyance and shook her head.

Jadine was relieved. "Well, they seemed reasonably friendly."

"Yes, almost too friendly to two women and a child alone."

"Anya, sometimes you are too cynical. We are fortunate. Another community might not have been so welcoming to strangers. At least we can assume that we will be left in peace whilst we stay here. I mean, they didn't exactly order us off their land or slay us as we slept."

"I'm not so sure," interjected Jodie.

"Oh, Jodie, your mother and I know when we can trust someone, and he seemed like a good man."

Jodie just shook her head and returned to drawing in the sand.

* * *

The next day, all three awoke to the sound of people nearing their camp. There were at least ten men. They made no attempt to disguise their approach. Anya recognised the brothers who had visited the camp the previous day. They appeared to be leading the rest of the party. Between them walked an older man. His skin was heavily wrinkled and his hair was white and thinning. He wore similar dress to the others, but his cloak was dyed a bright ochre colour. His neck was obscured by strings of beads. In his hand he held a weathered old staff.

Anya stepped forward to greet them. She did not feel the need to protect Jodie this time.

"Back so soon?"

"This is our elder. We do not use names as such. We

have symbols tattooed at the tops of our arms. We have references that we are permitted only to use within our community. For ceremonies... or for more formal purposes, you understand." The speaker pointed out an owl on the elder's neck just above the highest ring of beads. "I am called Anya. This is Jadine and my daughter, Jodie."

The elder's face lighted up as he surveyed Jodie.

"How are we to refer to you if you do not use a name?"

The elder spoke. "There is no need. Names single out individuals and divide people and communities. They can be barriers to dialogue, so please think of us as one, as a tribal group that looks after the needs of all its families. We work as one, celebrate as one and grieve as one. I am the elder and I lead ceremonies, but I am not the leader. I have learnt that you are on your own in this world, and that your tribe has gone, that you have become nomadic. Too bad, too bad for all of you!" He shook his head before he turned his attention once again to Jodie. "You're a sweet little thing, aren't you? Do you know how many summers you've seen? "

Jodie just shrugged.

"It seems that you're just shy. No matter." The elder adjusted his stance to face Anya. "We will leave you in peace now, but rest assured that we will come and check on you from time to time. Stay as long as you like." Abruptly, he turned to leave.

The simple man who had accompanied his brother on the first visit turned to wave, and they were gone.

* * *

That afternoon, Jadine took Jodie exploring. "Jodie, we need to collect more firewood and find some stronger branches that we could use to make our new shelter. If we walk further up the bank, we can survey the tree line for suitable sites."

"Are we staying here, then?"

"Perhaps… If we do decide to stay on, it would be useful to know how far we would have to go to get building supplies."

"Could we not just move and set up camp wherever we find the wood that we need?"

"If it was far, we could do that, but I like where we are now. The vegetation is not too dense, and the clearing gives us a sense of space and security."

"Hum…." Jodie did not seem convinced.

They were at the river's edge now. Jadine was twisting and turning as she walked. Sometimes she walked sideways, occasionally backwards.

Jodie copied her actions, looking back at the trees. "What exactly are we looking for?"

"A clump of trees that will provide us with wood of the thickness we need. All but the youngest palms have trunks that would be far too thick to cut. These bushes with purple flowers have no long, straight branches. We need to find something else."

Jadine was now looking at Jodie, who was still scanning the tree line. "Would those do?" Jodie was pointing to a clearing where palms were absent, having been replaced by an altogether different species.

Jadine turned and looked up. "Yes, I think they just might."

They began to cut inland through dense undergrowth. Jadine had to use her long knife to cut her way through the vegetation. Jodie followed on several paces behind.

The lush, dense growth began to thin and they found themselves in a small clearing. Sunlight streamed down through the canopy above.

"These will do fine," confirmed Jadine, studying the

foliage around her. "I could cut these, and it would not be too far to drag them back to our camp. It might even be easier to haul them back through the palms."

"Shall we see?"

"You mean walk back to your mother through the trees?"

"Yes, let's!"

"Okay, then, Jodie, but you must stick close by me. It would be easier than you think to get lost and disorientated in here."

Jodie's shorter stride made it difficult for her to keep up in the dense undergrowth. "I will, but don't walk too fast!"

Jadine grabbed Jodie's hand. "Don't worry, I won't leave you."

They were nearing the point at which the palms regained their position in the tree line, where Jodie hoped that progress would be easier. Jodie and Jadine were so focussed on not tripping over whatever lay on the ground that they failed to see what was hanging down from the branches right before them. That was, until Jadine walked right into it. At first, Jadine did not realise what she had stumbled into. As she peeled a cobweb away from her face, Jodie let out a scream loud enough to be heard as far away as the opposite riverbank.

Jadine stepped back in horror. "What is it?" she exclaimed.

"Look!" Jodie was pointing. Her voice was trembling. "Is it real?"

"Oh! How awful! Yes, I think it is. Look away, Jodie."

Before them were the remains of what had apparently been the body of a young woman. Some flesh remained on the bones, but the majority had been stripped off by the creatures that inhabited the woodland. Clinging delicately to her skull were strands of long black hair in braids. Her hands had been lashed together before someone had placed a rope between her wrists and used the upper branch of a tree to lift her no more than an arm's length off the ground. Jodie was repulsed although she could not resist the temptation to take a closer look. The shaft of a spear was protruding out of the corpse's left shoulder. The tip of the blade was wedged under the collar bone. Jodie knew that although such a wound would be very painful, it was unlikely to cause death immediately. As she stepped in front of the corpse, she could see that insects and spiders had taken up residence in the ribcage. There were no other clues as to how the girl had come to be there.

"Jadine, Jodie! Are you all right?" Anya's voice was some way off.

"Yes, we're over here," shouted Jadine. "Beyond the palms." Jadine stepped around the hanging body and pushed and chopped her way out of the vegetation.

Jodie followed closely. Suddenly, everything seemed so dark. Jadine saw a flash of Anya's body as she ran through the trees.

"Over here." Jadine did not feel the need to raise her voice as much this time.

Jodie could see her mother clearly now. "Come and see what we found in the trees."

Anya was panting. "I heard a scream. I knew it was Jodie."

"We're okay." Jadine's tone was reassuring. "We've just had a fright, that's all. There's the body of a young woman over there, tied to a tree. It looks as though she was deliberately bound, then killed."

* * *

During the days that followed, nobody came to their camp. At least, none of the visitors disclosed their presence. From time to time Anya and Jadine sensed that they were being observed. However, Jodie knew that they were there for certain, but said nothing. One day, she even waved in the direction of the taller brother, but he did not acknowledge her. Through the hours of darkness they were left alone, although Jodie wondered if this would change as the moon grew in size and offered down more light.

Four days after his first visit, the elder returned with the brothers and two more companions. The two strangers were silent, burly men who constantly scanned their surroundings. Anya surmised that they had been invited along only to protect the elder. He had brought with him gifts for Jodie, comprising a golden necklace, a tiny jug and a carved wooden doll.

"Here you are, little one." As he presented them to her, he began to chant incoherently.

It only lasted a few moments, but this clearly unsettled the women. The elder was unmoved.

Jodie accepted the gifts rather coldly. "Thank you."

The elder then momentarily took back the gold chain before tenderly placing it around Jodie's neck, gently smoothing her hair from her face. To him, this child was precious. She stepped away, carrying the doll in her left hand and the jug in her right.

Anya wished they had brought some food with them instead. The large fish that they had caught the previous week had, with the exception of a few scraps, been consumed. What remained was beginning to decay. After a number of attempts, Jadine very much suspected that her previous triumph was beginner's luck. She had taken a few very small fish in the shallows, but these were nothing but a snack or an accompaniment. They had also picked most of the nearby berries and fruits. The time of year meant that their stock would not be replenished immediately. Even their early morning forays had failed to provide them with any game to roast.

Anya considered mentioning the body in the woods, but thought better of it. Instead, she opened with what she hoped would be a more productive line of conversation.

"We have been rather less successful with the fishing these last few days. Have you got any wise advice for us?" The elder contemplated Anya's request for a few moments. "We use a net. If you like, I can get one brought over to you. Think of it as a loan. You could copy its design and make one for yourself."

"Thank you. That would be useful."

"That would be great," added Jadine enthusiastically. "More fresh fish would be appreciated. I am fed up with eating fruit and berries."

"Food is plentiful here if you know where to look." The elder did not elaborate. "We must be going now. You take good care of the little one. We will return shortly. Please stay on here. It would not be wise to leave. There are many unseen threats beyond this plain."

The other visitors were already moving away.

As the elder turned his back, Anya shook her head. She did not feel any safer now than on the night of the first visit. She could not shake the vision of the body in the wood from her mind. She began to contemplate their options as the visitors disappeared from sight. Another brief visit had ended.

10

Anya and Jadine sat near the riverbank enjoying more fresh fish. Not wishing to wait for a net they had tried their luck again with the hook and line soon after the visitors had left. On the third cast Jadine found success. Their catch was much smaller than the huge fish they had landed on their first attempt; however, it was more than adequate for several meals. Jodie had finished eating and was playing with some discarded branches that were destined to be firewood.

Anya tossed aside what remained of her meal. "Something is just not right with the people who come to visit us. They say they will give us space and mean us no harm, but I do not trust them. I see the way that they look at us, Jodie especially. They say that they are happy for us to settle here, but... I don't know, maybe I'm wrong, but I don't feel comfortable. Why is it unwise to leave? Do you understand what I'm saying, Jadine?"

"I know exactly what you mean. I have felt uneasy since that night they first came to us from the tree line. I think that they tolerate us because we are not a threat, but I don't know if they have our best interests in mind. They have never invited us back to their settlement. At first, I thought that they wanted to give us space and not interfere with our lives, but they have visited us on numerous occasions now. Perhaps they mean well with their gifts for Jodie, but there are other things we need more, and they must realise that." Jadine rose and came face to face with Anya. She glanced around before continuing in a whisper, "We cannot just tell them to leave us alone. If their intentions are bad, it will not make any difference. However, we know that they are watching us most of the time, so leaving unnoticed would be very difficult. Even if we did manage to get away, they might come after us. They know this terrain far better than we do."

"Jadine, I think we should try to leave. We need to get away from here and soon. Yes, I understand that nowhere is going to be safe for two women and a girl, but I sense something threatening, something ominous."

Jadine turned away from Anya, letting out an ironic chuckle as she shook her head. "Are we not just frightening ourselves? After all, they have not harmed us, and it would have been easy for them had they intended to. The body that we found must be far from their village. They probably had nothing to do with it."

Anya sprang forward, grabbing Jadine by the arm and spinning her around so that, once again, the two women were face to face. Jadine stared deep into Anya's sad eyes.

"Jadine, you have always been dear to me. I will not let anything bad happen to you, not now, not here. I must protect Jodie, too." Anya tried her best to hide her concern from anybody who might be watching. Her voice was lowered to a hiss rather than a whisper. "We must get away. The moon is near full. I do not think they watch us after dark. We could pack up and leave. Why not tonight?"

"Anya," whispered Jadine, "we will leave, but not tonight. I spotted movement up the bank a short time ago. He seemed to be moving away, but I fear that they might still be watching us."

"If they are keeping a vigil over us today, what will be different tomorrow?"

"If we departed tomorrow, we would have time to

gather some more food and group our belongings together."

"But we cannot reveal to them that we are planning to leave."

"No, Anya, we must not, but we hunt and gather anyway. All we need to do is to group our possessions so that, after dark, we can pack them quickly and move out."

"Okay, Jadine, we will leave tomorrow?"

"Agreed!" Jadine nodded thoughtfully. She did not know why they had come to this decision, but she was convinced that it was the correct one.

Jodie had been making drawings in the sand with her sticks. As well as a number of wavy lines and shapes, she had sketched several fish and a bird. She was quite pleased with her efforts. As she shaded the feathers on the bird's wing she glanced over to see if her mother and Jadine were looking. They were some distance from her. Jodie could see that they were talking, but she was too far away to hear what they were saying. She added a great crest to the bird's head and some long tail plumes. She picked up a rounded pebble and placed it on the ground to represent an eye. Two more were used as fish eyes. Now she was pleased. Her masterpieces were almost complete. The final addition was a curved line that covered all the pictures within her montage.

As Jodie ambled over, Jadine and Anya exchanged a glance before forcing a smile as they turned towards her. Jodie waited until she had walked right up to her mother before speaking. "Is our departure a secret? I think it would be wise to keep it that way and leave soon."

* * *

That evening, those who had made regular visits to Jodie, Jadine and Anya, lighted a huge pyre in celebration of the forthcoming events. The nights were warm by the great river, so the dark skins of those that danced and chanted around the fire were heavy with perspiration. A drummer beat out a hypnotic rhythm with his hands. Their ceremony was fuelled by fermented fruit drinks, anticipation and excitement.

The tribe could also distil alcohol, a skill that had been passed down through many generations. A tribal elder was drinking the distillate and spraying a huge mouthful over a flaming torch. The results were spectacular, set against the dusky sky. As he did so, there were shrieks and cheers from the crowd that had congregated. The entire village was present. Almost everyone was dressed only in a short hand-woven skirt made from reed leaves and grasses. They had painted their torsos using a dark grey paste made from ground charcoal embers and river water. The dark base coat was overlaid with stripes made from saffron, henna and turmeric. The sagging breasts of the older women flopped around as they danced. The younger girls had white-painted nipples to emphasise their fertility. Both men and women wore tight braids and beads in their hair, but it was only the men who held knives aloft. The women wore long, decorative earrings made from brightly coloured, polished semi-precious stones. A ceremonial pipe was passed around. The leaves that they smoked added to their euphoria.

The men were now chanting in unison following the lead of the elder. The women bent over to expose the naked gap between their legs. The drumbeat became much slower and more rhythmic, as the men went over to their partners and mounted them from behind. This was not some random orgy, but clearly a well-rehearsed ceremonial pillaging of the village women. Each man thrust in unison to the drum beat whilst concentrating to control his breathing. Clearly, none of the participants wanted to be the first to ejaculate, but after quite some time, several men did so almost simultaneously. The ritual ended for both them and their partners. Gradually, each duo ended their coupling and fell to the ground until the last pair remained. At this point, the beat speeded up into a crescendo. The only man standing grabbed the woman's breasts as he pumped away frantically until finally his load was spent into an apparently grateful partner.

The elder, who had been seated next to the now silent drummer, rose to address his tribe. He held a decorative spear aloft and declared, "Now we must take the life blood to ensure our seed is fertile. We have no written word, so we must tell our children, and our children's children to follow this ritual so that life may continue. Our people, as those who have gone before us, know that we must appease the gods of our world if we are to continue to enjoy prosperity."

There was a loud and enthusiastic cheer when the speaker paused.

"Let us prepare our sacrifice to the god of the river and the god of fertility, as, without either, we know that we cannot exist." The elder raised a large curved knife aloft beside his spear.

There was another great cheer, followed by the sound of running feet as the men raced into the trees.

The marauders from the tribe covered the ground quickly, high on drugs and alcohol, as well as the endorphins generated by their recent ceremonial experience. Soon, they came to the riverbank. From here, it was just a short journey following the river upstream to their prize. The older women were not important. They would dispose of them immediately. It was the girl that they needed. Indeed, the elder would not accept their return without her, as she was crucial to the completion of the ceremony.

The visitors did not travel as a group. They were spread out over a considerable distance by the time the faster runners approached the clearing. Had they not been planning an attack on two women and a child, they might have been better co-ordinated. As things were, each and every man wanted the honour of claiming the trophy. A group of three had raced away from the others. As they neared, they could smell the campfire's aroma and see the smoke rising against the moonlit sky. Finally, they slowed momentarily to survey the area. It was late and they assumed that the women would be sleeping. However, the first man to arrive could not see them on their reed beds. The other two separated to flank the site. They could hear the other members of their tribe approaching, so all three dashed into the central clearing to search for their prospective captives. They were nowhere to be found. There were fish bones, a single carved wooden bowl and the doll that the elder had presented to Jodie, but the women were gone.

The others arrived singly and in small groups. They soon realised that their quarry had evaded them. For many this was a sobering thought. The taller brother took charge. Clearly, they were not long gone. He organised his comrades into small units and directed them to spread out and search. He reminded them that only the little one was important and should not be harmed. The ceremony demanded the sacrifice of a fit and healthy child. A sick or injured offering would be an insult to the gods and bring about bad fortune.

Men were sent out in all directions, both into the trees and along the riverbank. A number concentrated on a detailed search of the immediate surroundings in case the women had heard their approach and were simply in hiding, but it was obvious to even the simple brother that this was a planned departure.

11

Anya's mind had been in turmoil. How did Jodie know of their concerns? Had she heard them talking? Impossible! She was too far away, but she obviously had had some insight into the intentions of the visitors. Jadine was right though, they were a threat, and they had to leave as soon as possible. Tonight! We must take our chance now. Pack up and flee these people forever!

* * *

Anya and Jadine held onto the floating logs that they had hastily lashed together. Jodie rode on top clinging tightly to the possessions that they wanted to keep dry. Tools and implements were strapped to the side. Their small makeshift raft was not at all stable so they avoided stressing the structure, as much as possible. As they paddled across the river they could see flickering hues in the distant sky cast by the visitors' great fire. The water was deep now. They had little idea just how deep it was, but it mattered not. They could easily drown. As they did not have the luxury of time, there was no opportunity to search for the narrowest point to cross. The river was vast; therefore slight variations in width probably made negligible difference.

They were a considerable distance from the bank, but Jadine still kept her voice muted. "I hope there are none of those big fish around here. I don't enjoy paddling through water when I can't see what's around me."

"Don't worry, Jadine," said Jodie, "they only eat plants and seeds. They would not bother us."

Jadine was impressed with her knowledge and maturity, but then realised that it was likely that other animals inhabited the river that did not thrive on a diet of vegetation!

"Shush!" prompted Anya. "I can hear something! There are people approaching our side of the bank. I wonder what they want."

"Us, no doubt!"

"I hope that we will never get to know. Now paddle faster!"

"I am going as fast I can! We have only just crossed the halfway point. We need to pace ourselves so that we don't tire before we reach the other side. The current has already taken us way downstream. If we stop paddling, we will drift away and who knows where we will end up."

Jadine lowered her voice to an absolute whisper. "They are looking for us!"

The voices of many men travelled across the water.

Anya glanced back. "I cannot hear what they are saying, but I am sure you are right. I hope they don't follow us."

"Ah!" Jadine struggled to contain a brief moment of terror as something brushed her leg and wrapped around her ankle. As she realised that it was just a strand of floating weed, the panic subsided and she felt a little foolish.

"Shush!"

This time, both Jodie and Jadine followed Anya's instruction until they neared the opposite bank.

"Look!" said Jodie, pointing to a pair of eyes reflecting back the moonlight. They were set far apart and were clearly not human.

"Oh, no!" It was out before Jadine could stop herself.

The beast propelled itself from the muddy shore and slipped into the water, sending just a few ripples radiating out. Jodie saw its long, knobbly and leathery tail enter the river last. Anya and Jadine kicked water in a frantic attempt to increase their progress. Jodie kept quiet and tried to track the route of their latest threat, but she lost sight of it as it submerged into the inky depths. At least they were out of earshot of the other bank, thought Anya, but it mattered little if the men who pursued them could hear them being eaten alive!

Anya was pulling from the front of the raft, so was the first to feel the riverbank coming up to meet her feet. Jodie screamed as she saw the eyes reappear just a short distance behind them. Jadine felt the mud and silt beneath her feet. Two more steps and Anya was half out of the river. She slipped and slid her way up the bank with one hand aiding her balance, whilst the other was used to haul out the raft out of the blackness. Jadine steadied herself against the bottom, grabbed a spear and in a single movement hurled it at the crocodile. The tip flew into its open mouth and penetrated the tongue, dragging the shaft through with its momentum. The beast shrieked and hissed in protest. It rolled over snapping off a large part of the protruding rod.

The raft was beginning to come apart, but it had fulfilled its purpose. Anya struggled to drag it across the muddy bank, but now Jadine was only hampered by ankle-deep water and the slippery surface and joined in to help. Jodie had jumped off the raft. She had fought her way across the mudflat and had reached the relative safety of the grassy bank. The injured crocodile lacked the determination to pursue its prey any further. Though its injury was unlikely to be fatal, it had had enough for one night. The three women were wet and muddy, but had made it to the opposite bank.

* * *

The dark skin of the hunters merged with the blackness of the river as they lined up along the bank. A thorough search of the area had failed to locate the women. There were no clear tracks to suggest that they had left on foot. "They must have fled via the river," declared the tall one. "It's not safe to go out into the water at night. We must go back and get the boats. It will not take long to cross and I'm sure they will make uncertain progress in the dark. We should be able to pick up their trail at first light. The current will have forced them downriver a little. If we cut directly across from our position, assuming they head upstream, we should catch them in no time."

"Their fate is with our gods. If they desire it, we will have them, but, tomorrow, the moon will no longer be full. We will not be able to perform the ceremony."

"We can hold the little one through the next cycle if we have to."

"Let's head back." This time, in unison, the men turned and began to jog towards their village.

* * *

Anya led Jadine and Jodie behind a thick clump of reeds. There were fewer trees growing directly adjacent to the river on this bank. Except for the tall grasses, most of the vegetation was low level. Anya crouched as she returned to survey the bank from which they had departed. Tracking back a considerable distance upstream she could just about make out the figures of the visitors in the moonlight. As she strained to focus on the distant shapes, she could tell that they were leaving the position of the encampment and heading back towards their village.

"Do you think that they will try to follow us?" Jadine

already knew the answer to the question that she had posed.

Anya considered their situation. "They live, hunt and fish by the river. Although we have never seen them do so, they must have some means of crossing over. If they do decide to come after us, our head start will be relatively small. They will be able to travel over the ground much faster than us. We should dry our clothes, gather our packs and move on as soon as we can."

"They may assume that we will head downstream, away from their settlement, but if we head upstream, their journey to intercept us would be shorter."

Jodie spoke for the first time since the encounter with the crocodile. "They will follow us, but we must head this way!" She was pointing upstream.

Jadine made a valid point, "If we run, we will not know if they are coming for us or where they are. We will always be looking over our shoulders. If we move up the riverbank and await their next move, we can assess how much of a threat they pose. We might be able to hide from them and put them off our trail."

"We must go that way," Jodie reminded them.

Anya was swayed. "Okay, we will head upstream, but we will stop a short distance away and find some high ground."

"And watch for them coming?"

"Yes. If they come, we will try to stay out of sight. We could never outrun them. We will tread carefully and try to cover our tracks."

"We will be all right," said Jodie. "Don't worry."

Jadine was not convinced, but she nodded anyway.

As they moved up the river, dawn was beginning to break. The sky grew lighter, although the full moon still shone brightly. They had elected to move away from the water's edge, hoping to leave less of a trail for an experienced tracker to follow. They would also be far less visible from the opposite bank.

After walking a considerable distance, they came upon a thick clump of woody palms, hidden from the bank by tall grasses. "Here will do," declared Anya. "We can hide our stuff amongst the palms and watch from the bank over there. If necessary, we could climb up into the tree to hide."

"How long are we going to wait?" enquired Jadine.

"If they don't come by midmorning, I'm sure it would be safe to assume that they are not coming at all. If we reach that point, we can move on safe in the knowledge that they are no longer a threat."

"Or never were? Anyway, that would be good to know. There will undoubtedly be other challenges ahead wherever we go, but it would be one less thing to worry about."

"Jodie, you go with Jadine to the trees. Take the packs and hide them as well as you can. Jadine, ready what weapons we have just in case they are needed. The sun is beginning to rise. I need to go to the river's edge."

Anya crouched as she approached the bank. She drew up behind the tall grasses and river reeds, careful not to disturb the leaves and give her presence away. Anya settled into a comfortable position, seated with her legs stretched out in front. She would have been happy to wait there all day. However, she did not have to sit very long to catch sight of the visitors. A single dugout canoe was being launched from the opposite bank. Onboard were a number of men. She was too far away to make out any detail, but she estimated that there were perhaps four or five on board. As they neared, Anya was able to see their spears being held aloft. She decided to wait for a while before moving. By the time the vessel reached midstream she was confident that they would not launch a second boat. Slowly and calmly, she backed out of her hide, again taking care not to disturb the vegetation and give herself away. Once clear, she ducked her head and raced towards the trees where Jadine and Jodie were waiting.

Jadine had laid her bow out. Next to it was a small collection of arrows. She busied herself using a knife to carve the tips on a number of makeshift arrows fashioned from a collection of sticks that Jodie had collected from around some nearby trees.

Anya arrived breathless and red-faced. "They are coming! A boat on the river! Five of them!"

"I know, Jodie told me."

"But how?"

"Never mind now. Help me with these."

"We don't have long. They will have reached the halfway point by now. Their heading suggests that they will land nearby. Oh, Jadine, what are we going to do? The palms are difficult to climb."

"We will do what we planned. We will hide in here. If they find us, we will do the best we can."

"And Jodie?" Anya's concern for her daughter was apparent.

"We must not let them take her. Whatever happens, do not let them take her."

Anya gulped, but she knew what Jadine meant. Jodie understood, too. She had told Jadine just a short time ago.

12

The two brothers had been sent out with three other tribe members to find the girl. As they approached the bank they discussed their heading.

"They won't have walked along the bank. Not if they have any sense. It would be too easy to track them if they did. I'm sure that they know that we are after them now. Let's head inland a bit and check downriver first. If we pick up their trail, we can take it from there."

"Okay then. This should be easy. Whichever direction they are headed, they can't have got far. Not with a child in tow."

As they neared the lakeshore, two of the men seated at the front leapt out, grabbing a rope secured to the bow. They splattered their way through the mud, unconcerned about the mess that it made. The boat was dragged up behind them once the other three had disembarked. With two per side, they carried their dugout canoe high up onto the bank. They made no attempt to conceal it before running off towards the tree line.

Instinctively, the tribesmen spread out to widen their search pattern. Each member of the team paused occasionally to check for tracks. The tall brother sighted a small clump of trees a short distance away. He lengthened his stride and headed towards them. As he approached, he drew out a long curved knife from the animal skin scabbard suspended from his waist. Ferns and grasses covered the ground. He could see nothing between the trees. Slowly, he made his way through. There were no broken leaves, no signs of intrusion. Moments later, he had emerged on the other side. Before him was an expanse of parched grassland.

It was at this point he wondered if finding them might be more difficult than they had first predicted. It seemed as if they could have set off in another direction.

A short distance across the flood plain was a similar clump of palms. These were a little taller than the ones he had just left. He glanced around. Most of the hunting party was invisible behind him. His brother, it seemed, had chosen to revisit the thicket he recently passed through. The sun had begun to climb high in the sky and it was baking hot. Sweat mixed with sand and mud trickled down his face. He put his knife away, wiped his brow and removed the water flask secured on the other side of his belt. He took a few swigs before replacing it and marching on to inspect his next objective.

There were more palms in this thicket and the ground was covered with low-level vegetation. He picked his way between the trunks, looking for any signs of a recent human visitation. Movement to the left attracted his attention. It was the last thing he would ever see!

* * *

Jadine watched and waited. She could see four of the five hostiles. She recognised the taller brother approaching. Hopefully, he would pass on by. Anya nestled amongst the ferns. She had her long hunting knife and a smaller filleting knife at the ready. Jodie was by her side. Still holding the hunting knife in her right hand she wrapped her arm around her daughter and grasped her tightly. Jadine settled by a thick palm trunk and readied her bow. She selected one of her best arrows and steadied herself. She fought to control her breathing. This is it, she said to herself. Had he seen her? His movement suggested that he was heading their way.

Jadine knew now that she must attack. She waited for a clear shot; one with fewer trees in between her and the target. He was some distance away. She aimed high, adjusting for dip in the flight of the arrow. The taller brother turned to look towards her as she released the string. Her projectile seemed to take an eternity to reach its target. It seemed for a fleeting moment that it was soaring too high. When it struck, it did so with devastating force. The arrow landed squarely in the centre of his left eye socket. It burst through the eyeball and passed straight into the brain. He fell to the ground without a sound.

Anya did not see what had happened, but she deduced from the two distinct sounds what approximated to an accurate account. A whistle followed by a dull thud could only mean one thing. Anya was reassured when Jadine reappeared in her line of vision. Jadine went over to check the body before moving off towards the edge of the tree line. Anya saw her yank the arrow out of the man's skull.

A second pursuer was nearing the thicket. He seemed unconcerned as he approached and did not call out to his friend. Clearly, he had no clue as to what had just taken place. Anya pulled Jodie's head into her chest. Jadine strung a second arrow on her bow. Before her was a narrow corridor leading to the edge of the thicket. She waited for the second man to enter. Let him get closer, a little closer, she repeated to herself. He was now out of view to the outside world. Not too high this time. He is much nearer. The arrow punctured his chest just below his sternum. He dropped to his knees as a crimson tide enveloped his chest. Moments later, he fell face down.

One of the remaining men was shouting and heading towards their position. When he did not hear a response his pace quickened. Jadine loaded her bow again. She allowed him to take three strides beyond the shadows cast by the overhanging foliage before letting go of the bowstring. The shaft tore through the muscle above his left shoulder. Its velocity carried it through and it became embedded in a tree behind. He cried out in pain, clutching his wound. Jadine fumbled for another arrow. She fired again, but missed. Three of her best arrows remained. Her next shot hit him in the throat and brought the third man down where he stood. The two men left behind heard the commotion and came running over. Jadine hastily reloaded. She moved towards the clearing. Her arrow sailed over the head of the nearest man. His right hand launched a spear toward her. It missed by some distance. He drew a knife. Jadine's next shot skimmed past his left arm. One good shaft remained, but he was almost upon her. Quickly, she fired. From a kneeling position, she hit him under the neck, stopping him in his tracks, but her remaining adversary had seen the man fall.

Jadine retreated backwards into the shadows. She could see that the remaining survivor was the smaller of the two brothers who had been present the first time that the men had visited the camp. He was now charging across the open ground toward their wooded hideaway. Jadine waited a short distance inside the tree line, jamming her spear against her foot and raising the tip as a last line of defence. No time to reload the bow. The man had reached the thicket. Suddenly, an arm arced around from behind a tree and a knife was embedded high up in the man's arm. Anya stepped aside, splattered with blood. Anya primed her bow with one of the makeshift arrows. The wounded man now stood before them. Blood was gushing from his wound. Clearly, a major blood vessel had been severed. He acknowledged two of his fallen comrades, but an evil grin remained on his face as he put his own knife between his teeth and pulled the blade from his arm and threw it to the ground. This did little to stem the flow. Anya circled around him to stand by Jadine. He removed the long curved knife from his mouth and coiled his good arm back over his shoulder, ready to strike. However, he advanced no further, content for the time being to enter into a standoff.

"Go and leave us in peace," demanded Anya.

"I need the child, not you."

"You must kill me first!"

"You have no need to take any of us! Walk away now, go back to your village, and we will spare your life," commanded Jadine.

He laughed. "I cannot. What have you done with my brother? Have you killed him, too?"

"Why us? Why Jodie? Why did you have to come after us?" Jadine let out a shriek as she threw her spear at the wounded man.

He dodged to one side and it landed harmlessly in the ground. He laughed again, put his head down and charged towards them, his blade now raised above his head. Jodie's crooked arrow veered off course, but, as the man jumped to clear a bushy fern, it slammed into his thigh. He screamed in agony. He knelt, clasping the shaft. He knew better than to rip it out. He began to sob. Through his tear-stained eyes, he looked up as Anya approached.

"I'm sorry. Please help me," he said. "We just wanted to bring about good fortune. My leg hurts, more so than my arm. Please get my brother." He sat back, with blood cascading down one side of his body and covering the delicate leaves surrounding him. "Please help me!"

"If he makes it, he'll be no further threat to us," said Jadine to Anya. "Give him some water. We'll leave him here. I can't kill this man in cold blood. Not him, not like this."

Anya was controlled. "Go back to your village. Do not attempt to follow us or I will kill you. Do not come after us or we will cast down bad spirits on you and your people and kill every last one of you."

"Thank you. You won't be followed." He tried, unsuccessfully, to stand and fell back to his knees.

"No!" cried a young voice from behind. "He cannot return!"

Jodie plunged the small filleting knife into the side of his neck and he slumped forward, his face hitting the ground with a thud.

13

Jodie seemed all right considering what had just happened. "I couldn't let him go. He would only bring back more of them to chase us."

"It's going to be fine. You did what you felt you had to do. They were bad men, anyway."

Jodie ran to her mother and buried her face in Anya's breasts.

"You were very brave," said Anya.

"What are we going to do now? Surely they will be missed?" It was Jadine who was rationalising.

"Not for a while. For all the others know, we could have set off on a hike up or down the river. They could have gone either way, maybe tracking up to a day in one direction before turning around and going back the other way. I am sure it will be several days before there are any concerns. In the meantime, we should hide the bodies. If they do send out another search party, the sight of their fallen comrades will only spur them on. If we wait until dusk, we can take their boat and slip up the river under the cover of darkness. Also, in doing that, we will leave no trace of where they arrived."

"I'm sure that other villagers would have watched them land here."

"Well, if nothing else, it should confuse them and buy us a bit more time, plus we can travel faster by canoe and we would leave no trail."

"If we head upstream, paddling will be harder and we would not progress as quickly, although Jodie insists we go that way. She has been right about most things lately!"

Anya was thoughtful for a moment. "Jodie, it's odd how sometimes you know what's about to happen, although I can't complain, as it has worked out very well for us so far."

"I can't always see things."

"I'm just glad that you saved us. We will go your way, but, right now, Jadine and I have things to do. Perhaps you could prepare some food?"

"Okay, I can do that." Jodie was happy to be included.

"Stay well away from the riverbank!"

Anya and Jadine contemplated a feast for the crocodiles, but decided that they might not be that hungry, and, anyway, they would miss bits and leave a mess. Burning the evidence wasn't an option, so they decided to hide or bury them. Jadine scouted the area directly behind the thicket that they had previously occupied. She found a steep-sided natural drainage channel where floodwaters had eroded the silt. Anya helped Jadine to drag their victims to the ditch and toss them in. It was hard work in the baking sun and the bodies had already begun to attract flies. Vultures roamed the nearby plains. This would be a dead giveaway to the visitors, so they moved as quickly as their stamina would allow. Once the bodies were in position, it was relatively easy to bury them. The dry, parched earth crumbled easily. They had to do relatively little digging with their makeshift spade as the mud and silt was easily directed on top of them. The sun would dry out the top sand in no time, making it difficult to detect. Jadine used a leafy branch to cover their footprints to good effect. Inevitably, there would be traces of the slaughter in the trees, but Anya used several flasks of water to wash away the blood as best she could.

In all this madness, Jodie had laid out some food on giant palm leaves. They could not risk refilling their flasks at the river's edge until after dark. However, a little more water had to be sacrificed in order to wash the blood and dirt from their hands before they ate. Jodie had grown up very quickly that day. Preparing the food had been a worthwhile distraction from the horror of it all.

* * *

It was now late afternoon. They had packed all of their possessions, including some items stolen from the visitors, and had readied themselves for another departure. Jadine now sported a long, curved knife held in a scabbard on her thigh. From time to time, Jadine and Anya had taken turns to creep down to the riverbank and survey the opposite bank from behind the reeds. Each time they had done so, they were relieved to find that no one was coming. Anya went through a mental checklist. "We need to wipe away any traces of our presence here. No remains of any kind, no footprints, no food scraps. Nothing is to be left behind."

Taking care to keep out of sight, they spent the final hours before dusk tidying the site.

The sunset was stunning. Blue hues merged and passed towards violet as reds and oranges reflected off the underside of a few passing clouds. Once the spectrum of vibrant colours had disappeared, the wait for total darkness was agonisingly long, but they could not risk being spotted.

Anya directed the evacuation. "Jodie, you carry what you can down to the canoe. Jadine, you bring the weapons and other heavier items. It should still float okay. It carried five of them here. Take care not to disturb the vegetation. I will take this pack and ready the boat."

Anya found the boat as the visitors had left it. Inside were four oars. She put the large pack in the middle of the canoe before turning the vessel so that the bow faced the water. A crude bench ensured that their possessions did not dip into the water lining the bottom of the hull. Anya glanced over towards the muddy shoreline. There were many footprints and, soon, there would be a few smaller ones. Jadine and Jodie arrived carrying the remainder of their cargo.

"Wait," said Anya. "Put the things in the canoe. Jodie, you get in. Jadine, help me push it down the bank. Try not to step off the grass. I will drag it across to the water's edge with you both inside. I will do my best to cover the tracks. Let's hope the crocodiles do the rest! "

Once again, Anya struggled to cross the mud. Fortunately, the smooth, flat-bottomed hull slid down to the water with ease. She used the current to flip the boat around, holding onto the rope and using it as a pivot. Before climbing aboard, she splashed water as far as she could to cover her footprints and filled her flask. Holding onto the hull two thirds of the way forward, Anya waded out into the river. Jadine moved to the opposite side in an attempt to counterbalance Anya's momentum, but, despite her efforts, Anya nearly flipped the canoe over as she hauled herself aboard. Jodie sat in the middle, Jadine at the stern and Anya took her place near the bow. An oar was deployed at either side. They turned the unsteady vessel around and headed upstream.

14

Progress was slow at first. Anya and Jadine were not used
to paddling a canoe. Fortunately, the lack of recent rainfall
meant that although they had to paddle upstream, there was
little current to contend with. Not wishing to pass directly
by the crocodiles that inhabited the river's shore, or to risk
hitting a sandbank or even a rock, they headed out a short
distance from the bank. However, the nearer they went to
the other bank, the greater the risk of being spotted by the
visitors. Anya had insisted upon absolute silence. In many
ways, they were fortunate that the clouds that had
contributed earlier to such a spectacular sunset had gathered
in greater numbers in order to obscure the moonlight. It
made navigating somewhat difficult, but at least it meant
they would be very difficult to spot.

Gradually, they began to find their rhythm and as the
canoe glided silkily across the calm water, their pace
quickened. As they rounded a slight kink in the river, they
were just able to make out a faint glow from a small
campfire located beyond the opposite bank. Anya wanted
to hold her breath, but she needed all the air she could suck
into her lungs to maintain their speed. Jadine and Anya
crouched down to lower their profile, even though the
village was a considerable distance away. Even Jodie was
relieved once the distant glow started to recede behind
them.

Now that their spirits had lifted, they turned their

attention to their future plans.

"Jadine, if we paddle on through the night, we should put a considerable distance between us and our pursuers. We could rest for a while, or take turns to paddle solo. What do you think?"

"I am happy to take turns. If we only make slow progress, it will be better than none at all."

"I could always help row," added Jodie.

"You might blister your hands," warned Jadine.

"I'll be okay if I take it easy."

"How far will we travel on the water? I mean, are we planning to ditch the canoe at some stage and continue on foot?"

"Let's just see. Although we're heading upstream, the current is slow now, and I think, overall, we are making better progress than we would on foot. Besides, Jodie's strides are shorter than ours."

"But I don't tire too easily," added Jodie.

"You have to admit, this is easier on the feet. It also feels safer, even at night. We have to mind the crocs, but nobody is going to jump out and ambush us here."

"Where are we heading? We have no idea what lies beyond this area. I hope that there are no tribes like the last one."

Anya tried to be optimistic. "Whatever lies ahead, it has to be better than what we have just left behind. We'll try to be ready for anything. Let's face it, we are a little vulnerable. We need to settle somewhere that we feel safe, somewhere that provides for all our needs."

"We will find our way," said Jodie. "I'm not sure what lies at the end of our journey, but I think that we are heading for a good place."

"How can you be so confident?"

"Sometimes I see things in my dreams. I'm not always sure that they will come true. I guess that sometimes they really are only dreams. Other times, I just have thoughts that I think will turn out to be real. If I try too hard, though, I can't usually see anything. It's best not to think about things too much."

"I see!" said Anya, although she didn't.

"It's like I get ideas, or even pictures, sometimes."

"Hmmm."

"Other times, I imagine someone talking to me. Sort of like a clever voice in my head."

"Yes, well, don't listen to it all the time! Your mother also knows a thing or two."

* * *

The sun was still well hidden below the horizon, but the black of night was once again beginning to give way to shades of deep blue. Jadine was napping whilst Anya continued to paddle. A stroke on one side and then the other. Jodie assisted by dipping her paddle in the water from time to time. The river had narrowed noticeably, but it was still a considerable distance from bank to bank. As dawn arrived, the landscape on either side began to change. Dense, impenetrable jungle gave way to parched grassland and rocky promontories. In no time, the sun's rays sought to combine with the high humidity to produce conditions so oppressive that Anya could no longer continue.

"We need to find some shade," said Anya, as she headed towards a sandstone outcrop that formed a natural jetty.

Jadine was barely awake. "What?"

"It's getting too hot to be out paddling in the sun. Jodie's hungry; we need to stop and rest up. If you help me get the canoe out of the water, we can shelter under that solitary palm."

Anya hopped out whilst Jadine steadied the canoe, then

Jodie and Jadine did the same whilst Anya reciprocated the favour. Together, they hauled the boat out of the water. After walking a short distance, they settled down under the tree and ate some of the food that they had brought with them. Anya's eyelids were heavy and, soon, she drifted off into a peaceful sleep.

It was past midday, and all three had rested.

"We should move on," suggested Jodie.

Anya was unsure if Jodie's statement was a product of another precognitive vision or simple foresight and common sense.

Either way, it did not matter as Anya agreed. "Yes, there is a bit of a breeze in the air now, so it should be a little cooler on the water."

"What's the plan, then?" asked Jadine, not for the first time.

"We should carry on as far up the river as we can get. When we near the source, the landscape should improve. Heavy rains must have created this vast expanse of water. Hopefully, we will find everything we need to settle once again."

"But that could mean travelling a huge distance!"

"We have the time and little else to do!"

Jodie interrupted, "I'm not sure we will find what we are looking for at the source of the river, but let's go and see anyway!"

"At least we have a little food and plenty of water. Later on, we could try to catch some more fresh fish," suggested Anya.

* * *

The trio continued their journey, battling with the fierce heat as they went. They spent three more days and nights on, or close by, the mighty river. The landscape had changed. At either side, there was a distinct absence of a fertile flood plain. A great desert stretched out around them. Huge red-brown sand dunes stretched as far as the eye could see. Every hour or so, at least one of them looked over their shoulder half expecting to see their pursuers. They now realised that it would be virtually impossible for anyone to track them by land. However, they were still concerned about their attackers; a team of determined men would be able to travel across the water much faster than they could paddle and perhaps catch up with them. They assumed that despite their efforts to hide the bodies of the men that they had slaughtered, it was a question of when, not if, they would be found. Anya had no way of knowing beyond her own imagination how they would react to discovering that two women and a girl had killed five athletic young men from their tribe.

On the fifth day of their river expedition, they awoke to the spectacular sight of a distant electrical storm. Forks of lightening arced across a darkened sky. They could just make out muffled claps of thunder.

They set off upstream as they had done on previous days. Although such weather was infrequent, it did not overly concern them. A short time later, the rumble of thunder got louder.

"It looks like we are heading towards this storm," remarked Anya, "or should I say that it is heading towards us."

"If it is, we should find a place to take shelter," stated Jadine. "We do not want to be caught out on the open water in a torrential downpour. Besides, the river might rise and cause the current to quicken."

"I think it may pass across us. Look, there are mountains in the distance!" Anya pointed towards the horizon.

"Yes, I see them. Perhaps that is where the river

begins."

"Probably! Let's watch it for a while. We should be able to tell which way the storm is heading. We'll keep paddling for now."

"Okay."

The display continued for half the morning. Angry rods of rain grazed across the sky from left to right. The thunderclaps grew even louder, but not a single drop of rain fell on their canoe.

The river had narrowed significantly and was now characterised by kinks, turns and eroded banks that were once again bordered by lush vegetation. The current had quickened, making progress much more difficult. As they rounded a curve they were greeted by a new sound. At first, they strained to discern what it was and therefore they were unsure of its origin. Gradually, it grew in volume as they neared the source. One more turn and they could see it in all its glory. Towering before them was an enormous waterfall. The river widened out to reveal a gigantic plunge pool into which vast volumes of water cascaded from the wide sandstone cliff above.

"Clearly, we cannot navigate that," stated Jadine.

Jodie smiled. "Wow... We'll have to go around it, won't we?"

"We can't climb those cliffs, either. We'll have to head inland and see if we can find a way past."

It was Anya's turn. "If we go up onto the bank, we can camp for the night and contemplate our next move. We just don't want to stay too near to all that noise and spray. Which side?" Anya was viewing both of the banks alternatively.

It was Jodie who answered, indicating that they should go to the right. "That way; we should go that way."

"There is a small clearing over there in front of the trees," said Anya, pointing out a crescent-shaped line of palms adjacent to the bank. "We can easily haul the canoe out of the water and hide it somewhere."

"Why not?" The rhetorical question came from Jadine. "I'm not sure that it matters, but, if Jodie prefers to head that way, then we might as well follow her advice. She's been right so far."

They were already steering the canoe towards the riverbank. Anya grabbed at the loose orange earth on the bank and hauled herself out. She helped Jodie and then Jadine to get out of the boat. They emptied it before hauling it out of the water. They dragged it a short distance into the trees and settled the canoe into a natural hollow. Whilst Jadine unpacked their belongings a short distance away, Anya busied herself collecting fallen palm leaves and other vegetation to hide the boat.

Their temporary camp was far enough away from the waterfall to remain dry, but they could not escape the continuous rumble of the falls. However, the view more than made up for the noise. Jadine surveyed it from the waters edge. Nearby was a shoal of long, narrow fish, most being about an arm in length. Quickly, she collected her spear. Holding it near the end of the shaft, she thrust it towards the nearest fish with both speed and accuracy. It passed through the fish near the tail end. It flapped as she drew it towards her. It would make a tasty meal.

"Look!" said Jodie, pointing at two canoes travelling upriver.

Still holding the spear with the fish on the end, Jadine whirled around to see twelve men, six in each canoe, heading their way.

15

Anya came tearing out of the trees to see what the commotion was about. Jadine used her foot to force the fish off the tip that had just taken its life. Then she ran for her bow. She only had eight arrows left at most and many of these were hastily made and substandard.

"What are we going to do? There are too many to fight this time and they've seen us."

"Gather whatever you can carry. We need to run and hide." Anya was forceful with her instructions.

The pursuers came within range. Jadine shot off her arrows one after another. The first two missed the vessels completely, but sent their occupants into a frenzy. They appeared to have only knives and spears. The third arrow slammed into the shoulder of the man at the front of the nearest boat, making him topple over his fellow crewmen and capsizing the boat, sending them sprawling into the water. Two of the men in the second boat hurled spears in their direction, but they fell well short. The occupants of the surviving boat seemed divided between helping their fellow tribesmen and pursuing the women. Jadine fired off a few more of her remaining arrows, hitting another one of the boatmen, this time in the leg.

Anya grabbed her hand. "Come on, we must go now."

The two canoes were side by side. The first one was now righted. Some men were helping others out of the water. In unison, those in and on the water and the three women on the bank stopped abruptly and looked up towards the top of the falls. There was a deafening roar as a huge surge of water charged over the top of the cliff face. Anya scooped Jodie off the ground. Jadine grabbed what she could from the belongings around them as they raced away from the river.

When the water from the cliff face hit the plunge pool, it caused a momentary depression sending water up and over the banks in both directions. The flow was unrelenting and an enormous wave swept down the river. The men in the canoes were powerless. The water smashed the boats into pieces, their occupants being swept under the surface, and then away with the current. Several of the pursuers tried in vain to grab the bank, but the sustained surge smashed them against the rocks, they were hit by debris, and, inevitably, the water took their bodies into its midst.

Anya held Jodie tight to her chest. She ran after Jadine who was heading through the trees, away from the deadly floodwaters. They were heading diagonally away from the river and towards a safer part of the sandstone rock face. As they neared elevation and safety, a knee-deep torrent of water hit them, knocking them off their feet. Anya dropped Jodie, who fell face first into the muddy water. Jadine grabbed Jodie's hand and pulled her up as she coughed and spluttered to clear her airway. Branches and debris slammed into them as they tried to gain their footing. One of Jadine's animal-skin sacks was swept away, but she made no attempt to follow it. Somehow, they were able to stand, bracing themselves against the current. Anya had managed to re-gather Jodie. They remained still for a moment, adjusting to the force, and then they began to shuffle forward, towards a collection of large rocks at the bottom of the cliff face. The body of a goat rushed towards them. It slammed into Jadine, and knocked her over once again.

Anya reached the rock face, climbing in between two

large boulders. She thrust Jodie up onto one of them before turning to help Jadine.

"Here, grab my hand."

Jadine was clearly limping. "My leg, I think the goat might have broken my fucking leg!"

Anya waded back towards Jadine. On reaching her, she hooked Jadine's right arm around her left shoulder and neck in an attempt to take the weight off the injured leg.

"Thank you, Anya."

"Oh, it's nothing! Always glad to help!"

Gradually, they made their way to where Jodie was waiting.

"Do you think any of the others survived?"

"I doubt it, but, if one or two did, I'm sure that chasing us would now be the last thing on their minds."

"Maybe you are right, but they would find it hard to return to the village having been defeated by us once again."

"We did not defeat them; nature did!"

"But I do not think their elders would believe the truth."

Jodie interrupted their conversation, "Don't worry; I am sure they are all gone now. I saw it, but I did not fully understand what I was seeing. It all makes sense now. The men who were chasing us are all dead. They will not risk sending any more."

"Okay, Jodie, I believe what you are saying, but that still leaves us out here in this, and now Jadine has hurt herself."

"Hurt myself?" Jadine was feeling her leg. A slight gash was visible just above her right knee. "It was a goat!" She had time for a wry smile. "But I don't think that it is broken. Lucky, I guess."

"Can you climb?" Anya wanted to get them to safety as soon as possible.

"I'm not sure; just give me a moment. It's probably just

badly bruised."

As the water continued to surge across the flood plain, Anya, Jadine and Jodie clawed their way up towards the plateau above. When they neared the top, they stopped to survey the scene below. The river had swallowed up a vast tract of land on either side. Trees had been uprooted and dragged to random locations. Dotted here and there were the bodies of a number of large animals that had been unable to escape the surging waters. Amongst them were several human bodies from the boats that had pursued them.

Once they had clambered over the top, they could finally see what lay before them. The landscape was bleak and desolate. Towards the horizon was an imposing mountain range. Orange and brown stacks jutted towards the sky, displaying very few signs of vegetation. The river tracked towards them cutting out its path through the bedrock across an inhospitable plain littered with large rocks and boulders of a similar appearance to the peaks beyond. The ground on the other side of the river was very much the same, but immediately to the right of their position, rocks gradually gave way to sand and dunes. As they gazed beyond these, the vista revealed the very tops of a clump of tall palms.

"Phew, that was hard," said Jodie. "I thought we would never get to the top. Are you okay, Jadine?"

"I'm fine, Jodie. The climb has loosened it up a bit." Jadine lifted the rag that she had tied around her leg to stem the flow of blood to see underneath. "It seems to have stopped bleeding now."

"Maybe we should rest here for the remainder of the day," suggested Anya. "I don't like the look of those mountains – very barren. Mind you, none of it looks too promising, compared to the river basin below."

"I think we should head out that way." Jodie was pointing to the dunes.

"It's just a vast desert out there. We'll fry in the heat and our water will run out in no time."

"No we won't; see, there are trees! Where there are trees there must be...."

"Water, I know, but we can't survive off just one oasis."

"Oh, I'm sure that there will be more. You'll see!"

"I'm not sure yet if we will, but we can't go back. I'm convinced that this region floods on a fairly regular basis and that we have not seen anywhere worth settling in the last few nights. Besides, we couldn't settle within the range of those tribespeople."

"So, we have to move on," stated Jadine.

"Okay. Let's walk over to the river and get some fresh water."

Their attention then turned to what they had managed to salvage. Jadine had a water flask slung over her shoulder. A large hunting knife was still tethered to her side, but her bow was gone, as was the fishing equipment and their cooking utensils. Over the other shoulder was a carrying bag, still dripping from the soaking it had received below.

"I have some food in here. I'll see what I can salvage. Maybe I can wash it off and we can eat it soon."

"I only managed to grab this small bag of spare clothes. I think there is a sleeping cover in here, though. We need to dry them. You fill the water flask and I'll lay these out." Anya was good at giving concise instructions when required.

"Jodie, do you want to help?" Jadine thought that Jodie should be included.

"Can I go down to the river with you?"

"Okay, but you have to be careful over the rocks. That surge will have made them wet and slippery. We don't want to risk another injury!"

Anya had a new plan. "If we are going to head out into

the desert, we need to load our bodies with water and head out just before dusk. We should be able to make it to those palms before the light runs out completely. We'll camp there overnight."

16

The hot, soft sand made for heavy going and, consequently, progress was slow. They reached the desert oasis a considerable time after darkness had descended. Fortunately, the glow from the moon silhouetted the trees against the horizon to guide them in. Their haven was situated in a natural basin in the middle of a dune field. Moonlight reflected off the surface of a small pool in the centre. All around the perimeter were tall palms, with smaller bushier varieties growing adjacent to the water. They had just enough energy to tear off a few palm leaves to bed down on. Exhausted, they all fell asleep almost instantly.

* * *

Jodie awoke in the dome. Now that she was finally there, she felt much more comfortable than she had on previous visits. There were no menacing entities nearby. She was in a bright, white room with no openings or portals of any kind. The room was empty, save for the soft, smooth mantle that she was sleeping on. At the far end of the room an image appeared filled with black, white and grey fuzzy dots. The dots began to arrange themselves into an image. The picture became a face. A strange face that somehow seemed unreal. "Hello, Jodie! If you come here, you will find sanctuary. Don't worry about the other things you have seen here.

They exist to protect us and keep this paradise safe from those who would seek to destroy it. They will not harm you. If you come here, you will gain knowledge beyond your wildest imagination. You will want for nothing. You will never be hungry again, and you will find companionship and comfort. You are most welcome to join us here. All you have to do is follow your instinct."

* * *

Jodie opened her eyes. She stared up at the interwoven triangles on the bark of the palm near her feet. A small gecko was on its way down having just eaten a mosquito. It was a hot and humid morning.

Anya and Jadine were already awake and bathing naked in the nearby pool. Their tanned skins had darkened on the journey. They would never normally spend so much time exposed to the heat of the midday sun. Jadine was slightly slimmer, taller and more athletic than Anya. Her breasts were small, pert and noticeably firmer. Unlike many of the women of their region, both had always worn garments that helped to support their figure.

They splashed at each other as they washed. It had been a while since they had indulged in any kind of fun. It developed into something of a water fight. Jadine advanced towards Anya moving as quickly as the resistance around her feet would allow. As she went, Jadine used both hands to scoop water and hurl it towards Anya. As she got nearer, Jadine lost her footing. Anya tried to catch her as she fell to one side, but ended up falling on top of Jadine. They both laughed at each other's antics. Jadine gave her a hug as they picked themselves up.

Suddenly, four heads appeared over the rim of the basin. Two were human, preceded by the heads of two large animals on which they rode. Jodie had never seen these

strange creatures before. They were light brown in colour
and their riders were astride saddles on a huge hump. Every
feature was exaggerated. It had long eyelashes, a big mouth
and large, flat hooves. Jodie noted that it seemed well suited
to negotiating the sand.

They rode straight towards Anya and Jadine, their arms
and hands raised, seemingly in a gesture of peace. The two
women raced to gather up their clothes. Anya sat and
hurried to cover herself. Jadine remained standing, but fell
over in her haste, banging her injured leg as she went. She
cursed to herself as she finished dressing. She adjusted the
bandage on her leg before rising to meet their guests. Jodie
sprinted over to join them.

The men laughed as they approached. One of them
spoke first to the other, and then to the three women in a
language that Jodie did not understand. As they neared,
Jodie cast her gaze over the strange appearance of the two
men. Both were draped in cool white robes secured with red
rope bands. Comparable garments covered their heads. Both
men were similar in appearance. Jodie thought that the man
who had just spoken had a kind expression. He looked
different from any man who Jodie had seen before, yet
somehow, he had a certain familiarity. Like his companion,
he had dark russet skin, with lines etched into his face from
many years' exposure to wind, sun and sand. They both
sported black and grey beards making them appear many
years older than Jodie's mother, but it was difficult to gauge
their exact age. At their sides, they wore long, curved
swords. The handles were brightly decorated, encrusted
with red and green polished stones. They wore long,
pointed black boots embroidered with red thread in a similar
design to that on the saddles. Anya looked at them
quizzically.

The first man spoke again. "Hello, I am Jed, this is
Zack, and what, may I ask, brings you here? Where are you

from?"

There was a momentary pause before Anya answered, "We have travelled across the land and upriver; we lived many days away."

"Are you alone?"

Anya looked around. "Er, yes, there is nobody with us now."

"Why do you do this?" He paused for a moment. "Pardon. What I meant to ask is where are the men who should be protecting you?"

"We can look after ourselves, thank you!"

"I am sure that you can, but it is unusual for two women and a young girl to be so far away from their people."

"We have no people! All of them were slaughtered. We are the only survivors of our community."

He shook his head and lowered it in sadness. "These lands have become very dangerous. I stand by what I say; it is not safe for you to travel alone. Especially if you choose to expose yourselves in such a way!" He was laughing again as he made an open-handed gesture towards the pool.

Blood rushed to Anya's cheeks and neck, but she remained serious, ignoring Jed's remarks. "Yes, we have seen for ourselves. A tribe that, at first, tried to befriend us later attempted to take my daughter. They pursued us upriver as far as the cliff face."

"And where are they now?"

"We were fortunate. There was a great torrent of floodwater after the storms and it took them."

"God be praised. He looks after you. You must have done something good in your lives. May I ask you where you are heading?"

Anya looked at Jadine, not entirely sure how to answer. They certainly did not want to reveal the fact that they were following the visions of a young girl to a place as yet unknown. Jadine spoke for them. "We were hoping to travel across the desert, far away from the river, in order to find a new place to settle."

Zack now joined in. "Moving across the desert is very difficult. It is hot and, from here on in, there is very little water. You will only find some if you know where to dig, and I doubt that you are equipped to do that."

"What lies beyond the desert?"

"The desert is vast. Our people are nomads. We are able to survive because we have camels and skills that have been passed down through many generations. We generally stay within its boundaries. It might seem like a difficult existence, but we are able to live our lives in peace. Nobody bothers us here."

Jed added his own comments, "From time to time, we go up into the mountains for a while, but we never venture over to the far side of the wilderness. Strange things are said to happen there."

"Such as?" asked Jodie.

"Ah, my little one. There are things we cannot understand and do not want to. We are a simple people who have survived for thousands of years in this way."

Jodie was not convinced that Jed had answered her question, but she knew that she was unlikely to get a better response. Instead, she decided to pose another. "Are you going to hurt us?"

Jed and Zack both laughed again and shook their heads. They did not seem embarrassed at Jodie's bluntness.

Zack answered, "We are a compassionate people who believe in an almighty God. It is not God's will for us to strike down our fellow man. We accept as true that we will have an afterlife and that we will profit only if we live good lives here in our mortal world."

"So that's a 'no' then!" Jodie chuckled and everyone joined in.

"What brings you here, I mean now, if you don't mind me asking?" enquired Anya.

"To get some good water," said Jed, pointing to several large containers tethered to the side of his animal, "and to check things out. We heard the storm from some distance away, but we never expected that it would bring visitors with it!"

"We are just passing through. We do not want to trouble you," stated Anya. "We will be on our way soon enough, and don't worry, we will not settle in your desert." She smiled as she ended her sentence.

"As I said, life is hard in this environment, but you would be most welcome if you wanted to stay."

"It seems that our options for travel are limited, so, if you could point us in the right direction, we will brave the journey to the far side of this desolate tract."

"I am not sure that such an undertaking would be wise," said Jed, "but we will do what we can to assist you if you are certain that this is a journey that you must complete."

"Thank you."

"Our families expect us to be away for no more than two days. There is a narrowing in the dune field near to a dry riverbed. There is an old building there, and I know we can find water nearby. We can take you there in just over a day if we push on. When we arrive, we will point you on a heading that should take you where you want to go."

"Do you want to collect your water, then?"

"Yes, of course."

Jadine interrupted, "My name is Jadine. This is Anya and Jodie."

Jed dismounted. "I am very pleased to meet you." He shook Jadine's hand before going on to greet Anya and, finally, Jodie. "I can tell that you are the special one! May God watch over you!"

Zack followed Jed in making the acquaintance of the

three women, and although he seemed slightly less enthusiastic, he was pleasant enough.

"May we help you fill your water carriers, then?"

* * *

They did not linger at the oasis. Jed was keen to press on. Anya and Jodie rode with Jed, Jadine with Zack. The men had helped the women to tie cloths around their heads to protect them from the sun's burning rays. Nevertheless, the heat was still almost unbearable. The camels seemed relatively slow across the sands, but, with their long-reaching legs, they made good progress. As the sun began to set, the sand turned red, accentuating the ripples that covered the surface of the dunes. The sky was a deep violet and the large crescent moon had already begun its elliptical pathway above the horizon. As they crested a peak, Anya could make out a clump of three or four palms in the centre of a small, flat and sandy plain.

"We will rest here during the hours of darkness. There is water if we dig. We need to save the supply that we have brought from the spring." Jed indicated by pointing.

When they reached the tiny oasis, Jed and Zack made the camels kneel so that they could all dismount, then, as all three girls guzzled down some of the water that they had brought with them, Zack tied the animals to one of the palms.

"No need to make a bed," said Jed as he motioned towards the ground. "Just sleep here."

Unexpectedly, Anya wondered if Jed would want to sleep next to her, but then she thought of Keon and felt very guilty. Zack dug down to get some more water for them all to share. After eating some dried fruit that the men had brought with them, Anya nestled down in the sand with Jadine on one side of her and Jodie on the other. The men kept a respectable distance.

"Do you think that these two are for real?" whispered Jadine. "Their generosity seems too good to be true."

"Yes, I do. Not all men are bad!"

"Shush, keep your voice down!"

"Okay. I just think that they have an honourable code that they live by. They have not been tainted by the world's past events."

"I hope that you are right. Jodie seems comfortable with them. That must be a good sign."

Jodie had already fallen asleep.

"For someone so young, I think she sees the bigger picture."

"Anya, what do you mean?"

"I think that she is determined to get somewhere. Maybe she sees Jed and Zack as a means to an end, so to speak."

"Clearly, she senses things that we can't. If they did intend to harm us, I would think that she would not have agreed to go with them."

"She asked them directly, didn't she? Perhaps she could tell the truth by the way that they answered."

"Perhaps…."

It was still dark when they were awoken by Zack saddling up the camels.

Jed came over to hurry them along. "We should go now. If we move on under the cool of the moon, our animals will make light work of the sand. It will be better for us, too."

"Will you still be able to navigate in the dark?" asked Jadine.

"The stars, the moon and our God will help us. You can rest at our journey's end."

"We will place our trust in you, then."

"I know, you already have!" Jed smiled.

Zack had coaxed the camels down, and once in the

saddle , they covered their heads and departed.

Another beautiful sky heralded the coming of dawn. The day grew hotter, but the morning passed without event. They paused occasionally to take a sip of water, but Jed was determined for them to push on so that they made their deadline. By early afternoon, a breeze began to blow from the south. Sand and dust whipped across the ridges of the dunes. Patterns on the sandy surface changed continually.

Jed turned to Anya. He seemed concerned. "I think that we might be in for one of our desert storms. Pull this right down over your face to protect your eyes. Help young Jodie with hers. Zack will be telling Jadine to do the same. As long as it does not get too severe, we will push on. Anyway, if we stay still for too long, we run the risk of being buried. The sands shift quickly under these conditions."

"As long as you know where you're going, I'll be fine."

Within no time, the sand was being tossed around by the wind with such vigour that visibility was down to a few paces, but still they pushed on. Jodie had covered her head completely. She was gently swaying with the movement of the camel and found herself in a trance-like state. She was in one of her 'daydreams', imagining that they had reached a vast desert oasis, a true utopia.

She had lots of friends her own age. Her father was there, even Remy. Everyone got on with their neighbours. Food and water were plentiful, and a massive wall surrounded their paradise that would withstand even the most determined attack by the visitors. They had found the true Fartherland foretold by their ancestors and life was beginning again in earnest.

Jodie was drawn from her fantasy when her camel stopped and she could hear Jed trying to shout something to her mother. They wind was so loud now that she had to strain to hear what he was saying.

"It is here in front. We have arrived."

Jodie pulled apart the slit in her veil and half closed her eyes to protect herself from the force of the storm. At first, all she could see was the swirling sand, but, as vast dust clouds began to shift, she could just make out one end of what appeared to be a huge stone structure. The flying debris was too much to see any more. Jodie pulled down the shroud and opted to wait until she could see.

A short time later, she felt herself being lifted down, presumably by Jed. The howling wind abruptly stopped and the light inside her veil dimmed. They were inside a building.

II
Not Going Back

17

Jodie uncovered her head. The first thing she noticed was the smell.

"Pooh! It smells in here."

"Ah, the bat droppings. Not good," said Zack.

"If we move further up the building, things will get better," said Jed.

They were in a vast entrance chamber. There were piles of rubble everywhere, and a deep layer of sand covered the floor. Exposed sandstone masonry made up most of the walls. However, here and there were areas that still retained their original decorative facade. Carved into the stone were symbols, birds, exotic animals, rams and stylised views of people. Some still retained inlaid colours, with ochre being the predominant shade. At the far end of the vestibule was a very large, but badly damaged statue, apparently depicting a human form with the head of a beast. Around the base plinth were more inscriptions. Further along the room there were two more similar structures, each in a worse state of repair than the previous. Fragments of them and other debris were lying all around. Much of the stone roof was still intact, but noise from the wind and swirling sand suggested that the adjacent chamber was less intact. At the far end were stone stairs, apparently leading to a higher level and rooms or chambers above.

As they headed towards the steps, the smell of bat dung diminished somewhat. Anya and Jadine removed their protective robes. It was warm and humid, but noticeably cooler than outside. Anya sat on the bottom step and looked down at her arms. As a result of holding tightly onto Jodie, Anya's forearms had been laid bare to the elements. Her skin was not just darker then ever, it had also been burnt by the sun and blasted by the sand. She realised they were, indeed, quite sore.

Jed noticed, too. "You should not expose your arms for a day or two. More of the same would make things much, much worse and you would then risk infection and fever."

Zack seemed reluctant to settle for even a moment. "We must leave soon. Our families will soon begin to worry."

"But what about the sandstorm?" asked Jadine.

"It is not so bad now. Such storms are common in this part of the desert. Once we distance ourselves, I expect to see an improvement."

Jed joined in. "We are used to travelling in such conditions. Do not fear, for God will watch over us."

"Won't you just stay and rest for a while?" Anya persisted.

"No. As Zack says, we need to rendezvous as expected and, if we stay too long, our animals will think that they have finished for the day and get lazy on us."

"Okay, so where should we head now?"

Jed surveyed Anya's face as if trying to read her thoughts. "If I can persuade you to change your mind, you could accompany us back to our settlement. Please, it's not too late; come with us. Let's turn around. With God's help, we can look after you."

Anya did not contemplate Jed's request for too long before responding, "Jed, we hardly know you. Thank you for your kind offer, but we need to reach our destination. We have made it this far and events have proven that we are able to take care of ourselves."

Jed glanced at Zack. "It seems like your mind is set."

"Yes, it is. All we ask is that you point us in the right direction."

"Then please stay here and rest a while. A day or two's recuperation will do no harm. When the storm dies down, you will see some palms to the rear of the building. Dig down and you will find water. Only when you are fit and rested should you head west. Follow the light of the brightest star when it rises in the early evening sky. It will move across the sky, so you must fix the original heading. Use the tops of large dunes as reference points. Three days' travel should take you near to where you want to be. Take plenty of water, but do not overburden yourself, as this would make walking even more difficult in this barren wasteland."

Jed and Zack were already looking to exit the building.

"Thank you for helping us," said Anya.

"Yes, thank you," added Jadine.

"You are most welcome."

Jodie ran forward and as Jed and Zack bent towards her, she jumped up in between them and hugged them both at the same time before running back towards her mother and Jadine.

"May the great almighty one be with you," declared Jed, who was now some distance away. "If you cannot hear Him, listen to the little one. She will help you find your way."

"Goodbye," shouted Anya, feeling rather perplexed about Jed's last comment. "I hope that we will see you again one day."

"That is very unlikely," muttered Zack, very much to himself.

18

The building and its remains were there to be explored, though the light would soon be fading. Anya and Jodie took a quick tour of the ground floor whilst Jadine climbed the stairs to discover what lay above.

Jodie seemed impressed. "I have never seen such a large building. Is it very old?"

"Me neither. I think that it dates back to a time long ago, way before established civilisation, before the time of machines, before our people even existed."

"Wow. How come it is still standing?"

"It looks very solid. I don't think that it has been used for its intended purpose for many, many years."

"And what would that have been?"

"Probably a place of worship. I think that these people built such great structures to talk to their gods."

"Do we have a god?"

"No, I don't think so. Our people have always lived off the land. They have made good fortune for themselves by hard work. I do not believe that praying to an unseen god would have prevented the terrible fates that befell us."

"Are all these pictures of different gods?" Jodie was pointing to more faded inscriptions on the wall.

"Perhaps, these people may have worshipped many different gods. Others revere only one."

"Sometimes, I see things in my dreams. There are often people there, but there are no gods. At least, I don't think there are."

"Do you think that you can see the future? What exactly do you see?"

"Often, I'm not sure. I dream about many things that I do not understand. Some things I see only once; other visions come to me again and again. Lately, I have even seen my father, or, at least, his image."

Sadness spread across Anya's face when Keon was mentioned. "What do you dream about most often?"

"I see where we are going; at least, I think I do, but often the dream is slightly different. Sometimes it's a bit scary; lately, it gives me hope."

"That's good. Even if we do not have gods or religion, we all need a little hope. This place that we are heading towards, what does it look like?"

"Oh, it's a dome, somewhere near the edge of the desert."

"What's inside, then?"

"I'm not sure. It changes often."

"I see... Maybe one day soon we will be able to find out for ourselves." Anya was a little more sceptical than Jadine when it came to Jodie's gift.

"Oh, I'm sure we will," replied Jodie.

"Wherever we go, we won't be leaving here so soon. Come on, let's go and find Jadine."

* * *

"Jadine!" shouted Anya. "Where are you?"

"Through here."

There were only a few long, slender openings on the inside wall, and the light outside was beginning to dim. Anya strained to see what lay ahead. When she stepped forward, she felt deep sand under her feet.

"Where?" As her eyes adjusted, Anya saw the room

before her. Though smaller than the one below, it was still
sufficiently large to house many families within. In the far
wall was a narrow doorway. Jadine was standing within its
frame.

"There is another room through here with a stairway at
the end leading off to one side. Below is a sheltered
courtyard, but the wind is still blowing in. It feels safe up
here, though, and there is very little rubble in the soft sand.
I think it would make a good place to settle for the night."

"I'll get our things, then. Jodie, you stay here with
Jadine. I don't want you risking a fall."

"We don't have very much food left."

"There is nothing we can do till morning, and then we
can't be sure of a good meal."

"Then we'll just have to ration what we have."

                          * * *

It was now past sunset and the wind continued to blow
hard outside. All three were exhausted. They had eaten a
little and were now settled in the far room. There was
nothing combustible and with no natural light it was almost
pitch-black. Anya began to wonder if staying in this first
floor room was such a good idea.

"Just sit tight," she said, as much to herself as Jodie.

However, Jadine was right in one respect. The warm
sand was very comfortable.

Jadine sat up and screamed. Her arm flicked out and
tossed whatever was crawling over her against the opposite
wall. Anya had just begun to fall asleep. "What was that?"

"A scorpion or spider, I think."

"Come on, let's go back down!"

"Don't be stupid, Anya! We cannot see. We could step
on one and that would be very bad, indeed. Besides, do you
think that there would be no insects down below! We

wouldn't be able to see the stairs, either. One wrong move and we could all go crashing down. No, just stay here. Remain very still and try to sleep."

Despite the heat, Jodie nestled closer to Anya.

* * *

Some time later, the wind dropped and they heard them for the first time. A low frequency note resonated through the building. It seemed to be emanating from somewhere outside. It lasted but a moment. However, it was soon followed by another and then many more. Each burst of sound had a slightly different tone. They were not very loud and could be likened to a haunting musical conversation using only the bottom base notes from a giant horn, although they sounded somehow synthetic in nature.

Jodie was sleeping. The hairs stood up on the back of Anya's neck. "What of all things was that?"

"I don't know. I've never heard anything like it!" Jadine began to shudder. She stood.

"Careful where you are standing!"

"I can't see a thing!"

Jadine moved slowly, arms outstretched in front, as if the power of sight had deserted her. She made her way towards one of the rectangular slits in the wall.

"I can't see anything out there. The moon is small and the wind is still churning the sand a little."

There was a momentary lapse before the sounds recommenced.

"It seems to be coming from all different directions. Anya, I think that someone or something is moving out there. I can't see shapes, just shadows!"

Anya did not want to leave Jodie, but she threw caution aside and rushed over, jumping as she went, hoping to avoid treading on any insects or spiders. She could just make out

Jadine's form in the window frame.

"What can you see now?"

"Nothing! I told you, it's very dark. I just thought that I saw some movement out of the corner of my eye."

"Let me see!"

"Okay, but there's only room for one."

Anya placed her head into the deep, stone chamber that framed a view to the outside. The sound was now very intermittent. "Which way were you looking when you saw 'whatever'?"

"I was looking towards the horizon, but I saw shadows moving in the foreground. There it is again!"

There was a single burst of sound, much like a low frequency hum this time.

"I heard it! It was off the left, I think."

"Is there anything there?"

"No, like you said, it's too dark."

Silence! Abruptly, the wind had been replaced by a gentle breeze. A cluster of trees was now clearly visible on the horizon beyond.

Anya stuck her head out and looked immediately left. She scanned along the bottom of the sandstone wall. A shape disappeared around the corner. "Ahhh!" Anya controlled the volume of her voice, but not the surprise.

"Did you see something? What did you see?"

"Shush!"

Jadine was now whispering loudly, "Was it a person?"

"No, I don't think so. It had no real form. It was more like, well, a large rock, I guess."

"A large rock? A big stone?"

"Yes, in an instant, it reminded me of the large megalithic stones that formed a circle near my birthplace."

"And it moved?"

"I think so."

"Move out, Anya; let me see." Jadine half guided, half

pulled Anya away from the window, and then squeezed her body in between the stones. "I can't see anything there."

"It moved around the corner."

"Do you think it will try to get in?"

"Well, if it does, there is little to deny it entry. There are no doors or barricades here."

There was another lingering hum. It was much louder this time and even deeper than all the others that had gone before it. The sound came from behind them, somewhere outside. Jadine rushed over to the top of the staircase. Anya went over to make sure that Jodie was all right. Apparently, she had slept through it all.

Jadine spoke softly. "I'll check down below."

"No, Jadine, we have the advantage of higher ground. We can defend the steps more easily."

Jadine once again fumbled across the vast room. She collected her knife and returned to her position at the top of the staircase. As if in reply to the sound at the rear, there was another reverberation emanating from the front of the building, this time perhaps an octave higher. Anya rushed back to the window. She looked left, right, below and out across the sand. Nothing! Her knees began to tremble. Her mouth was dry and she wanted to urinate. She could hear her own heartbeat as her blood was pumped through the vessels in her ears. Sweat dripped onto the sand below. She held her position.

Time moved on, but there were no more sounds. Once more, they found themselves agreeing to take turns to form a watch. On this occasion, Anya remained awake to see in the morning. As the light outside increased, she was able to see more of what was around her, but she waited until the sun had risen above the horizon before waking Jadine. Anya didn't want to alarm her daughter. Jodie had been through enough of late, so Anya allowed her to sleep a while longer to enable her to discuss the events of the previous night with her companion.

* * *

Jodie was flying across the desert. It didn't take long for her to see the dome ahead. As she glanced to one side she noticed a hooded man flying beside her. She could not see his face. Good of him to join me, she thought, whoever he is. Jodie re-focussed her attention on the dome. As she neared, she could see a vast field of grey stones, rather like those the she had seen inside. They were arranged in neat rows like a vast cemetery, but they were much more menacing, like a legion of soldiers waiting to go into battle. Suddenly, Jodie was afraid once more. Using the power of thought alone, she was able to guide herself down and land on a dune ridge overlooking the gigantic army of stone warriors. The hooded figure landed beside her. He remained silent.

"I don't want to go any further this time; I don't want to go in!"

"But you must!"

"No, I don't like the look of it anymore. It's not safe."

"Of course it is. Here, you will always be safe."

"No, I think I will go back now."

"You have to go to the dome. You will receive all that you have ever wanted if you settle there, but be warned, if you refuse to go, we will come and get you!"

19

Jadine felt a gentle nudge on her shoulder, and so, opened her eyes. The room was still dim. Jadine squinted until her pupils adjusted. "Did you manage to stay awake?"

"Yes, I have been awake since I took over from you. Not even a nap, I promise."

"Did you hear any more 'sounds'?"

"No, nothing, and, as far as I can tell, no one, or anything else, for that matter, has entered the building."

"I gathered as much.... We're still here, aren't we!"

"Um...." Anya did not seem very convinced about her safety.

"What do you suppose was out there last night?"

"I have no idea. I have never heard anything like that in my life."

"Are you still convinced that you saw something?"

"Yes; at least, I think so."

"You're not sure? Last night, you claimed to have seen an immense stone moving across the sands."

"I told you what it looked like, but the light was poor; all that I could see were shadows. Maybe the light was playing tricks on me or something."

"What you described didn't sound credible, but how do you explain the sounds?"

"This is a large, irregular building that we haven't fully explored. You don't suppose that it was merely wind blowing through its various nooks and crannies?"

"I'm not sure. The sounds were so deep. It didn't sound like gusts of wind to me."

"Are we not just imagining things?"

"Anya, you seemed pretty scared to me last night!"

"I know, but being left here alone is frightening in itself."

"That's true enough!"

"I wish I knew where we were going or what exactly we expect to find at journey's end."

"Well, we are committed now. We can't turn back. We'll just have to see when we get there."

"Shush! Jodie's waking." Anya was pointing. "Hello, my little one. How are you this morning?"

Jodie rubbed sand out of her eyes and yawned. Her face was very dirty. Water marks suggested that she had shed a few tears. "I'm okay…"

"You don't look okay. What's wrong?"

"I'm fine. I just feel a little uneasy. I must have had a bad dream or something, but I don't remember. I have that feeling, you know, the one you get when you wake up and you think that your nightmare was real, that bad things are true. It'll wear off."

Anya was a little taken aback by Jodie's mature summary of how she assessed her own feelings, but chose not to highlight it.

Jadine walked over to the stone window frame, leant in and peered out. "Blue sky and no wind! It'll be hot again, but anything's better than a sandstorm."

"Can you see anything else?" Anya sounded genuinely inquisitive.

"Just the trees that we saw last night. That must be where the water is. We should go over and get some whilst we can."

"Yes, we should, but I just want to have a quick look around here first."

"I could take Jodie out with me and dig for water while you explore the building."

"That's not such a bad idea. Be careful, though, and keep a sharp lookout."

"Don't worry, I will."

"Any sign of trouble, give me a shout and get back here as fast as you can."

Jadine was grimacing. "I said, don't worry. Do you want me to wait for you to come with us?"

"No, it's all right. You go ahead and get some more water. I would do well to stay out of the sun today." Anya pointed to her sunburnt and blistered arms.

Jadine took Jodie's hand and led her down the staircase, across the grand hall and, after pausing a few times to examine the stone artefacts, out through the doorway.

Anya followed close behind, through the second room and down the stairs. As Jodie and Jadine left via the doorway, Anya stopped to study the images carved into the stone. There were many different birds, animal, lines and symbols. Some of the hieroglyphs were faded and eroded, but many had survived intact. Anya searched the sand that lined the floor of the room for signs of everyday artefacts, but there were no jars, vessels, tools or weapons to be found. She shook her head, presuming that they had long since been removed. Anya would have liked to have known more about the people who had built this great temple. Perhaps, she thought, there might be more clues in some of the other rooms, so she decided to venture into adjacent chambers.

Anya stepped out to one side. Stone from the first floor littered the floor. Above that, the roof was damaged sufficiently to see clear blue sky above. She clambered over the stones, stumbling as she went, towards a dark opening at a right angle to where she had entered. When she reached the doorway, she discovered that it led directly into an apparently featureless passageway. Inside, progress was easier. Fewer stones littered the floor. The exit was dimly illuminated by light from the next chamber. Just before she reached the end, Anya noticed that there was, indeed, a small compartment set into the wall on the right, just large enough for a few people to stand in. She glanced inside. It was empty, but she could just make out that the entire surface was covered with many neat, carved inscriptions.

The next area was weakly illuminated by the absence of one large stone, missing from the upper portion of the wall to her left. Anya spotted something next to the missing stone at its base and went nearer to investigate. Protruding from underneath the sandstone block lay a near-complete human skeleton. Most of the bones from the neck down were visible. The shoulder blade and the top of the right arm were badly damaged. It did not take an expert to deduce that the stone had fallen, killing its victim, but Anya thought it odd that such a large, heavy stone could just fall out of the wall. She leant over the remains. Most of the clothing had turned to dust. The remnants of some sort of animal hide footwear protruded out of the sand next to what could be seen of the larger foot bones. As Anya shifted to gain a better view, she felt something under her knee. Carefully, she put both hands down into the sand and felt around the buried object. Moments later, she lifted out a pointed knife, obviously designed for use as a weapon. As the light was so poor, she used her sense of touch for a preliminary investigation. The handle and blade were crafted in metal. The cutting edge was still sharp enough to slice skin, so she continued her examination carefully. At the top of the shaft was a rounded metal ball that gave the weapon perfect balance. Anya did not want to slip the blade into her belt for fear of injury, so she clung to it as she stood to survey the rest of the chamber. Apart from the corpse, there was nothing remarkable, so she moved on.

The smell of bat dung was strong once again and began to overpower her senses. Anya went into the next long chamber. This room was illuminated by light from a large opening at the far end. Decorative hieroglyphs lined the walls. Many retained a degree of colour. Blues and reds predominated. Anya walked through and stepped outside into the courtyard Jadine had mentioned the previous evening. She turned and looked up the stone staircase. Most of the steps contained worn hollows towards the centre. Some were chipped and crumbling. She turned to face the opposite wall. Along the façade were eight stone pillars. The outer two were intact; the others were in various states of decay. Above them were the remains of a single-storey roof that part covered the last remaining great chamber at the end of the building. Anya passed through the courtyard and entered through one of the two gateways into a large bright space. Here too, stone slabs littered the floor; in the centre of the room was a massive stone plinth. As Anya neared, she noticed that the centre had been hollowed away, the outline and size of which roughly represented that of a human body. Anya brushed away the sand at one end of the slab. Anya shuddered as she attempted to picture what had taken place here many years before. Before leaving, she stopped to examine the remains on the floor. She hoped to find more artefacts, but she soon realised that the sand was far too deep.

Anya headed back into the courtyard and ascended the steps into the room that adjoined their sleeping quarters. The walls were constructed of smaller sandstone blocks. Near the entrance, a row of these stone bricks were missing. Anya could see them lined up towards the middle of the room. It was as if these had been ripped apart from the others and cast away from the solid structure in a single violent event. All the building blocks within this massive structure appeared to have been cut and honed to very fine tolerances. Each stone was shaped precisely to fit around the adjacent blocks. Anya had no idea how these stones had come to move or why anyone would want to move them.

* * *

Jadine and Jodie stepped out into the bright world outside their sanctuary and strode towards the trees. The structure was so immense that they had to walk a considerable distance before they could turn and fully appreciate its scale.

Jadine was in awe. "Wow."

Jodie was impressed, but she knew that she had seen it before in her dreams. She acknowledged that it looked much bigger from down on the ground. Intact columns lined the aspect that they were viewing, extending up to stone promontories at the edge of the vast flat roof. They had exited through a doorway about one third down the building. Clearly, it was too small to have been the primary entrance. Any external detail or decoration had long since been weathered away. Jadine gazed up at the narrow openings through which they had surveyed the surrounding landscape. On looking along the façade, she noticed a row of missing blocks. Other parts of the building were beginning to crumble and decay.

"Why do you suppose that no one has made a home here?" asked Jodie. "It's a great structure and would be easy to defend."

"Yes, but just look at what surrounds this place. What would people eat? You couldn't grow crops here, and I don't know of any domesticated animals that you could rear under these conditions. We'll be lucky to get some water for ourselves, and, if we don't move on soon, we will surely starve!"

"Let's go and dig for some water before it gets any

hotter."

When they arrived at the mini oasis, they looked back the way they'd come. They were in a natural dune valley with traces of an old dried-up river bed running close to the palms. They could not see the roof line of the building they had recently left. Jadine quickly set about replicating the process that Zack had demonstrated the day before. After a while spent digging and scraping, both women were somewhat surprised, and very relieved, to see liquid appear at the bottom of their hole. Jadine, ably assisted by Jodie's smaller hands, dug a little deeper and a small pool developed beneath them. They splashed their faces repeatedly, then sucked up as much water as they could take before filling their flasks.

Every once in a while, Jadine stopped to look up and scan their surroundings. Nothing moved. Away from their immediate position, sand was all that surrounded them. The temperature was rising rapidly.

"Come on, let's get back," suggested Jadine. "Grab some of these dried leaves, as many as you can carry. They might come in handy."

As they turned and began to walk away a large grey bird swooped down and landed by the waterhole. Without hesitation, Jadine dropped the water flasks, pulled out her knife and hurled it towards the potential meal. With such a small target, she was always likely to miss, but, to her astonishment, the blade slammed through the centre of its chest.

Jodie jumped up and down, clapping. "Well done, Jadine! Meat, we'll eat meat today!"

"That was one piece of good fortune that we needed!"

The bird slumped backwards. Jadine ran over, picked it up, and carried it away from the water source before gutting it. "Now we can return to Anya with a smile on our faces and hope in our hearts."

"I'm so hungry," declared Jodie.

As they approached the ruin, Jodie took the bird and ran in to give her mother a cheerful greeting, dragging the leaves behind. Jadine veered of to one side, heading towards the other side of the building. She noticed that it was roughly symmetrical. It was now apparent that they had entered and exited through a side doorway. Located at the front elevation were two impressive sets of steps cut into the structure and leading up to the roof. Between them was a large archway that marked what would have been the main entrance. It was bricked up. The stones used differed from those in the main construction. Jadine presumed that the main access had been blocked off for some reason, at a later date.

Jadine ran up onto the roof. Aside from the stone edging, it was flat and featureless. Towards the far end, there were holes and damage to the stone. One corner was crumbling away. Jadine skipped down the steps and returned to ground level. She walked around to the opposite side from where they had entered. It was, unsurprisingly, very similar. Stones were missing here and there, but there was no doorway. Jadine circled the perimeter, noting more damage at the far end. From time to time she turned to gaze out into the desert. It was featureless, except for the dunes. Jadine felt the sun beating down on her exposed skin. She realised that she was still carrying the water, so decided to return to Anya and Jodie.

"Helloooooow," shouted Jadine.

"In here," came a muffled reply from Anya. "In the courtyard."

Jadine followed the trail towards Anya's voice, finding herself in the outside courtyard. "You wasted no time preparing the bird, then. You lighted a fire, too."

"I had a flint and some straw. The leaves are starting to burn, but we might need more. There is nothing in here to burn." Anya was plucking the bird.

"I'll run down and get some more. There might be a little dry wood or bark, too."

Jodie placed the feathers on the fire, causing it to smoke intensely. "I'll go and help Jadine," declared Jodie.

"No, stay here, please. I don't want you going off on your own."

"But why?"

"We've met people along the way. Some good, some not so good. You never know who'll be around."

"I'll run fast!"

"No! I meant what I said."

Jodie put her arms down by her sides, shrugged and started to sulk. "I'm nearly a grown woman now. You never let me do anything."

Anya stifled a laugh. "You are very mature for your age, although you are still but a child. You have much to learn. Be patient; you have your whole life ahead of you."

"Hmm!" There was silence for a while. However, as Anya pulled out the last few feathers Jodie spoke up. "How are we going to support the bird while it cooks?"

Anya had already cradled the fire in a collection of small stones. "Go through there and bring as many of these rocks as you can."

"Okay." Jodie was still brooding.

Jadine returned. "This is all I could find. We won't be able to make another one."

"If we can just get that log burning, it'll be sufficient."

"Shave some bits off it and pare it down."

Anya pulled out the knife that she had found earlier.

"Where did you get that?" asked Jadine.

"In one of the rooms back there. There is an old decayed body. I'll show you later."

Jadine seemed a little concerned, but went on to break up the dried palm leaves that she had brought with her.

"Very old?"

"It's just a pile of bones. Poor man had one of those great stones fall on his head."

This did little to allay any fears that Jadine might have. "That's a well-crafted knife. I wonder who he was."

"I've no idea. It hasn't been used in an age, but it's still very sharp."

"May I see?"

Anya skilfully flipped the knife over, caught it by the blade and passed it to Jadine. Jodie returned, struggling to hold onto an assortment of stones. Anya rushed over to help.

"I've made a small pile that I collected. I just couldn't carry them all."

Anya took three of the larger ones from her daughter. "Thank you. You did well."

Jadine glanced over. "It's certainly a fine knife." She threw it so that it landed blade first in the ground. "You go and help. I'll get the fire going."

"Come, let's go and get some more." Anya headed through to the room with the great slab to gather smaller rocks from the rubble.

They waited a while before loosely covering the fire with the stones that they had gathered. Anya cut the prepared carcass in half so that it would cook quicker, and then laid it on top. Anya and Jadine sat back in the shade of the doorway and waited for it to roast. Jodie was restless, though. "Can I go back in there and play?"

"Okay, but be careful. I don't want you tripping and falling over that rubble."

"I'll be careful." Jodie sped off.

"Don't worry, she'll be all right." Jadine sensed that Anya was concerned.

"This is no life for someone so young. Just look at us. We're in the middle of a vast desert. We have no idea where we are going and we are just about to consume the last of our food."

"We'll get by. We always do. You have to be positive, Anya. This morning, we had no meat. Now we have this great bird to eat. Something always comes along."

"Today, you were lucky, but you said yourself, there is nothing more to burn."

"So? Our next meal will be eaten raw. Not a great prospect, whatever it is, but we will survive."

"For what?"

"Be positive, Anya! Be positive, for Jodie's sake."

"My arms are a little better this morning." Anya pulled them out from under her robe.

Jadine glanced down. "Hardly!"

"Tomorrow, we should head out away from here and move on. I'll keep my arms covered as best I can. We should leave before sunrise. We should sleep after we've eaten and save our energy for whatever lies ahead."

Anya flipped the two halves of the bird to cook the skin on the outside and ensure even cooking. "I think it's done. I'll pull it off and let it cool for a few moments."

Jadine produced a green palm leaf that she had collected earlier. "Here, lay it on this."

Anya obliged.

Jodie returned from play. "I'm starving!"

"You're just in time." Anya began pulling the meat off the carcass. "Although it's a large bird, it doesn't have very much flesh on it. I doubt that there will be enough left over to take with us."

"To take with us," repeated Jodie. "Are we leaving this place today?"

"No, tomorrow, before dawn," replied her mother, quite matter-of-factly.

"All right," said Jodie. "Let's eat."

After their meal, they settled back and talked for a while

about the prospects for their journey and the direction that they would take.

Anya began to feel a little more optimistic. "Come on, let's gather our possessions together and sleep while our bellies are full."

"You promised me that you would show me something." Jadine was keen to remind Anya.

"Later. Let's return to the room upstairs. We'll pack and rest first."

* * *

Earlier, Jodie had listened to her mother's words of caution. In the end chamber, she had hopped and skipped about, taking care to stay clear of the larger piles of rubble. Then she had seen the large stone slab in the middle of the room. She had hitched herself up and laid down in the centre of the hollow. She had gazed up and viewed the sky through the holes in the roof. She had felt at peace and closed her eyes for a few moments. What she had failed to notice, was a large, dark, elliptical stone at the end of the building that had not been present earlier. There was a deep indentation near the top of its form, like a single, dark, lifeless eye.

20

Jadine woke first. It was nearly dark. She sat bolt upright. Anya and Jodie did the same moments later.

"What sort of sound was that?" asked Jodie in a loud, uncontrolled voice.

"Shush!" hissed Anya.

The noises from the previous night had returned. However, this time, they were louder, and there were more of them, like a cacophony of low frequency horns echoing around the room. Jadine headed for the opening in the wall. Anya scooped Jodie up in her arms.

"I'm scared!"

"Me too, Jodie, but we'll be fine. It's just noises."

Jadine was looking out. "There are so many of them! Down below and spread out across the dunes. What are they? What do they want?"

Still clutching Jodie, Anya dashed to the opening. "What do you mean, Jadine?" Anya had reached the gap between the stones.

In the half light of dusk, she could see what now occupied a previously empty landscape. An array of stone megaliths stood before her. Each one was taller than a man and obviously many times heavier. "What are they, indeed? I told you what I saw last night, but you wouldn't believe me!"

"They're just so unbelievable, but they're out there, they are real!"

"Let me see." Jodie fought against her mother to lean out and take a peek.

"No, Jodie, stay out of sight." Anya pushed her daughter down by her feet.

The din continued. Each stone apparently emitting a pulse of low frequency sound at random.

Jadine leant forward. "What could they be? Where did they come from?"

"I have no idea, but what's more important is what do they want from us?"

Jadine pushed forward and looked out at the megaliths down below, near to the wall of the building. "They just look like giant, rounded pebbles, but how could they move?"

Anya did not have any answers. "It's just as though they are waiting for something. Stones cannot see, but it appears that they are all gathered around, just watching us. Go across and look out the other side."

Jadine ran across to one of the openings. "It's just the same, twenty or thirty, maybe more." In the gloom of the building's shadow, Jadine detected something out of the corner of her eye. "They can move. I saw one move. It just shifted sideways very slowly. It just seemed to glide over the surface of the sand!"

"Most of these are moving, too," shouted Anya.

"Let me see!" Jodie forced her way to the opening. "Wow.... I've seen them in my dreams. Not here, though, but several times recently."

"What are they, then?" asked Anya. "What do they want?"

"I'm not sure. I think that they are some kind of army." Jodie thought for a few moments. "I think that they want to drive us away from here."

"Not now. We can't leave here. Not with them outside." Anya glanced down. "They're all moving now, coming towards the building."

The megaliths edged forwards. Their progress was slow, but relentless. Several moved towards the entrance. Anya tracked their progress, but was distracted by Jadine running back into the centre of the room. She began to gather their meagre possessions once more.

Anya glanced outside once more. "The two by the opening, I can't see them anymore."

Jadine went towards the stairs.

"No, Jadine, stay up here; they won't be able to get up," cried Anya, taking hold of Jodie once more.

"I want to face them, to see what they are and what they want from us." Jadine pulled out her knife.

In the dimness of twilight, Anya saw the flash of the blade. "That won't do much good against a huge rock. Stay here and sit tight."

Jadine sheathed her knife. "No, I need to see them." She was gone.

Abruptly, the constant barrage of sound ceased.

Before Jadine reached the bottom of the steps, she realised it was pitch black. She could not see a thing within the great hall. An eerie silence greeted her. She had nothing with her to make a torch. Nothing to help her see what was around or lurking at the bottom of the stairs. All her courage deserted her. She did not like the dark.

A single low frequency thud filled the lower chamber. It was so intense and resonant that it hurt Jadine's ears. It stopped her in her tracks, two steps from the bottom. Her arms and legs began to shake uncontrollably. She shook her head and forced herself to slowly retreat up the stairs backwards. When she reached the top, she turned, terrified, and sprinted back through the first room towards Anya and Jodie. Up here too, the light was all but gone, but Jadine managed to locate her two companions who now huddled under the window.

"Did you see one?" asked Anya.

"No, it was too dark." Jadine's voice was now down to a whisper and she was trembling. "But I'm sure that they're in there. One let out a deafening pulse of sound as I approached."

"They are silent now."

"Yes, I wonder what that means?" asked Jodie.

"It might mean that they are leaving," suggested Anya.

"I don't think so," replied Jodie.

Jadine looked out towards the desert. "Most of the stones are still visible; they are just creeping nearer and nearer."

Anya held tightly onto Jodie, and Jadine stared down at the megaliths as they made their way inexorably towards the ruin. Darkness had descended in earnest, but, fortunately or not, the crescent moon provided sufficient light to illuminate the landscape beyond. Together with the stars, it cast a bluish hue over the orange desert, creating a long shadow wherever one of the stones was situated. The silence remained.

"Where are they now?" Concern was apparent in Anya's voice.

"Just a little closer than before," snapped Jadine.

Anya leant out to see for herself. "Quite a few of them are pressed up against the wall below. They seem to be making little attempt to gain entry, if that's their aim."

"I know. I'm sure more will be collecting on the other side, too."

"Shall I go and see?"

"No, don't bother. What's the point?"

A wave of sound shook the building. Everyone inside instinctively covered their ears. There was a brief interlude of silence, followed by strong rhythmical pulses. The ancient cement around the stones began to crumble and give way. The floor below them began to shake. A layer of powdery sand rose up from the ground. There was a huge rumble accompanied by an almighty thud as several of the blocks comprising the main wall of the floor below were ejected into the building.

Jadine grabbed a water flask in her right hand, and Jodie's hand in her left. Anya grabbed Jodie's free hand and together the two women hauled her to her feet.

"We need to get out," cried Jadine.

They ran towards the exit leading to the courtyard at the far end of the building. No sooner had they moved when six or more of the blocks around the window frame were hurled into the room, creating a massive dust cloud. All three women briefly glanced over their shoulders, but kept on running. They squeezed though the opening into the next chamber just as more blocks were knocked inwards as if hit by a giant invisible hammer. The rhythmic sounds continued relentlessly, each one accompanied by more and more damage to the surrounding structures. As they were about to exit into the open night air at the top of the stairway, they were halted in their tracks. The roof rapidly cracked and caved in before them. Anya and Jodie leapt backwards, dragging Jodie with them. Had any one of, or even a part of the huge slabs hit one of them, it would have undoubtedly been fatal, but they were spared. The top part of the end wall fell away and finally they could see the stars above.

"One moment," shouted Jadine. "Let it settle!"

"Come on, this way." Anya was now giving the instructions. "Over these stones! Climb down to the courtyard below. If we can't climb out directly, we can exit through the wall of the final chamber."

"The water!" Jadine had dropped the flask.

"Forget it! Right now, our lives are all that are important!"

"Without it, we won't have a life in the desert!" Jadine

ran back into a rapidly deteriorating situation. She struggled to see her hand in front of her face. Instinctively, Jadine dropped down to her knees and began to feel her way through the sand on the floor, reaching out in all directions to locate the flask.

"Give me your hand, Jodie." Anya was attempting to lead Jodie to safety.

They clambered down the top few steps onto the rubble that littered the courtyard below. They glanced over at the end chamber. From what they could see, all of it remained intact, as did the side walls enclosing the courtyard. As they reached ground level, Anya turned, expecting to see Jadine. She waited a few moments before attempting to overpower the rhythmic pulses with her own voice. "Jadine, are you okay?"

Silence was the reply.

"Jadine!"

"Go on. I'll catch up to you. I'm still looking," came the muffled reply.

Anya searched for a breach in the wall that would allow them to escape out into the desert directly, but there was no such opening. Although she really did not want to enter into another part of the building, she finally conceded.

"Jodie, through here!" Anya pointed to the entrance before them.

"I don't want to," declared Jodie as Anya dragged her into the doorway adjoining the vault.

"It's our only chance. Quickly, through the room and let's get out on the far side. We'll wait for Jadine out in the dunes."

"But..."

There was a very large, very loud synchronised blast of energy and sound. They both looked back in time to see the far end of the building totally collapse. Anya pulled Jodie back against the wall behind the opening to shelter from the blast. A cloud of rubble and dust passed by them.

"Jadine!" cried Jodie.

Anya's voice trembled, betraying her true feelings. "She'll be okay. Watch your legs as you go."

It was very dark. Jodie began to cough. Anya took her hand, gently this time, and led her through the chamber. Jodie continually glanced back over her shoulder. Through the swirling haze, Anya could see a dim orange light in the middle of the room emanating from the floor where the vast stone slab had stood. She looked beyond for an exit at the far end. Silhouetted against the blue light of the outside was the terrifying sight of an elliptical stone. The single 'eye' in the centre near to the top of its bulk began to glow, giving off violet hues. Very slowly, it began to advance towards them, pushing aside large rocks and stones that were in its path. The deafening pulses of sound had now ceased.

A second, then a third megalith appeared at the far end of the chamber, forcing their way through the outer shell of the building. Just as Anya turned to flee in the opposite direction, a flaming torch appeared, seemingly out of the ground. This was promptly followed by the arm that held it, attached to the body of a young man wearing nothing but a ragged cloth hanging from his waist. "Quickly, in here!"

Anya collected Jodie, staring at the man, bewildered. "Who...?"

"In here, now! There is no time to explain. We are risking everything exposing ourselves to them like this."

A myriad thoughts and images flashed through Anya's mind. Was this man a saviour or a captor? Was he, too, in danger from the stone creatures or might he control them? Who was he and where could he have come from? Were there others like him? Where did 'down below' lead and where would he take them? Would they be safe? Should they go, and what about leaving Jadine behind?

The man rushed forward and grabbed Anya's arm. His

flickering torch illuminated the chamber and the three large megaliths that were advancing ever closer. Anya felt very weak, but allowed her body to comply with the man's direction. After all, she thought, he was, at least, human. Moments later, they were descending down a staircase below the ruined building. Their new companion pulled a lever at the bottom of the steps. Metal grated against rock and the vast stone plinth above sealed them in the passageway below.

In no time, the tunnel narrowed considerably. Anya realised that, even if one of the megaliths was able to descend after them, it would not be able to fit through the tight corridor. At least that was something. Jodie and Anya obediently followed their guide. Anya was forced to stoop, while there was just sufficient headroom for Jodie to pass upright. The walls appeared to have been cut out of the solid sandstone. The tunnel was rounded, but the centre line of the floor was flattened. It was neither straight nor continuous. Every so often, there was a junction or passage leading off to the left or the right. In some sections, water trickled or seeped around the walls and over the floor. Most parts were, at least, damp. Both women were now completely disorientated and had no idea where they were in relation to the ground above.

They had now been scampering along for some time and had covered what seemed like a considerable distance underground. The ceiling in the passageway gradually lifted and all three could now stand freely and move upright. Anya panted and her lungs heaved due to the relentless pace that their escort was setting, compounded by the dank, stale air. Jodie began to falter.

"What about Jadine?" Anya's question went unanswered. "Can we please slow down?"

At first, there was no response, but, a few strides later, the man slowed.

"Our friend, Jadine, she is trapped back in the building," stated Jodie.

"I know," was his only response.

"Well, can you go back for her?"

"No, we must go on."

Jodie stopped walking. "We have to save Jadine. She is everything to us!"

"We cannot go back. Not now; it is most unsafe. I have never known them do so much damage."

"Do you know what they are?" asked Anya.

"Not exactly," replied the man. "We have avoided them for generations, but, I must confess, we have not seen them here for quite some time. My name is Niahli." He put out a hand towards Anya.

"Anya, and this is Jodie." Anya looked over at the man who stood before her.

He had pale olive skin, stretched over a very thin but muscular frame, brown eyes and glossy, black hair. On his face were the early showings of a thin and patchy beard that usually adorned a young male who was still undergoing puberty, but the skin of this young man suggested that he was a little older.

"I am very pleased to meet you, though I wish that the circumstances were different. Come, we must make progress towards our rendezvous."

"How much further have we to go?" Anya's tone suggested a combination of frustration, anger and fatigue.

"Not far now. You will be safe."

Once again, they set off at a measured pace. Not for the first time that day, tears pooled along Jodie's lower eyelids, blurring her vision. It was all she could do to prevent herself from breaking down into a fit of sobbing. Be brave, she thought. We must get though this.

21

Niahli's pace slowed, and now Jodie thought that she could hear voices. The passageway opened into a large underground vault. Jodie marvelled, as clearly it did not appear to be a natural phenomenon; it must have been built by the hands of man. Though largely lacking in internal structure, in many respects, Jodie thought it more impressive than the building that they had recently vacated above ground. There were similarities, too. Symbols and shapes adorned most of the walls, but, unlike those above, many of the decorations were brightly coloured and clearly defined. Jodie examined what lay ahead, and realised that the cavity was indeed stepped. After a few more paces, she could see vast stone steps cut into the rock leading down to a larger lower level. There were people. Twenty, thirty, perhaps more, most were gathered in a large central circle, with several small groups congregating elsewhere around the floor. The vault was lighted by burning stone-based lamps that were located along the walls at regular intervals. In spite of a little smoke, the air was clearly fresher than in the tunnel, prompting Jodie to conclude that it must be ventilated in some way.

As Niahli approached, a number of the people who were congregated below, facing the steps, noticed his arrival and advanced hesitatingly towards them. He raised his hand, palm out flat, in gesture of greeting. As the onlookers raised their own hands in response, the rest of the group turned to see who had entered their world. Jodie paused to survey the scene from the upper level. Most of the gathering was dressed in long robes. Some robes were white; others clearly used to be. A few wore brown. Those who were children wore clothes similar to that of Niahli. Of the adults present below, there was roughly an even distribution of men and women. Anya followed Niahli down the steps. The crowd advanced en masse and restructured themselves to form a semicircle around the bottom step. One man with greying hair and a closely cropped beard stepped forward to great Niahli. "My son, you have done well. You are a brave young man."

"What of my brother?"

"Why, is he not with you? Then, he has yet to return!"

"When we arrived at the temple, it was chaotic. We assessed the situation and were forced to separate."

Jodie ran down the steps towards them and brushed past Anya. A young girl came forward. She was three or four years older than Jodie. She too had black well-groomed, long straight hair and a complexion similar to Niahli. Her warm smile revealed damage to her teeth and gums, perhaps through neglect, but a poor diet and malnutrition were likely to have contributed. Jodie glanced down and noticed that the little finger was missing from her right hand.

She spoke to Jodie in a soft and friendly voice. "Are you from above? My name is Simone. Welcome to our underground domain."

"Yes, I have come down from the desert. What is this place?"

"This is where we live."

"Jodie! Manners," said Anya in a scolding voice.

"Sorry, my name is Jodie, and this is my mother, Anya."

Anya interrupted, "Thank you for rescuing us from

whatever was happening up there, but we have to find our companion."

"Yes, Jadine went back to get the water, but I think that she may be trapped," said Jodie with an anguished look.

Simone sighed and shook her head. Niahli's father held onto Simone's shoulders and pulled her towards him. "My dear, my elder son, Salim, is out now looking for the other woman." He turned towards Anya. "Jadine, you say? Sorry, my name is John, John of Simian. My two sons went out to the temple when we realised that you were in trouble. He is still out there. If he fails to return soon, I will go out and search for the two of them. They might have had to lay low if their exit was blocked."

"We must go back," declared Niahli.

John turned to one of the other men. "A new torch, please."

The man complied immediately, bringing a second for Niahli. The two men hurried up the steps and quickly disappeared into the darkened tunnel at the end.

Anya and Jodie looked around the underground chamber and over at the people gathered before them. They were clearly not used to visitors and stared intensely. Several of the women standing nearer the front became aware of their behaviour and glanced down politely when Anya met their gaze. They were both around Jadine's age, and had well-groomed shoulder-length, straight black hair, wide set eyes and a prominent, chiselled noses. When they raised their heads again, one of them smiled at Jodie and she reciprocated the gesture.

She stepped forward and knelt to greet Jodie. "Welcome, Jodie, my name is Novae. I am Simone's mother and companion of Salim."

"Happy to meet you," replied Jodie respectfully. She glanced across to Anya for reassurance. A trusting glance was all she required to continue. "Are you all related?"

"I guess we are, in one way or another. This is my sister, Niamh."

Niamh nodded in Jodie's direction. "Hello!"

"And these are our people."

"How long have you lived down here?"

"I guess it must be several generations now. John was not, but Niamh and I were born down here, as were all of the younger people who you see before you."

"But why, why do you choose to live underground?"

"Jodie!" interjected Anya.

"No, it's okay. She can ask all the questions that she wants. After all, we have nothing to hide. We do go topside from time to time, mostly to hunt or gather food, but it is much safer down here. A controlled environment, if you like."

"What made your people come down here?"

As if to negate her previous response, Novae seemed uneasy and responded more to Anya than Jodie. "Our people used to be part of the nomadic tribe that roamed these regions. Our fathers told us that people began disappearing. One or two from year to year, but then the disappearances become more frequent. Those who vanished were never seen again. From time to time, they'd see the stones. We are still not exactly sure how the two are related, but we do know is that they pose a threat to whomever they come into contact with... and then there are the lights in the sky. We mainly see them at dusk or dawn, but, in general, we try to avoid them. They fly low over the dunes. We do not know what they are or where they are from. Needless to say, birds don't glow like that!"

"So your elders decided that it was safer to live down here?" Anya's eyes widened as she waited for Novae to reply.

"Our people had visited the temple many times. On one such occasion, they were searching for items in the sand when they found a trapdoor. When they eventually found the courage to go through and explore, the tunnel below led them here. John was just a boy then, but he has since described divisions within the family. Soon after its discovery, his father's brother disappeared. It was John's father who decided, together with three other families, to take refuge within these caverns. One night turned into a week, a week to a month, and so on...."

"And you are descended from one of those families?"

"Yes, but, since the original families decided to live down here, others have joined us. Most have come from other nomadic groups that had similar experiences out in the desert. You are not the first outsiders who we have simply found wandering amongst the dunes."

"We were not just wandering about aimlessly. In fact, it was two of your desert nomads who brought us here."

"Brought you here?" Novae was taken aback, but then surprise turned to reason. "Did they not mention us? They must have known that we were here."

"No, they were helping us on our way."

"Helping! Helping by leaving you alone in the temple? Maybe they did so because they knew that we would find you. Do you remember their names?"

"Zack and..."

"Jed?"

"You know them?"

Novae ignored the question. "Where were you hoping to get to?"

Anya faltered. "Our people talked of a 'Fartherland', a place that has retained some of the advantages of the old world. A place where we could go to be safe."

"Why should it be that two women and a child should be the ones to seek such a place?"

Anya explained how it had come to be. From time to time, Jodie interjected with the odd correction or addition.

Novae, her sister and their families listened intently. Predictably, Anya once again became upset when she described Keon's disappearance. Anya was very open with her newfound friend; however, she neglected to tell them anything at all about Jodie's dreams and 'visions'. That, she decided would just be a little too much to reveal to a virtual stranger.

When she had finished, Anya found that Novae was holding her hand.

"If it is any consolation, I do not think that the slaying of your people is in any way linked to the strange things that happen here. It does not fit the pattern and, anyway, your home was many, many days away. I am very sorry for your loss, particularly that of your companion. Everyone here has known such a loss."

"I thought you said that it was safe down here?"

"Everything is relative, but our 'losses' are very infrequent and usually result from a visit above. Sometimes there are accidents...."

Anya wanted to ask Novae to define 'accidents', but felt compelled to turn as she heard voices coming up behind her. Anya recognised all three, but one of them was much more familiar!

* * *

Niahli led them in. Jadine could barely walk. She was supported on either side by John and Salim. Novae rushed forward and kissed Salim on the cheek. Jadine's body was covered in dust. There was a gash on her right shin and the toes on that foot were crushed and bleeding. Bruising was already beginning to appear on her temple. Over her left shoulder was slung the water flask that she had returned to retrieve. They led her down and lowered her so that she was able to sit on the bottom step.

Anya greeted her with a hug. "I'm so relieved to see you. I thought that we'd lost you forever!"

However, Jadine did not reply; she just stared at Anya blankly and shook her head.

"What is it? What's the matter, Jadine?"

Jadine raised her arms, that showed additional signs of bruising, and pointed to the side of her head.

At first, Anya did not understand, then she realised what Jadine was indicating. "You can't hear me, can you?"

Though it might have been a somewhat pointless question, Jadine seemed to understand. She shook her head and looked down at the floor.

Niamh disappeared then reappeared moments later with a cloth ball and some water in a bowl. A sprig of leaves had been added to the solution. Jodie assumed that they had antiseptic properties. Novae began to assist Anya in cleaning up the battered and bruised body that was barely recognisable as Jadine. Niahli, John and Salim were a little dusty, but otherwise, they appeared unharmed. Novae looked grateful for the safe return of Salim. However, Salim covered his ears with the palms of his hand. He cupped them tightly and then proceeded to use them as plungers as if to clear a blockage in his ear.

John grabbed one of his wrists and speaking very loudly, he said, "It's no use. The ringing will pass in a day or so. Can you still hear me a little?"

Salim nodded.

John turned to Anya. "I am not so sure about Jadine's hearing. She had to withstand a sustained bombardment. They transmit enough energy to shatter solid rock, so one cannot be sure what it has done to her inner ears. If she is fortunate, she may regain some or all of her sense of hearing. We will just have to wait and see."

As Anya paused for thought, she, too, could hear a continuous high-pitched whine in her ears. She presumed that Jodie would have the same.

John then turned his attention to Niamh and Novae. "Would it not be more dignified to clean her up and dress her wounds in a bit of privacy? This is, after all, a public place."

"Sorry," replied Novae. "We just wanted to prevent infection."

"Very well, Niahli, help Niamh and Novae to carry her down to the spare quarters. Take Anya and the girl with you. There is room enough for all of them in there, and Jadine will be away from the gaze of what are, to her, a bunch of strangers."

Anya thanked them all once again before picking up Jadine's water flask and following the lead of Novae who already had hold of Jodie's hand.

Jadine appeared shocked and bewildered as Niahli scooped her off the step and cradled her carefully in his arms. Niamh stroked Jadine's cheek reassuringly before picking up the bowl of water and departing.

John clapped loudly before declaring to the other onlookers, "That's enough for now. Give them some space! We can all gather later this evening and I will update you on their progress." He turned to Niahli, put a fatherly arm around his shoulders and led him away. "I'm afraid that we have much to discuss when you have rested."

After a short walk down a corridor leading off the large cavern, they entered a rock-walled chamber that was lighted by several stone lamps. Smoke billowed up into a ventilation shaft a short distance above. Niahli gently laid Jadine down in a wide-berthed hammock made of woven dried palm leaves. On it was laid a clean, white linen sheet.

"Most of us sleep on plinths cut out of the rock. We soften them with leaves or whatever we can find," pointed out Novae.

"I'll come back later when you have finished tending to

her," said Niahli, guessing that what was about to happen was required to be conducted away from a man's gaze. "If you will permit it, I will take the little one with me."

Jodie appeared unhappy about the prospect of being separated from her mother.

After their experience at the river, Anya too, was more than a little concerned. "Well..."

Niahli sensed this and added in a reassuring voice, "Do not worry, I will bring her back in a while." Niahli knelt so that his eyes were in line with Jodie's. "Would you like to see how we make the torches and lanterns?" He offered a hand, and Jodie cautiously took it.

Niamh carefully removed Jadine's belt together with all that was attached. She paused for a moment to study the knife, sliding it out of its sheath. She took a section of cloth, dipped it in the water, and proceeded to clean the blade. Novae took the knife from her and began to slice through what remained of Jadine's clothes.

Anya stood close by for reassurance. Jadine's eyes were open, but she was barely conscious. In no time, the rags that had clothed her had been removed and were heaped in a pile on the floor. Jadine lay naked on the sheet. Anya surveyed her friend's body. The head wound that she had sustained at the river had left a scar that was now flanked by bruising and a large swelling. Her torso was covered in scrapes and more bruises. The gash in her leg gained at the flood was healing, but the wound to her lower shin looked sore and continued to ooze blood. Her foot was badly swollen and she was very, very dirty. So much so, that the fine dust particles that adhered to her skin had lightened her complexion several tones.

Niamh and Novae set about cleaning her body and dressing her wounds. From time to time, one of them left for a while to get some more clean water, some soap solution or another length of linen bandage. They did not hurry. Jadine seemed to understand what they were doing, and, after a while, she drifted into a troubled sleep. When it seemed that they might have finished, Niamh smiled and whispered something to Novae who returned a grin and nodded. Niamh produced a small tan leather case and looked towards Anya for approval. Anya was not at all sure what it contained, but, given the level of care that they had provided for her friend, she simply nodded anyway. Niamh pulled out a tiny brush and a small blade with a matching wooden handle. She used the brush to lather the soap solution, giving of a distinctive scent of palm oil, and applied it around Jadine's pubic area. Niamh carefully shaved away all the glossy black hair that joined the tops of Jadine's legs. Novae assisted by moving Jadine's legs in whichever direction was necessary. It might all have been embarrassing had Jadine not remained asleep. Later, Niamh would reveal that they had given her a mild sedative. When they had completed their work around her groin, they set about Jadine's underarms. Anya watched with fascination. Although battered and bruised, her friend's sleek, clean body was once again a thing of beauty. Jadine's small, rounded breasts were flattered by her reclined posture, rising up like two mini hummocks from the top of her chest. Anya was almost disappointed when they covered her over with a second sheet. To complete the makeover, Niamh and Novae washed the hair on Jadine's head before combing it back and trimming off the ends. Before leaving her to sleep, they brushed through a small quantity of light oil that had the scent of jasmine.

Niamh turned to Anya. "When she wakes, she will be sore and aching, but a woman always feels better when she is clean."

Anya's face was glowing with a sort of embarrassed smile. "Can you do the same for me?" There was a momentary pause. "Although I think that I can manage to shave myself."

Niamh smiled. "Of course we can."

Anya was led over to the far side of the room, where she disrobed.

* * *

It was Niahli's turn to make the torches for his family and refill the numerous stone lamps that adorned the chambers. Within the maze of underground passageways was a small, almost circular room. The segment opposite the entrance was partitioned by a low wall, behind which was located a natural trough. It was in this pit that the oily tar for the lamps and torches was sourced.

Niahli described to Jodie how the design of the stone lamps varied slightly. A lot depended upon the shape of the rock that they had to work with, but many were square. Most were of simple construction with an open reservoir and had either a floating or sunken wick made from knotted rope. The square stones in the large communal chamber were mounted on top of poles. They had a small hole at the bottom of the reservoir for the placement the wick. In addition to these, they used hand torches made from thin pieces of resinous palm saplings, which were coated with thicker tar from the edge of the pit, held between two rocks, and wedged into the crook of a stick.

Jodie passed the time accompanying Niahli as he went from chamber to chamber, refilling the reservoirs, using oil from a large jug. From time to time, they would return to the tar pit to refill the jug. Jodie was amazed by just how much he took. Niahli reassured her, "The fuel comes from the earth above. Do not worry, it will never run out; we have used this trough for many generations. It always replenishes itself. We simply take our turn to refill the lights and we do not leave all of them burning at any one time."

Every so often, they would pass people as they made their way to the next lamp. Everyone they met seemed to know who Jodie was and either said hello or greeted her with a friendly smile. Indeed, she recognised many of them from her arrival in their underground world. After a number of trips to and from the pit, Jodie met Simone again as they entered the living quarters that belonged to Niahli and his father's family.

"Hi, Jodie, do you remember me?"

"Yes, of course I do. You are Simone."

"Yes, that is correct. I am so glad that you remembered my name. Would you like to see where I sleep?"

"Okay. Is that all right, Niahli?"

"Yes, of course it is. You can stay here with Simone tonight if your mother approves."

Jodie beamed. "I'll ask her as soon as I see her. Is she still with Jadine?"

"I expect so. We can go and check in a while."

Simone took Jodie by the hand and led her over to her bed.

"How did you lose your finger?" asked Jodie.

"Oh, I got it trapped between two rocks and it was crushed much worse than Jadine's toes. It went black, so my father had to cut it off."

"Ahh! Did it hurt?"

"Afterwards, it hurt a lot, but, at the time, they gave me something to take away the pain and make me very sleepy. I think they have given Jadine some of the same. Strangely, it made me feel quite happy. It is not a problem now."

Before them was a small stone table and on it were a comb and two hair brushes, some necklaces and bracelets, and a selection of pastes that Jodie imagined were used to decorate Simone's face. The bed was laid out on a stone plinth. On it sat a thick mat woven from palms and stuffed with dried leaves.

"There is plenty of space here for two."

Simone was keen to make room for Jodie. She reached below the bed and picked up what was, to Jodie, a strange-looking object. It was made from wood and consisted of at least two pieces. Down the front, strings were fixed tightly in place by wooden pegs at the top. Simone strummed the strings with one hand whilst holding the others near the top of the instrument with her good hand. To Jodie's amazement, it played a tuneful melody.

"I practice whenever I can. Most of the people here have learnt to play something. Would you like to try, Jodie?"

Jodie was hesitant at first. "Maybe later."

"Go on, have a go now. I will teach you a few notes."

"Okay then, how do I hold it?"

"Like this." Simone went around and behind Jodie, pulled her back and sat her down between her legs before placing the instrument in her lap and showing her how to hold it.

Jodie spent most of the morning learning how to play. She felt a bit clumsy at first, but decided to persist and soon mastered the art of playing a simple tune.

"You must be tired. You've had no sleep." Jodie looked towards the doorway.

Anya was standing before her. It was conceivable that she might have been listening to Jodie's attempts to produce a tune for some time.

Jodie studied her mother for a few moments. Something was different. "You look... You look all clean and tidy."

"Indeed, I am. Niamh and Novae helped me tidy myself up. They even cut my hair. They have done the same for Jadine, too."

"How is she?"

"She is sleeping right now, as you should be! I don't

think that her injuries are too serious, though. It might take her a few days to get over our latest ordeal."

"Can she hear yet?"

"No, I don't think so. It's too soon to tell. We'll have to wait and see how that goes."

"Do you think that she will ever hear again?"

"I couldn't say for sure. I hope so. Niamh says that there is another woman here who was subjected to the same barrage of sound. She regained most of her hearing within a few days. She still suffers from a little ringing in her ears, though. I guess that's a small price to pay. If Jadine had been hit more directly by one of those large rocks...."

"I know. We should be grateful that she is still with us."

"Yes, we'll find out later exactly what happened, from Niahli."

Niamh appeared at Anya's side. "Do you want to sleep now, Jodie? You could just lie on Simone's bed."

"Not just yet, thank you. If I nap now, I know that I won't sleep later."

Anya interjected, "I think that Jodie is just excited to be here. We have had little interaction with friendly people for quite some time, and I know that she misses her family and the rest of our community."

"If you wanted," said Niamh, "I am sure that John will let you become part of our family. The more we are, the stronger we become."

"But what about food and other resources?"

"We will get by. We always do. Anyway, you and Jadine can hunt, can't you? And I am sure that you have other talents between you."

"Thank you for such a kind offer, but we'll have to wait and see. We have barely arrived. I still feel a little disorientated down here and I need to know how Jadine feels. Perhaps we will still have our ultimate goal in mind."

"No problem! Let us just take each day as it comes for

now. There will be plenty of time to plan your future. You might consider changing your mind once you get to know us all a little better."

Novae had now joined them. Jodie re-focussed her attention on playing Simone's instrument.

"Listen to this!" Jodie went on to reproduce the tune that Simone had been teaching her almost note perfect, humming as she went.

"You are a natural," exclaimed Simone.

Anya, Niamh and Novae clapped in applause.

"Sorry to interrupt," said John, with a friendly smile. "We can all eat together later, in the main chamber, and it will give us the opportunity to have a chat about the day's events. Salim's ears are a little better now. There is still some ringing, but he will be able to tell you exactly what happened up there. If Jadine is awake, she may join us, too, but I fear that she might not quite be up to it." He gazed down at Jodie. "That was excellent for anyone's first time, not least someone as young as you."

Jodie beamed wider than Anya had seen for a long time.

"Anya, would you like to take a tour of our world?" asked Novae, positively glowing with excitement.

"Yes please; why not? After all, I have nothing better to do! Lead the way."

"I will just get a fresh torch; some of the corridors are very dark," said Novae with a smile. "We can go around almost anywhere. We just need to respect the privacy of certain individuals within our community. Jodie, do you want to stay here with Simone or are you going to join us for a look around?"

"I will stay here if that is all right. I would like to practice some more."

"You go right ahead and enjoy yourself!"

Novae began the tour by leading the way back to the large underground crypt.

"This, we presume, was once used as a burial tomb for people who lived many generations ago. It must have taken many years to hollow out the chambers and passageways, but we suspect that this, the largest of all our rooms, was modified from a natural occurrence within the rock. Once they had completed their building, they set about decorating the walls. See here." Novae pointed. "It depicts many scenes of worship, life and death. The colours are almost as vivid today as they were when they were made."

Anya was silent for a while whilst she studied the painted engravings. "Are they present in most of the rooms?"

"Some, but not all. It is as though they sealed this place up before they completed their work. If we walk through here to some of the other living quarters, we can see that the walls of some of the chambers are smooth, whilst others are coarsely chiselled, as if they were abandoned before they were finished."

"Are there any possessions left over from the people who lived here?"

"We have found a few, but we suspect that most things were taken long ago. Who knows, there might even have been great treasures down here. We did find a gold bracelet once. Niamh keeps that very safe!"

"Novae, may I ask a question?" Anya tentatively enquired.

"You may," replied Novae, somewhat cautiously.

"Does Niamh not have a companion? I mean, at first, I thought that she was with Niahli, but I know now that that is not the case."

Novae blushed a little. "My younger sister should have taken a man long ago, but I think that she waits in hope that Niahli will one day fall in love with her. He, too, is old enough to have children of his own, but, for some reason, he waits."

* * *

Novae went on to show Anya the tar pit, and a number of smaller chambers that were occupied by families living down below. As she met people on the way, she too was surprised by how friendly their greetings were. Could this underground village be the utopia they had been searching for, she wondered. However, despite the people's welcoming nature, it was apparent that this was not the Fartherland, the paradise that Anya yearned for. Food was clearly in short supply, and a life of perpetual darkness would not be good for the mind.

One noteworthy site on Anya's excursion was a seemingly blind-ending passage at the far side of the labyrinth. When they reached the end, Novae pointed upwards. Stone rungs had been cut into the sandstone. With the torch held aloft, Anya could see a considerable distance upwards, but the portal clearly ascended much further.

"That goes topside," Novae informed her. "It comes out near to the oasis where you gathered water."

Anya looked a little surprised.

"Yes, we were watching you. There is an opening that surfaces between some of the trees. It is covered by a hatch. We have concealed it by using thick tar to stick a layer of sand onto the cover. We tend to exit here when we want to go up into the outside world. Once you step out over the top, you can safely survey your surroundings before leaving the security of the trees."

"I must say, Novae, your language and use of words is far better than mine. I assume that your people are well taught?"

"We like to practice conversation; in any case, we have the time!"

"Are there any other ways up?"

"Besides the way you came in, just one, but I am not

allowed to show you. Most of our people don't know that it exists."

"Why do you keep it a secret?"

Novae smiled. "We have few secrets and are open about most things, but I am afraid that I cannot answer that question either!"

Anya was not bothered by this denial. "Okay, I won't ask again, but I am curious as to why you even told me of its existence."

"Perhaps I should not have mentioned it, but I am sure that one day we will be able to tell you. In the meantime, I would appreciate it if you kept silent about what I have just mentioned."

"Of course I will, Novae; my lips are sealed!"

Novae led Anya back to check upon Jadine. As she approached, she altered the pitch of her body so as to tread silently across the stone floor. Jadine was still sleeping peacefully. Anya tip-toed back to the door where Novae was waiting. As they walked away, Anya asked, "What did you give her to make her sleep so long? I didn't think that she was so badly hurt that she would not regain her consciousness after all this time."

"We used to trade some leaves with the nomads that visited this site for water or a place to rest. From time to time, they gave us the seeds from the plant. We planted some near the edge of the trees and now we have our own supply. They like the sun, but also thrive on water, so we have to visit them most days. We dry the leaves and the seeds, and then cook them in oil and eat them. You can also smoke them if you prefer. They help you relax and make you feel happy. They help conversation, too! The seeds are much stronger. They take away pain and, if you take a lot, relaxation turns to sleep. We fried some of the ground hemp from the store room and gave it to Jadine when we dressed her wounds. It is better if she sleeps. It will give her body an opportunity to heal."

Anya nodded. "Her body will heal without doubt, but I hope that her hearing returns."

"She may just need a little time."

22

Anya and Novae had returned to their family's quarters. Jodie was still attempting to play a tune on Simone's instrument.

John stepped forwards. "We will be eating soon, if you would like to join us?"

Anya was hungry and thought that she was left with little choice. She wondered why the question had been posed, but decided that it was simply polite to ask. "Will the others be joining us?"

"Er, yes, we usually eat together in the main hall two or three times a week. It preserves a sense of community."

Anya forced a smile. "I'd be happy to."

"The little ones will come, too. Do not worry, Jodie will be close by."

"And Jadine, is she still sleeping?"

"She will be better left to rest. I am sure that she will awaken in the morning, though she may be a little hungry."

"I am, too. I'd love to share a meal with you."

"We have a goat. We usually save them for special occasions. It was slaughtered a short time ago and preserved in salt. It seems a good time to eat it now. Do not worry, there will be plenty left over for Jadine tomorrow."

They made their way to the large entrance chamber. Some of the other dwellers had prepared the room. A great dish had been placed in the centre. On a vast bed of rice was half of a roasted goat. Beside it, was a silver jug. As Anya neared, she saw that it contained a brown liquid, presumably to pour over the meat and rice. There were cushions scattered about over the floor. Some were occupied. Most of the group was already present, the remaining members were arriving. Niamh handed out a mixture of stone and wooden bowls. Many were similar, but no two were the same. Everyone waited until the last of the group had arrived.

John addressed the assembly, "Please begin. Enjoy the food; we will honour our guests later."

With that, everybody waited patiently to take their turn for a handful of rice and a shred of meat. Anya looked hesitant, not knowing quite what to do, and feared that she might offend someone by not following etiquette.

John turned and said, "Please, my dear, help yourself. There is no protocol here."

As Anya rose, she noticed Niahli by her side. He leant forward with her and tore off a strip of meat and put it on Anya's plate. Anya helped herself to rice and poured some of the brown liquid to one side of her dish. She tasted it. It was rich, meaty and spicy. Anya wished that she had taken more. Niahli grabbed the jug and poured some on her plate, and then he turned to help Jodie. Someone was missing; Salim. Where was Salim?

Anya could tell by the smiling and happy faces that this was something of a treat. Most of the people before her tried not to rush their food, but she could tell by their expressions that many were ravenously hungry. John though, clearly exercised control. He paused between mouthfuls, speaking to those around him. Niahli was a little less controlled, but he took the time to look and wink at Anya.

"Where's Salim?" she asked.

"Oh, he said that he was a little tired, but, if you ask me, I think that he just wanted to avoid answering questions about his trip up top to help rescue you three. He is very modest."

"Modest?"

"Yes, it means that he does not like to boast about his brave actions. I do not think that he is happy with being cast as a hero."

"But we are very grateful. If it was not for his efforts, we would have lost Jadine …."

At that moment, Salim walked up to them and sat beside Anya. His father glanced over. Salim nodded in acknowledgement and took some food.

"How is your hearing?" asked Anya woefully.

"Pardon?" asked Salim loudly. He was smiling. "Actually, it's okay now; just a bit of buzzing. I can hear well."

Anya felt confident and relaxed, so she placed an arm on his shoulder. "Tell me, Salim, what happened up there?"

Suddenly, there was silence. The whole group stopped and looked towards Salim, but he turned, and spoke only to Anya "I knew that Niahli was going to get you through the main hatch. I saw Jadine go back into the building and I knew that I had to get her out. I've never seen them do so much damage. Part of the building is in complete ruins. I was crouching in the corner of the lower courtyard. As you headed towards Niahli, I cut back in through the lower level and rushed up the stairway. Although the sound was intense down below, when I reached the upper level, I thought that my ears were going to explode. Without a torch, I had to feel my way across the floor until I found Jadine. She had been hit by falling debris and was barely conscious, but I was relieved to see that she was still alive. I pushed away some of the stones that had fallen on her prostrate body and, somehow, was able to coax her to her feet. She had managed to find and cling onto her water flask! By this time, you were safely below. In fact, at that moment, the noise stopped abruptly. I tried to get her out, down what remained of the outside stairs, but they had collapsed and the rubble below looked unstable. It was too dangerous, so we headed back into the building. I had planned to take us out into the desert, to get back via the oasis, but the stones had encircled the entrance. I feared what would happen if we tried to pass, so thought it best that we lay low for a while and wait for their next move. We had seen one or two of them enter earlier on the far side, but they must have left to join the others in the barricade."

"Is that when John and Niahli returned to find you?"

"Yes, they risked everything by returning with torches and calling out to me. My ears were ringing; I could barely hear their cries."

"There were stone creatures near the entrance to this underworld. How did you all get past them?"

Salim glanced across at his father nervously. "They had destroyed most of the chamber, but, somehow, we found a way past."

Anya sensed that Salim was hiding something, but did not think it appropriate to question him further. "Wow, you are a very brave man. I am most grateful for what you did to rescue my friend."

John added his version of events. "When we broke cover, the cacophony of sound resumed, but Salim had the briefest opportunity to call out, and we headed towards him. He managed to bring your friend with him to meet us as they sent more stonework sprawling across the site. Our greatest fear has always been that they would have some way of pursuing us down here. Maybe their size prevents them. They somehow glide over the sand above and have the mysterious power to generate enough sound to blast apart solid brickwork. They are able to bury themselves in the loose topsand, but it seems that they are not able to tunnel this far below. Anyway, we managed to secure our escape and return here without sustaining further injury."

"How...?" Anya wanted a little more detail, but John raised his hand with the flat of his palm facing her.

"Let us enjoy the rest of our meal."

Gradually, everyone present entered into their own conversations.

If Anya felt tired, Jodie was exhausted. Bags had developed under Jodie's eyes and her eyelids had begun to close whilst she was still eating. Novae approached Anya offering to take Jodie back to their sleeping quarters to spend the night with Simone. Anya felt that she could trust them, so was happy with the proposed arrangement. She was anxious to check on Jadine and knew that a peaceful night's sleep would do her no harm either.

* * *

There were several beds in their sleeping quarters, but Anya decided to lie beside Jadine. She did her best not to disturb her friend, but Jadine began to stir and became conscious of Anya's presence. Half awake, Jadine looked up at Anya and smiled for a few moments. Anya cradled her in her arms to comfort Jadine before she returned to a restful and peaceful slumber.

Jodie had to be carried back to her chamber by Novae. As much as she might have envisaged frolicking around with Simone at bedtime, she fell asleep instantly.

Novae ensured that both Jodie and Simone were tucked up in bed before heading back to be with Salim and the rest of her family. On her return, she found her companion deep in conversation with his brother and father. They were obviously talking about the temple rescue. They stopped abruptly when Novae approached.

"Hello, Novae." Salim was welcoming with his greeting.

"Hi. Simone and Jodie are sleeping. It has been a long

day for them both. Were you talking about what happened topside?"

It was John who responded first. "Yes, we are a little concerned by what all this activity means for us. People have visited the temple many times before. The stones have never reacted like this before."

"We were wondering why two women and a girl would be attacked with such ferocity," added Salim.

"I am considering taking a trip up to see if they are still congregating around the building," declared Niahli, showing no apparent concern.

"Don't you think that you've seen enough of them for one day?" asked Novae.

"We need to know what their intentions are. If the stones have any understanding of our world, they will know that the women are here."

"Why don't you wait until daybreak tomorrow? If they are still present in numbers, then we know that we have a real concern."

"I agree," said John. "We will wait until the morning, then go up to the surface at first light. We should all go and get some rest soon. We might need it!"

* * *

Anya awoke to find Jadine still cradled in her arms and that she had a stiff neck from sleeping in a semi-upright position. As soon as she tried to move, Jadine stirred.

"Anya? Where am I?"

"You're safe!"

"Jodie?"

"She's safe, too. You can hear me!"

"Yes, but there's a loud ringing in my ears! What happened?"

"Don't you remember being at the temple? The

megaliths?"

Jadine struggled to recall the last two days. "The building... I remember going back in to get the water...."

"Yes, Jadine, the stones were attacking us. They brought the building down around you. We were rescued and brought down here below the sands of the desert."

"Ah, my leg, my foot. My whole body aches."

"How is your head?"

Jadine gingerly touched the bump on her head with her fingers. It was beginning to subside. "Ouch! Actually, it's not too bad. What happened to me?"

"I think you were hit by falling stones. You are fortunate that they didn't kill you!"

"Right now, I don't feel so lucky!"

"Well, you should!" Anya's tone was harsh.

Tears welled up in Jadine's eyes.

"I'm sorry." Anya hugged her friend. "I just didn't want to lose you."

Jadine straightened up. "I'm so hungry. I could eat one of those camels all by myself!"

"I think that food is a little scarce down here most of the time, but I'm sure that they will be able to prepare something for you."

"They?"

"Novae and Niamh. Novae is with Salim, who rescued you. They dressed your wounds and cleaned you up yesterday."

"Oh.... I see. That was kind of them."

"Yes, it was. Jodie is with Simone, Novae's daughter."

"Is she truly safe?"

"Yes, I think so. These are good people."

"Good morning!" There was a shadow in the doorway. Novae stepped forward. In her hands was a large plate. "I know you're hungry! I promised Anya that I would bring you some of the leftover meat from last night's meal. I have wrapped it in fresh flat bread. We get a supply of flour from the traders. There should be plenty for both of you."

"Thank you. I was just telling Anya how hungry I am."

"I understand. We gave you something last night to calm the pain and help you relax. Unfortunately, it has this effect when it wears off."

"I'm sure that I will devour the lot, but first I need to pee!"

"Of course, follow me. It's just next door."

* * *

Whilst Jadine tucked into her first meal in two days, John and his two sons had already reached the oasis exit. The sun had yet to emerge from behind the dunes. John led them out of the tree line before trudging up the hill towards the temple. They approached the ruined building with caution, scanning the horizon as they walked. There was no sign of the great megaliths. The right side of the temple was almost completely destroyed, but most of the rubble had fallen within its boundary. After stopping to survey the scene from the outside, Salim was the first to go in through the main entrance. It was still very dark inside. He lighted the torch that he had extinguished earlier. The large internal stairway was mostly intact. Salim climbed the stars two at a time, closely followed by Niahli. John stayed behind to survey the lower floor.

Salim found that most of the upper floor remained as he had last seen it. However, the far chambers were now impassable. The stone roof had collapsed after the walls had been forced to implode. Salim recognised the spot where he had found Jadine. Within her outline were two large boulders that had been ejected from the wall. Niahli looked out over the desert. He was grateful that he could see nothing but sand.

They returned to the ground floor to catch up with their father. They found him in the chamber beyond the great hall. Unsurprisingly, this area was a scene of total destruction.

He turned to his sons and said, "I think that we were wise to approach from the oasis, but we need to check the crypt entrance. We cannot gain access to the courtyard through here. We will have to go out through one of the side openings and try to gain access around the far side."

Niahli and Salim turned and headed for one of the smaller rooms off to the side of the main chamber. John followed them into the one containing the remains of the body with the crushed skull. They climbed out of an opening in the wall and jumped down onto the soft sand.

After a short walk, they found themselves adjacent to a pile of rubble that had once contained the courtyard. Beyond this was the chamber containing the crypt, below which was the other entrance to their underworld. Most of this part of the building remained intact. There were no openings in the side wall, so they had to try to enter through the original doorway. Slowly, they picked their way over the rubble. A support slab, engraved with script, by their feet marked the way in. There was no way through. Without speaking, John pointed towards the roof. Salim nodded and pushed his father up, enabling him to grab hold of the top. Niahli did the same for Salim, and then John joined with his elder son to pull Niahli up to join them. Predictably, the stone roof was breached. Niahli dropped down to the left of the central slab that covered their entrance. Salim and John remained on the roof.

The torch was spent so Niahli had to manage with the available light that streamed in from above. He was relieved to see that the stone slab remained in place. As Niahli looked towards the far end of the chamber, he could see daylight through a large gap at ground level. He sighed as he realised that scaling the building had been unnecessary. As Niahli approached the opening, he suddenly stopped in his tracks!

A huge semi-elliptical stone appeared to be guarding the exit.

Niahli peered into the darkness to scrutinise its form. He had a sense of déjà vu. It stood before him motionless; the dark sunken 'eye' near the top was lifeless and indeed, as Niahli edged closer it could just have been any old stone. It was not! Niahli was about to dive through the hole in the brickwork when a violet light began to glow in the centre of its 'eye'. He hesitated for the briefest moment of time and his opportunity to escape was lost. The sand shifted below his feet and the megalith moved to block the exit. Niahli let out a loud cry and fled, terrified, in the opposite direction. Slowly, but relentlessly, a second megalith followed him.

"Father, Salim! Help me! Get me out of here!" Niahli looked up to see his father's head silhouetted against the daylight above.

His father held out a hand. Niahli jumped up, but he could not reach it. He looked behind him. The megalith was approaching. It began to pulse out regular low-frequency sounds. Niahli looked up again. John's head had gone! The stone was a few feet away.

"Niahli!" It was his father's voice.

He was suspended in the gap. Held out below him was a white tunic. Niahli crouched low, then leapt up and grabbed for the cloth. He missed. He stepped to one side and jumped up giving it everything he had. Salim lowered his father by the ankles. Niahli grabbed his brother's garment with one hand. He had sufficient strength to haul himself up enough to grab the cloth with both hands and he began to haul himself towards the hole in the roof. The robe lengthened as fibres began to tear. Niahli glanced below. The megalith was positioned directly underneath, waiting for him to fall. Using both hands, whilst trying not to jerk the cloth sharply, Niahli scampered up and grabbed his father's hand. At that moment, Salim ran backwards dragging them both out into the open air. Salim's robe drifted down onto the stone. Niahli picked himself up, supporting his weight on his grazed knees. He glanced back down, in time to see the megalith rocking to and fro in a frantic attempt to remove the veil that obscured its view of the world. There was a loud thud that shook the stone beneath their feet as the megalith fell backwards and crashed to the ground. The pulses stopped and there was silence.

Niahli stood and looked at his brother. He was naked. They both laughed. They turned to follow their father off the roof.

"We must get back before the other one follows us," said Niahli.

"Careful! We do not want any more injuries," remarked his father as they hurriedly picked their way back over the rubble.

Salim was the first to reach the desert floor on the front elevation, but he helped his father down and waited for his brother to catch up. "Let's get out of here!" Salim set off at speed towards the oasis.

He had travelled no fewer than five paces when he tripped and was sent sprawling face down into the sand. As he went down, his body was subjected to a huge jolt of energy. His legs were numb, but he managed to push his torso up using his arms to look back and see what had felled him. John and his brother saw immediately. The top of a grey stone obelisk was protruding from the sand. The moment Salim had passed over it; they had seen an arc of blue light hit his leg.

Salim slowly got to his feet; perspiration had moistened the sand causing it to stick to his body. His legs were still shaky, but he managed to stand and examine his surroundings; a cold shiver ran down his spine. Around the building's perimeter were many more stone tips spread out like a minefield before them, and they were now rising.

John and Niahli were with him now, hurrying Salim along. There was sufficient space between the rising stone mounds to navigate their way between them and they soon found themselves fleeing up the dune towards the oasis and safety. When they reached the entrance to their sanctuary, John had one last look back before securing the hatch. Nothing! They had not been followed.

23

As John, Niahli and Salim descended the stone ladder, they began to discuss which version of events they should tell their friends and family.

"We should not tell the others what happened today," suggested John. "It would only cause unnecessary concern and we do not know that they pose a direct threat to us down here."

"Yes, but what about our ventilation system? Most of the air in our quarters comes from the shafts that run up to the ruin. Part of the building has already been demolished. If they were to block the vents, either accidentally or deliberately, we would suffocate."

"No, but we are not solely reliant upon them. We would not suffocate immediately; we could unblock them."

"Unless they prevented us from doing so!"

Niahli joined the discussion. "Even if they leave us alone in our underground world, their mere presence here will restrict our movements. We cannot enter or exit through the building, and avoiding the site would restrict hunting opportunities and trade."

"My sons, you are missing the underlying issue. We need to understand why they are here and what they want. Why have they suddenly come to this site in such numbers? Why do they remain? Is the arrival of our visitors a coincidence?"

Despite his lack of clothing, Salim waited at the bottom

of the shaft for the other two to join him before continuing the conversation. "Are you suggesting, then, that the stones have come here seeking the three women who are now in our midst?"

"I'm just saying that we must consider the possibility."

"We cannot know for sure. Perhaps we should ask them to leave and see if the stones follow them."

"No, we must not take that course of action. These women would not be able to survive alone in the desert in their current state. It would be inhumane and I could not bring myself to do that."

"But, Father, by not doing so, you put all of us at risk."

Niahli interrupted, "Salim, you are getting ahead of yourself. We cannot be sure that the stones are seeking our visitors and, if they were, with whatever intelligence they have, I'm sure that they know where we are, and that the women are with us."

"My brother, that is my point, too, and I fear for what may happen to us all."

John tried to calm what was quickly becoming a heated debate. "They must have arrived here for a reason. We have chosen to take them in and, therefore, have a moral responsibility for their well being. Niahli is right. They know that the women are here. We must wait and watch for their next move. Perhaps the stones will remain. Perhaps they will leave. Time will tell. Let us make our guests comfortable and 'restrict' what we say to the others for the time being. Just tell them that we have our suspicions and that one of the stones is guarding the temple."

"And what do we do in the meantime?" Salim seemed impatient.

"We must take turns to watch the site. I'll speak to Momo and Sayid; they will help us and be discreet."

"And when do we begin our observations?"

"We'll go back and report our findings to the others.

Salim, you must get some clothes and return shortly to act as the first lookout. I will organise your relief in due course. Perhaps Niahli should take the next watch…. Please, do not mention any of this to our visitors. It would make them uneasy with our people at a time when we should be doing our best to welcome them."

"But…."

"Please, Salim, follow my instructions. If we need to modify our plan, I will have no hesitation."

* * *

John and Niahli returned to their chamber to find Anya and Jadine with Jodie, Novae and Simone. They told them the 'agreed' version of events. After enquiring about Jadine's hearing and general well being and promising to update the rest of the settlers, they made their excuses and departed to seek out Momo and Sayid, two of John's closest friends and founder members of the colony. Salim had dressed and was already on his way back to watch over the temple.

Jodie was happy. She had slept well, Anya had returned with Jadine, who, in spite of complaining about ringing in her ears, aches and pains plus a very sore foot, was otherwise well. There was another important factor contributing to her good mood; she had company. Since leaving her settlement on that fateful day several months before, Jodie had not had an opportunity to play with someone of similar age. Simone was fun and Jodie loved to play with her musical instrument. Even the perpetual darkness and a need to take care with the torches did not dampen her enthusiasm.

Novae had introduced Jadine to various members of the group. Niamh had offered to give Jadine an extensive tour of the caverns and chambers. Jadine declined due to her injuries, happy enough just to keep the weight off her feet and talk to the girls. Niamh had told them that she hoped to see them all later before she went off to see her friends. Anya had also awoken that morning feeling a little stiff and sore. She too was glad of the company and was content just to sit and chat.

* * *

Momo was quite conspicuous. He had dark oily skin and a tall, lanky frame. He shaved his head to disguise his baldness. Such was his height, he was forced to stoop as he made his way through some of the lower corridors. Wherever Momo went, Sayid was usually close by. They were the best of friends, and had been since the early days of the settlement. They both had companions and growing children who also got along well. In such a compact underground community, tolerance, understanding and forgiveness were essential qualities.

Sayid's appearance was very different from Momo's. He was a great deal shorter; his skin was significantly lighter, although more orange in colour and despite the limited availability of food stuff, his waist was rotund. He kept a long beard and had long, matted glossy black hair. Despite his compact and rounded physique, he was as strong as a camel. He particularly enjoyed trips up topside with Momo's boys as it was always an opportunity to have a wrestling match. He thought nothing of lifting them above his head and throwing them up a sand dune. Momo did not mind. He saw it as character building. The most important things in Sayid's world were his two daughters, Novae and Niamh.

John and Niahli found Momo and Sayid playing a board game in the corner of the main vault. There was a group of women towards the centre of the room who were sitting in a line as they worked on a tapestry depicting the desert at sunset. The assemblage included Momo and Sayid's companions, and Niamh, who had just joined them, and several younger members of their extended family. John acknowledged everyone whilst Niahli walked straight over to the two men and sat at a right angle between them. John eventually took his place opposite his son.

In a hushed, controlled voice John proceeded to tell his friends what had happened that morning. He told them of Salim's current whereabouts and their plan to keep watch over the megaliths. Momo and Sayid coolly continued to play their game. They understood the need not to cause alarm amongst their population. From time to time, Niahli added detail, but tried not to interrupt his father's flow. When John had finished he asked Momo and Sayid if they had any questions or misgivings. Despite looks of concern, they both shook their heads. John's wishes were implicit. Momo offered to take the next watch just after midday. It was agreed that Sayid would be the next lookout, followed by Niahli. Finally, John would take the night watch as he would not be missed.

* * *

Anya decided to ask Novae about Jed and Zack. "You said that you know of Jed and Zack?"

Anya had to wait for a response. "Yes, we know them. Several generations ago, we would have all been part of the same nomadic tribe. We have chosen to live down here whilst they have chosen to risk their very existence by remaining up there! Though, we are grateful for what they do. You see, they trade with us and bring supplies."

"You trade with them? Whatever have you got that they would want? Sand?" Anya's question was rather sarcastic.

"Actually, you are closer than you think. At the far end

of one of the passageways, we have discovered a layer of rock containing hard gemstones. They polish up clear."

Novae lifted her necklace to show Anya. "I believe that they were once the most prized possessions throughout the world. Some of the people who Jed and Zack trade with still value them. They are nice, but we are more than happy to exchange them for food and other essential supplies."

"Are they the only people who you trade with?"

"Oh no, we have a number of other visitors, and, when it is vitally necessary, we have people who venture far into the outside world, but Jed and Zack like to visit us fairly frequently."

"At the time, they seemed very kind and I thought that they were happy enough to assist us. I'm not so sure why they left us here without mentioning you."

"I cannot be sure, but I guess that there are several reasons. Firstly, in return for an unrelenting supply of diamonds, we have made them promise never to reveal their source. We want as few people as possible to know that we are down here. Secondly, they fear this region and the wide dune plateaux to the west. They are unlikely to venture much past the ruin."

"I have seen why they have such fear, but they did little to warn us about the strange megaliths."

"To be fair, no one has seen much activity of late, and perhaps they respected your determination to reach your final destination. Anyway, Jed is a deeply religious man. He believes that your fate is predetermined. That everything is 'Gods will'. I'm not as sure about Zack. Deep down, he is a good man and is always keen to demonstrate his loyalty to Jed, but, basically, I suspect that greed might get the better of him from time to time."

"Well, they have brought us this far, and we have met you. For that, I am thankful!"

* * *

Momo made his way up the ladder to the oasis. He was forced to squint and shut one eye as he stepped out into the bright sunlight. It was exceedingly hot. He knew that Salim would be grateful when he took over the watch. Momo could see Salim's flattened form lying near the top of a small dune facing the ruined temple. Salim did not move. Momo jogged over to where he was lying.

Salim spun around, knife at the ready. "Oh, it is you! Hi, Momo."

"Hello, Salim." Momo took up position beside his friend. "I don't see anything. Where are they?"

"That's the thing! They are almost entirely buried in the sand," said Salim, pointing. "See, there's the top of one, near the entrance."

"Yes, I see."

"It is as if they are sleeping or waiting for something. When I returned this morning, I did not know what I would find. As we left the temple and woke them, they started to rise out of the sand, but now it would seem that they have just burrowed their way back down."

"Why do you think they are here?"

"I am not at all sure. I am not even sure if they have intelligence or a consciousness. If they have, they must know that we are here."

"This position is very exposed."

"There is no natural cover in the desert. One cannot see what is happening from the oasis and it would seem that the building is out of bounds."

"You must be hot and thirsty by now. Go back and I will take over the watch. Please remind Sayid to take his turn later this afternoon."

"I will. Thank you, Momo."

Salim edged his way back on his elbows and knees

before retreating to the sanctuary of the shaft.

Later that afternoon, Sayid took the watch. The handover was equally uneventful with Momo having nothing much to report, and little to say other than to complain about the heat.

* * *

It was early evening. Though not as lavish as the previous night, a communal meal was shared in the main chamber. Anya sat between John and Niahli; Jadine sat on the end next to Niahli, facing Jodie and Simone. John was not asked by the larger group about his earlier trip outside and he did not volunteer any information. No one missed Sayid as he was prone to doing his own thing.

Anya turned to John. There were many things that she wanted to ask him, but decided that a personal question might actually be easier for him to discuss than some of her other subject matter.

"John, you have two great sons, but what of their mother?"

"It has been a while now…" John looked thoughtful. "…Since Beatrice passed. Several years, I think."

"If you don't mind me asking, what happened?"

"No, it is permissible for you to ask such a question; after all, you told us about the sad loss of your companion."

John seemed quite comfortable with the thought of recounting a tragic event. "About three years ago, it had rained. There was a sudden and torrential downpour. We were worried that our chambers were going to flood, as water seeped in through the exits. As I remember, the roofs of our tunnels and chambers dripped or cascaded water a day or so after the rain had stopped. Anyway, recollections passed down through many generations and my own personal experience suggested that, soon after the rain came, some parts of the desert would become fertile and green. We knew that seeds would germinate and that certain plants would bear fruit. Gradually, over a period of days, we saw signs of growth. Several months later, it was a bonanza for all of us living down here. The oasis was like the Garden of Eden. Every morning, a party would go up topside and collect whatever was edible. Beatrice went up on the fourth such day. She set out alone early in the morning. A friend found her body face down in the sand just before noon. To this day, I am not sure how or why she died, but I have my suspicions."

"Who or what do you think killed her? What killed Beatrice?"

"At first, we thought that her body was unmarked, but, when we were preparing her body for cremation, we noticed a mark on the side of her head, hidden under her hair, a sort of burn, I guess. That was the only hint as to how she died. I know a human could not do that. There were other clues in the sand. Strange tracks that were not made by man or beast. It had to be the stone creatures.... Since then, we have seen very little of them; until the last few days, that is."

"Why do you suppose they are here now?" Anya seemed to presume that they were still up there.

John leant towards Anya and reduced his voice to a husky whisper. "I have no idea. I am sure that it may be just a chance event. It seems that the temple may be their focus of attention for now, but, hopefully, they will leave soon. We will keep an eye on them, but I do not want to concern my people unduly. Understand?"

Anya simply nodded. She had gleaned some of the information that she originally desired.

John stood and addressed his community, "Let us be entertained!" Then he turned to Jodie and, in a softer, warmer voice, said, "If you will be patient for a few moments, I am sure that you will enjoy this."

Niamh and four other younger women scampered off. When they returned, they were wearing long flowing costumes. On their faces, they wore brightly coloured masks themed around characters that could be seen carved upon the many walls of the chambers. Simone had brought her instrument and began to strum a tune. One of the other young men joined in playing a set of hand drums. The troop began to re-enact an imaginary ritual from a time long ago. Jodie was thrilled with the performance, but Anya noticed that Jadine was now in some discomfort.

Anya leant behind Niahli to ask, "Jadine, are you okay?"

"I'm just stiffening up some from sitting here. Nothing to worry about. I just need to move around a bit."

"I'm aching a little myself."

Niahli overheard what they we discussing. "If you come with me before you retire, I will ensure that you both have a good night's sleep."

"What about Jodie?" asked Anya, more out of politeness than concern.

"I am sure that she would be happy to spend one more night with Simone."

Anya checked the sleeping arrangements with Jodie, then Novae and Simone, before saying goodnight to John and joining with Jadine to follow Niahli.

When they reached Niahli's quarters, he reached up to a shelf and pulled down a bell-shaped pipe and a small cloth pouch. He took out what looked like some dried leaves, stalks and stems and began stuffing them into the pipe.

"Jadine, this is similar to what we gave you when you first came in. It may be smoked for recreation, but we tend to reserve it for medicinal purposes."

Niahli lighted a fine taper from the wall torch, and then

used the taper to light the material in the pipe. He took a few puffs then passed it over to Jadine.

"Thank you." She inhaled deeply, then coughed and spluttered. Undeterred, Jadine took another drag. She began to smile. "Anya, you must try some!"

Anya took the pipe and obliged. She managed to hold the smoke in. "Wow, my head feels light."

Niahli intervened, "Now take the pipe back to your room. Take this pouch and use a little more if you want. The smoke will make you feel good and numb any pains that you may have. You might find that you become extremely talkative. I suggest that you try not to stay up too late and allow it to help you sleep."

Jadine and Anya burst out laughing as Niahli led them towards their sleeping chamber.

Niahli left them at the doorway, pulling across a shutter made of dried palm leaves. Anya joined Jadine on one of the beds as she repacked and relighted the pipe. Jadine filled her lungs with the acrid smoke, and then proceeded to blow it out through her nostrils before passing the pipe to Anya. Anya tried to do the same, but ended up having a coughing fit. As her coughs subsided, they turned to giggles. Jadine was already laughing hysterically.

"Shush!" said Anya, putting a finger to her lips whilst making more noise whilst doing so.

"You shush!"

"We need to be quiet." Anya tried to lower her voice to a whisper, but continued to titter.

"We need to be quiet." Jadine was now mocking Anya by repeating her every word.

The frivolity continued for some time until Jadine finally declared, "Let's set the pipe away now and put out the light. We should try to get some rest. Come here and lie with me."

Anya extinguished the torch that lighted their room and

took off her robe. Jadine opened out the thin blanket that had been folded at the bottom of the bed, dropped her tunic and pulled the sheet over them.

They were lying side by side. After a few moments of silence, Jadine slid her hand over and began to caress one of Anya's breasts. Anya giggled and moved her hand down to stroke Jadine's outer thigh. Jadine lifted the palm of her hand and used her fingers to stimulate Anya's nipples before moving on to explore areas lower down her friend's body. Both of the women continued to giggle as Jadine's hand found its way to the smooth skin at the top of Anya's inner thighs.

"I was a little shocked to discover what they had done to me. I don't remember much about it, but Novae told me what she did. I'm pleased, though."

"I enjoyed it," said Anya, smiling as she recalled the experience.

Jadine's fingers gently forced their way into the gap between Anya's legs. Jadine was somewhat surprised to find that the warm, fleshy folds were already moist, but then seized the opportunity to massage some of the warm, sticky secretions a little higher, towards an eager clitoris. Anya's hands went back behind her head as she moaned with pleasure. Whilst lying on her side, Jadine patiently used her long, slender middle finger to bring Anya to a shuddering climax. When the tingling had subsided, Anya leant over and kissed Jadine firmly on the lips. Her tongue briefly intertwined with Jadine's. "Would you like me to do the same for you, then? I could go one better if you like!"

24

After saying goodnight to Anya and Jadine, Niahli had headed up to take over the watch from Sayid. Darkness had long since fallen like a cloak over the desert landscape. The moon was waning so what little light there was, was provided by the millions of stars in the night sky. Niahli had found Sayid, as expected, gazing down on the ruined temple. Sayid had told Niahli that nothing had moved, that nothing had changed and that he had spent what seemed like an eternity staring down at nothingness! Niahli had told Sayid to go and get some sustenance.

Having dozed for few hours, John emerged from the trapdoor, surprisingly eager to take up his lonely vigil. A subterranean existence meant that his eyes did not require time to adjust to the low levels of light.

Niahli turned as he anticipated his father's approach.

John crouched as he neared the dune ridge. The handover was predictable. Niahli echoed the sentiments of Sayid before him.

As Niahli turned to head back to the settlement, he was distracted by a bright light moving through his peripheral vision. "Father!" It was as much of a shout as a whisper. "Look there!" Niahli's finger tracked across the horizon as he pointed towards the distant orb.

"So, my son, it seems that we are not alone in this desolate wilderness."

"What is it?"

"It is a light. Surely even you can see that."

"I know, but what do you think is producing such a glow?"

"I have seen these lights many times over the years. Sometimes white like this one. Sometimes there are different colours. Have I not told you about them before?"

"Yes, Father, but this is the first time that I have seen one with my own eyes."

"Anyway, I am not sure how such light is produced or, indeed, how such a thing glides across the sky, but I know one thing for sure: they are bad news. Such appearances always coincide with strange events and disappearances."

"Maybe we should head back down?"

"No, you go if you like. I want to stay here and observe it for a while. Besides, it is my watch. We still need to keep an eye on the living stones around the temple."

"They have not moved since this morning. Even if they did, there is no guarantee that you would spot them in this light."

"You underestimate your father's vision. I am not too old, you know. The trick is to look away slightly. In the dark, you see more out of the corner of your eye than you do if you stare at an object."

"Look, it is heading this way! The light is changing. There is red and blue!"

"Shush! Before we know it, it could be on top of us!"

"It is heading for the temple!"

"Yes, I'm sure that you are correct. Just keep your head and voice down."

The white orb appeared to grow in size as it approached the temple from a position directly opposite. Towards the base, a circle of light radiated red then blue. It stopped and hovered directly above the ruin. A narrow beam of violet light cut down towards the roof of the building. It scanned across the stonework as if reading and recording every feature, before moving onto the desert floor surrounding the building. The beam traced its way around the whole of the periphery before disappearing.

Gradually, the air began to fill with the muted sound of sand shifting over rock. The night sky did indeed provide sufficient light to illuminate the events below.

"Look, Niahli, they are moving!"

As if orchestrated from above, every one of the megaliths began to rise up out of the sand. Once on the surface, they began to move out in either one direction or another. Their flattened bases cut a path through the dunes as they slowly filed around behind the ruined temple and headed out into the desert beyond. It was some time before that last one had dipped out of sight behind the building. All the while, the glowing orb remained in position overhead as if to direct the operation.

The light went out momentarily as the orb shot towards the two men on the dune. It stopped dead above them. Niahli and John found themselves bathed in a blinding white light. Niahli covered his eyes with his hands. He could almost see the bones of his fingers through his eyelids. As abruptly as it had appeared, the light went out. The two men opened their eyes, but saw very little at first. The bright white light was then replaced by the violet beam. It tracked painlessly over their bodies. Then, in an instant, it was gone. There was a great rush of air as the unlighted orb sped off into the distance.

* * *

Jodie awoke to deep pulses of sound beating through the chamber like a slow heartbeat. She looked around and was frightened to find herself all alone. She called out loudly for her mother, but nobody came. Then she called out to Novae, Simone, Salim and finally Jadine. Still no one. She got up out of the bed and tip-toed to the doorway. Slowly, she edged her head out and looked left, then right. Nothing! Jodie closed her eyes tightly for a few moments hoping that the sound would go away. It did not. She reopened her eyes, and then proceeded to step out into the passageway. The air was unusually cold and damp. The pulses of sound seemed more distant now. Jodie began to run, heading for the large main chamber. She arrived to find rubble and debris everywhere. Chunks of stone were breaking off from the roof of the vast cavern and crashing down around her.

Jodie retraced her steps then branched off towards the room where her mother and Jadine had been staying. The palm screen was lying trampled on the floor. The chamber was empty. Back out in the corridor, the slow rhythmic pulses once again began to grow in volume and intensity. Jodie attempted to head away from the sound as she tried to navigate her way through the labyrinth of passageways and tunnels. Finally, she found herself back at the imposing entrance chamber. Fortunately, no more rock was falling from the ceiling. The tiled floor was now barely visible. Jodie made her way up the grand staircase towards the passageway that led out to the temple. She knew that the complex had been deserted and that she had to get out.

The rock face before her began to shudder and rumble. Once more, stones began to cascade down from above. One of the megaliths emerged out of the tunnel before her. It was larger then the dimensions of the passageway, but somehow it managed to force its way through. A shaft of violet light emanated from a deep indentation centred in its upper quarter. The beam was broken when Jodie's slight frame passed across it. Jodie stood frozen to the spot. The megalith came to a halt and the debris shower subsided. The room was soundless. Instead of fleeing, Jodie turned to face the giant stone.

"What do you want with us? What have you done to

the people?"

There was no response. Again, Jodie asked the same questions. Again, the stone remained silent.

Jodie stepped forward, and then to one side, attempting to pass around the megalith. Her fragile body was hit by a bolt of energy and she was catapulted across the chamber. She was stunned for a moment. Her back and elbows were grazed and bleeding. Slowly, she got to her feet and dusted herself down. The stone obelisk began to advance towards her. She screamed and took off in the opposite direction. The corridors were dark now. Jodie could hardly see as some of the lanterns had gone out. In a state of panic, she hunted for the one that would lead her towards the stone ladder and up to freedom. Without looking back, Jodie climbed up as fast as her hands and legs would allow. As she reached the top, she pulled the lever and the trap door swung open. The intensity of the daylight momentarily blinded her and she almost fell back down the shaft. She managed to snatch the lip of the supporting beam to steady herself. Tentatively, Jodie opened one eye, pulled her battered body up over the lip and hauled herself out. A second lever closed the stone hatch behind her.

Jodie wandered wearily out into the centre of the oasis. She was extremely thirsty and decided to pause for long enough to dig down and take in some water. When she had quenched her thirst, she stood and looked out at the desert landscape. Jodie scanned the full three hundred and sixty degrees around her. She did not want to go to the ruin again. In the opposite direction was a vast sand dune. Jodie had never seen beyond it, indeed, she had never climbed to the crest. She wanted to see what lay ahead, so she trudged off in that direction through the soft, warm sand. With each footstep, she made little progress. As the dune steepened, the sand fell away and her standing foot slid down and backwards. Soon, Jodie was reduced to using her hands and arms to drag her body towards the peak. When she eventually reached the crest, she threw her elbows over the other side and used her belly to flatten down the sand. She was able to use her right hand to shield the glare of the sun from her eyes. Jodie looked out into the distance. Before her was a vast, almost featureless desert plain. Halfway to the horizon was a large group of people. Jodie watched for a few moments. They were definitely heading away from her, but they were corralled like cattle, surrounded by twenty or more slow-moving megalithic stone creatures. Jodie sensed something, and turned to see two more, just below the dune ridge behind her.

25

Jodie awoke once more. Simone was standing by the bed looking down at her. Simone's face was etched with real concern.

"What's the matter?" asked Jodie.

"Are you all right?" asked Simone. "You were calling out and crying in your sleep."

Jodie gathered her thoughts. "I was having a bad dream. You know, one of those that seems so real that it can stay with you for the rest of the day."

"What were you dreaming about that was so bad?"

"Oh, it doesn't matter. It's over now. Where is your mother? I would like to go and find my mother and Jadine. I need to check and make sure that *they* are all right."

* * *

Anya awoke from her slumber to find herself staring at Jadine's feet. As she began to recall the events of the previous night, she felt regret tinged with guilt as her thoughts turned to Keon. Concerns over her own morality were soon overtaken by her ravenous appetite. Anya sat up and reached over to prod Jadine's shoulder.

"Good morning, Anya," said Jadine in a sleepy tone.

"Come on, we must get up. I think that we've slept in late again."

"What's the hurry? It's not like we have some place to

be!"

"I want to go and find Jodie. I need to see if she's okay."

"She will be; don't worry."

"I have to worry; she is my daughter!"

"Anya, calm down. What's the matter? Are you ashamed about what happened last night?"

"I'm never going to smoke that stuff again...."

"It's me!" Jodie was at the door. She pushed the palm partition to one side and ran towards her mother. Anya met Jodie with a huge hug that lifted her clean off the floor.

Novae appeared behind them. "I think that Jodie wants to be with her mother. She had some kind of nightmare last night. Simone said that she awoke screaming, but she seems fine now."

"Are you okay now?" asked Anya, concern showing on her face.

"I'm fine. I just missed you; that's all."

"What did you dream about that was so bad?"

"Nothing much." Jodie looked around towards Novae. "I'll tell you later."

"Thank you, Novae."

A few moments later, Niahli appeared with a tray of food.

"Niahli!" Jadine moved her arm to cover her naked breasts. "Anya, pass my robe, please."

Anya grinned before obliging.

Niahli turned away as Jadine slipped on her robe.

"There, you can turn around now."

"I thought you might be hungry. It is not much, but, if you are staying, you will have to get used to the way that we ration our food."

Anya walked over and took the tray. "Thank you, Niahli, but I'm not sure that we will stay with you for much longer."

Jadine threw her a questioning glance.

"Actually, what I meant to say was that we haven't yet decided how much longer we wish to take advantage of your kind hospitality."

Niahli went over and sat on the other bed before continuing, "The stones have gone. We watched them up and leave last night. They filed out into the desert beyond the temple. Salim has gone out with my father to check that none remain, but I am confident that they will return with good news."

Jodie stared at Niahli. "I dreamt about the stones last night. I dreamt that they came down here and took everyone."

"Jodie, they can't come down here. They have all gone away. We are safe now."

"I hope so. I like it down here. I like to be with Simone."

Anya reached for some dried fruit. "Jodie, let's eat, and then we can go and find Simone. Maybe she will introduce you to some of the other children."

"Yes, I would like that, but, tonight, I want to sleep with you."

"That's fine, Jodie. Of course you can." Jadine did not mind, either.

Niahli stood and looked as if he was about to leave. "Jadine, would you like to join me while I do my chores?"

"Why not?" Jadine followed Niahli out of the chamber.

Holding a flaming torch, Niahli led Jadine down an unlighted, narrow passageway that appeared to terminate in a blind ending. Niahli passed the torch to Jadine, then crouched down and slid his fingers under a slab of stone on the floor below. Niahli hauled the slab at one end and it swung up as if hinged on the opposite side. He then took the torch back from Jadine and climbed down into the shaft using a rope ladder. He beckoned Jadine to follow him. As Jadine neared the bottom of the short descent, Niahli offered his arm to steady her. Jadine found herself in a damp chamber, where she could barely stand upright. Niahli lighted a second torch fixed to the wall.

"Look here!" exclaimed Niahli, picking up a small, pointed hammer from the floor.

"What is it?"

"This is where we gather the precious stones that we trade for food and supplies.

Jadine looked at the seam in front of her. "Are these white bits of rock what you prize?"

"Yes, but only insomuch as they are currency to our people. Most of us have one or two that we have attempted to polish and have mounted as jewellery, but they are sought after by many people in far-off lands."

Niahli proceeded to chip away at an area of rock in one corner of the chamber. "The stones themselves are very hard. You cannot damage them with the hammer."

A small lump of rock dislodged itself, shattering on the floor. Niahli picked up a portion and held a light to it to examine it further. Attached to a black portion of rock was a frosted crystalline structure. Niahli held the stone to the floor and severed the two pieces with several precise blows.

"Here, take this. We cannot cut these stones, but I will show you how to polish one a little, using a paste made from sand and sap from above. Be warned, it takes forever!"

"Thank you, Niahli. It already has a raw beauty all of its own."

"Likewise!" Niahli gestured using his outstretched palm towards Jadine, whose blush was evident even in the half light of the chamber.

"Nonsense, I am bruised and battered. Not a pretty sight at all."

"Your bruising is already beginning to fade, but any man blessed with the gift of sight can see your splendour within."

Jadine blushed some more. "Niahli, do you not see the beauty that surrounds you every day?"

"What do you mean?"

"Niamh! I have been here for such a short time, yet I can see the way that she looks at you."

Niahli laughed. "Her sister is with my brother. I think it is more a case of brotherly love."

"I don't think so."

Niahli shrugged. "I love Niamh as my own sister, but I do not have any feelings for her beyond that."

"A pity, I'm sure. Is there anyone else?"

"I do not think so." Niahli seemed somewhat unsure.

"Anyway, may we go and polish my stone?"

"If you wish."

Jadine headed for the ladder.

Niahli glanced down at the short, cropped robe that Novae had given her to wear. "To save further embarrassment, it might be better if I climbed up first."

Jadine took a moment to comprehend his meaning, then blushed for a third time. She stepped back. "After you!"

Niahli extinguished the second torch, then climbed up and out of the cavern.

* * *

Whilst Niahli was apparently unfazed by his early morning encounter with the glowing orb, his father was much more concerned. John and Niahli had returned together and described their experience to Salim. John had sent a message via Salim to Sayid and Momo to inform them that there was no longer a requirement for them to keep watch over the temple. John decided to allow Sayid and Momo to rest before seeking an audience to discuss that morning's events. This also allowed him time to return to the temple with Salim to check that it was indeed, no longer occupied. They had decided to risk a return using the internal trapdoor. John was unsure whether or not this entrance would be blocked by fallen stones, but they elected to try it anyway. They were relieved to find it clear of any obstructions although the mid-section of the building around the courtyard was clearly irreparably damaged. After a careful survey of the ruins, John was reassured to find no trace of the stone creatures, and crucially, that all three of the known ventilation shafts seemed intact.

On returning using the same route through which they had departed, John and Salim found Sayid with Momo, playing their regular board game.

"So they have departed." Sayid's question was more of a statement.

"Yes, we saw them all rise and move out into the desert en masse, but there is more to it than that." John proceeded to tell Momo and Sayid about their experience with the glowing orb.

"And you and Niahli were both unharmed?"

"Yes," replied John. "For a moment, I feared the worst, but we are clearly still alive to tell the tale. Perhaps it did not see us as a threat or maybe it was looking for something or someone else."

"What have you told the others?" asked Sayid.

"Simply that the stones have gone and that we are safe for the time being."

"And do you truly believe that?"

"For now, yes. Our existence in this desert wilderness and these underground chambers has never been without danger. Maybe in the future they will return. Who knows what other challenges we will face, but, for now, we must continue with our lives as usual."

* * *

Niahli returned with Jadine.

"Look, isn't it beautiful?" Jadine held out a partially polished diamond. "I still have some way to go before it will be finished."

John frowned. His expression denoted that he was unhappy with his younger son for revealing where they kept their most precious resource.

"Surely, Father, we can spare a single gem." Clearly Niahli had missed the point of his father's displeasure.

"Jadine, Niahli ought to have gained our permission before taking you to see where we mine our gemstones. However, what's done is done, but might I ask you not to flaunt your prize in front of our people?"

"I am sorry, John. Of course not! I did not know that I was not meant to see. Do you want it back?"

John shook his head. "Take it and keep it safe. You are not to blame." He glared at Niahli.

"You should lighten up, Father, and be thankful that the threat has passed."

"Enough!" John dismissed Niahli with a sweep of his arm and a flick of the wrist.

* * *

That evening, as was customary, everyone gathered to share a meal. John confirmed to the chambers' inhabitants that the megaliths had, indeed, departed. There was rejoicing and optimism amongst the people. Jadine sat next to Niahli and Anya immediately noticed the change in behaviour that had beset her companion. Anya was a little surprised at Jadine's sudden affection towards her male companion, but she was also somewhat relieved. Anya glanced around at the faces of those close to Niahli, wondering if they too had picked up on what was taking place. It was clear by the way that Niamh coldly eyed Jadine that she had indeed noticed and was less than pleased. Niamh caught Anya's look and forced a smile.

Afterwards, instead of spending more time with Niahli, Jadine decided that it would be wise to return with Jodie and Anya. She too, had sensed Niamh's disapproval. Jodie climbed onto the bed to lie beside her mother whilst Jadine settled down on the leafy mattress opposite.

"Are you comfortable, Anya?" asked Jadine.

"What a difference a day makes."

"Pardon?"

"Oh, never mind. Good night, Jadine."

"Night."

"Sweet dreams," said Anya to her daughter.

Jodie looked serious. "Last night, I dreamt that I awoke to find myself down here alone, and that the stones had come and taken everyone away before returning for me."

"Yes, but it was only a dream."

26

Jodie was flying over the sand. Below her were people, scattered like cattle in the desert, being driven forward by the living stones. She tried to go lower. She wanted to shout down to her mother and Jadine, and to John to ask him to come and rescue her, but she could not. They were behind her, controlling her flight. She could not see them. They had prevented her from even looking around. As she flew beyond the last person, she began to lose hope. They forced her on towards the horizon. She pleaded with them to release her. Suddenly, she was unable to speak. They were cold and merciless, and she knew that they were never going to release her.

* * *

Jodie awoke with a jolt. The last thing she remembered was the sensation of falling, falling and spinning as she struggled to regain her balance. Her sudden movement woke Anya, too. Anya looked across the room. In the flickering torchlight, she could see that Jadine's bed was empty.

Anya helped Jodie change her clothes before changing her own. Anya had no idea if it was day or night, such was the perpetual challenge of underground living, but she was eager to get out of the chamber and find some other human company. For some reason, she too, felt uneasy. Carrying a spare torch, Anya headed towards John's chamber. She wanted some answers. As she approached the juncture of the main passageway, Anya heard familiar voices. They were laughing and joking. She knew at once it was Jadine and Niahli.

"Good morning, Jodie. Good morning, Anya." Jadine's greeting was cheery.

"Well, hello there." Anya was at least pleased to see someone.

"Good morning, Jadine." Jodie's greeting sounded more formal. Maybe she was a little jealous.

"We are going topside," said Niahli. "Jadine needs to see daylight."

"She's not the only one, but I thought I might have a chat with John first."

"Would you like us to wait for you?"

"No, you go on. I'll catch up with you later."

"Okay, I'll see you in a while." Jadine skipped off as if all her woes had been lifted by the company of a single man. Her foot was clearly much better.

Anya continued on with Jodie in tow. First, she went in to find Novae and Simone, hoping that they would mind Jodie whilst she talked to John.

Anya found Novae rubbing the sleep from her eyes. Salim was up and having a drink of water. He was wearing the skimpiest of undergarments. Anya tried not to stare.

"Would you like some?" Salim offered his cup to Jodie

"Thank you."

"Pass it onto your mother when you have finished."

Novae let out a huge yawn. "I'm sure that the sun is yet to rise. It's a little odd, but, even though we live down here, our bodies tend to keep in rhythm with the world above."

"We just passed Niahli and Jadine heading topside to get some fresh air."

"Yes, I am sure," exclaimed Novae.

Niamh arrived from her quarters in the adjacent chamber.

"I heard voices. It is still very early, I think." She paused for a moment. "So Niahli has gone up with Jadine?"

"Er, yes," replied Anya.

"I see." Niamh did little to hide her displeasure.

"She just needed to see a little daylight." Anya's offer was somewhat unconvincing.

"Salim, may I have a drink please?" Niamh stepped forward towards Salim to accept a second cup.

The atmosphere was tense so Anya decided to change the subject. "Novae, would it be all right if I left Jodie here with Simone for a while so that I can have a chat with John?"

"No problem. Simone missed Jodie last night."

Anya was glad that Novae did not ask what she wanted to talk to John about, but assumed that she was just being polite. "Jodie, I'll see you in a while, then."

"Okay, see you later!"

Anya was relived to find John up and dressed.

"I was just about to go out and see the morning. Would you like to join me, Anya?"

It was if John knew her purpose. "Yes, it would be a pleasure."

"Shall we head out to the oasis, then, before it gets too hot?"

"Lead the way...."

A short time later, they arrived at the bottom of the stone ladder. Anya looked up and was surprised to see the natural light flooding in. *Had Jadine and Niahli failed to secure the hatch? Had someone or something else opened it?*

Anya glanced at John whose was head was also tilted back. When she returned her gaze towards the opening, the sky above had been partially obscured by Jadine's behind.

John called up so as not to surprise them, then they waited for Jadine and Niahli to descend. John had hung his torch on the wall. In the dim glow that was cast by its dying embers, Anya could see that Jadine looked flushed, but happy.

After an awkward silence, Niahli was the first to speak. "She is tired. Jadine is yet to fully recover from her injuries. We will head back and rest."

"Did you enjoy the 'fresh air'?" Anya's tone was ironic.

"Yes, I did. It was good to see the sky again," said Jadine with a telling smirk.

Niahli had relighted his torch and was already on his was down the passageway when his father turned and said, "Oh, Niahli, it would be a good idea to put your tunic on the right way around before your return."

When Anya and John emerged from the hatch, dawn was breaking, painting the sky with graduated tones. As they stepped out of the trees, John pointed towards a large dune beyond the oasis. "Come; let us walk to the ridge. A bit of exercise will do us no harm."

Anya became breathless as she laboured towards the peak. Progress was slow in the soft, dry and warm sand. She turned to see that John was just a few paces behind. If he was struggling, he did not show it. Anya had remained on her feet, but, as she neared to within a few paces of the top, her hands found the warm sand. She paused to catch her breath and admire the majesty of the vast crescent of sand that stretched out on either side. After a final push, she was there.

The view of the desert plain with the orange orb of the sun rising over the horizon was quite spectacular.

John joined Anya and sat at her side. "So what is it that you wanted me to come and talk to you about?"

"Did I say that I wanted to talk to you?"

"No, you did not, but I can see it on your face as plainly as if you had asked me."

"Then you must also have an idea of what I want to

say."

"Indeed, I do, but I would rather you asked me straight out. We do not want any misunderstandings or ambiguity."

"Ambiguity?"

"It means vagueness or uncertainty."

"Ah, yes. Well, firstly, I'd just like to say that I hope you won't be offended by what I've got to say. After all, you helped to save our lives and you have offered us shelter and hospitality. For that, I will be eternally grateful...."

"What is it, then? Whatever you want to say or ask, I am sure that I will survive. Believe me, over the course of my life, I have faced far worse than a few questions from a woman!"

John's tone was not at all hostile, and his response brought a smile to Anya's lips. Anya turned to face her companion. "John, I sense that you have withheld information relating to some of the recent events, both from me and the rest of your people. Would I be right?"

Anya's question brought a wry smile to John's lips. "Yes, you are correct, but I did it not deliberately seek to deceive anyone; my tact was designed to prevent undue alarm."

"John, I need to know the truth. Is the community threatened by recent events? By our arrival?"

"Perhaps, though I cannot be sure either way. This is one of the reasons why we decided to withhold complete descriptions of some of our recent experiences. Your arrival might just be coincidence. Over the years, I have witnessed many things and it is true to say that mysterious, or even threatening, events sometimes occur not in isolation, but in clusters of time."

"Please, then, John, give me a fuller description of all that has happened."

"I would be happy to, but I do not want you blaming yourselves in any way. It is not my intention to scare you off."

"Please, John...."

John proceeded to relate recent events, from the original temple rescue to his encounter with the orb in the sky. This time he omitted nothing. Anya listened intently, interrupting occasionally to qualify the odd fact or remark. When John had finished he folded his arms, almost in resignation, but it was clear by Anya's body language that she had not finished yet.

"John, what do you know of the older world, not the people who built your dwellings, but the more recent civilisation of the machine world?"

"Our ancestors were somewhat removed from humanity at that time. In truth, those who claim to have knowledge of the past believe that we owe our existence to that very fact. I know that man cultivated ever more complex technologies, but it was his eventual reliance on the machines that brought about his eventual downfall. It has also been said that the machines' plan to bring about the extermination of mankind almost led to the destruction of our planet as a living entity. However, as a consequence of their actions, most of the machines were themselves destroyed."

"But machines do exist?"

"Yes, I described to you the glowing orbs. I have never been so close to one as I was two nights ago, but the sheer intensity of the light that it cast meant that I was unable to study its form."

"And what of the living megaliths?"

"Many of our people believe that they are cursed, misguided life forms. I am not so sure. I would suggest that, inside, they, too, have the heart of a machine."

"Have you ever tried to capture one?"

John chuckled. "The sounds they emit can move solid objects, destroy a man's hearing or worse. They can hit out with a bolt of energy that can throw a man off his feet or stop his heart. If we did get close enough to attack one, our blades would simply bounce off them."

"John, do you think that someone or something controls these entities?"

"Yes, I am sure of it!"

"Who? What?"

"Something beyond the confines of the desert; exactly what, I am not sure."

"My people believed in a 'Fartherland'. A place where the old technologies coexist in harmony with man, a place where life is easier and better."

"Am I to deduce that you and Jadine were seeking this place?"

Anya looked deep into John's eyes. "Yes, I believe we were, except our circumstances dictated that we had to move on and find a new place to settle, regardless."

"You have been accepted by our people. We have no old technologies, but you are welcome to settle."

Anya considered her response. "Thank you, John. I appreciate wholeheartedly what you have done for us, but I am not sure if we can stay. Above all, I don't want to put your people at risk, and, if I'm honest, I do not think that I could live most of my life in perpetual darkness."

"We believe that a lack of daylight is a small price to pay for our security."

Anya shook her head. "John, I don't think that it is a sacrifice that I could make."

"You mention a legendary land of paradise. Do you have any idea what form it takes?"

Anya shrugged as she answered, "Not really. Jodie claims to have seen it in her dreams."

"I suspected as much...."

"You suspected what?"

"There have been little clues here and there. Things that Jodie has said to me; the way she talks when she is with

Simone. I have met others over the years with similar skills of precognition. However, they were adults who had been able to hone their skills."

"I was sceptical at first; sometimes she gets things wrong, but Jodie has done enough to convince me that she has a gift that sometimes allows her to predict the future. That is why I think that our presence here puts us all in real danger."

"Am I to assume that Jodie has made a prediction about our fate?"

"A dream… Jodie told me about a dream that she had the night before last."

"Ah, yes, Novae told me that Jodie awoke very distressed. Did she go into detail with you about what she dreamt?"

"Not really, but she implied that everyone was rounded up and taken away by the stones."

"Anya, you must remember that Jodie is still young. She is unlikely to be able to discern with any certainty the regular dreams and nightmares that we all experience from genuine visions of the future."

Anya nodded slowly. "Yes, but sometimes I think she has her visions in her waking hours. John, these people who you have met who possess a similar talent, do you know what became of them?"

"In truth, no, but they all had one thing in common. They were seeking a special place. They all went in search of the dome."

"Does the 'dome' exist?"

"Yes, I am sure that it does. Perhaps it controls the machines; perhaps it is your 'Fartherland'. I have never seen it for myself – there are few who have. However, I think it is true to say that most people who choose to go there are never able to return."

* * *

The oppressive heat signalled that it was time for John and Anya to go back to the shelter of their subterranean world. They returned from the dune in good spirits despite the serious nature of the subject matter they had discussed. On their way down, John revealed his opinion about Niahli and Jadine's relationship. Anya was surprised to learn that Niahli used to be attracted to Novae and that he was terribly upset when his elder brother took her as his companion. As a consequence of his feelings for Novae, Niahli had always been no more that a close friend to Niamh and changing such a relationship had proved too difficult in such a close-knit community. John did little to hide that fact that he welcomed 'new blood' into their society.

* * *

The days that followed were uneventful. Niahli began to spend as much of his free time as possible with Jadine, and their budding romance did not go unnoticed. Niamh either glared at or totally ignored the pair of them. Eventually, Niahli decided to take Niamh aside for a chat. He attempted to explain his feelings for Jadine and how he would always value her friendship, but Niamh quickly became despondent and refused to discuss the matter further. Though Salim was positive, even encouraging, with regards to his brother's relationship, ironically, Novae took her sister's side in the matter and warned Niahli about rushing into a companionship with someone whom he knew very little about.

On several occasions, although half asleep, Anya became aware of Jadine sneaking out of their chamber in the middle of the night, only to wake to find her back in her bed by morning. Finally, a week or so later, Jadine finally plucked up the courage to announce to Anya that she would be moving in with Niahli. Jadine was taken aback when Anya seemed quite enthusiastic about her relocation. Jadine told Anya that Novae had said that her close friend also disapproved of the new relationship. Anya soon put an end to any suggestion that she frowned upon Jadine's newfound happiness.

Anya was content with the extra space and privacy within her dwelling. Even Jodie seemed to understand Jadine's need to be with Niahli. Novae soon began to adjust, but it was obvious that Niamh would take more time. She had been hurt, and perhaps the deep emotional wounds would never heal. Notwithstanding their reservations and the scarcity of food, all three of the new arrivals gradually began to adjust to a life lived predominantly underground.

27

Jodie opened her eyes. She was unsure as to how long she had been asleep, but her eyes were encrusted and she sensed that she had been in bed for a considerable period of time. She rubbed her eyelids clear, using her forefingers, and then raised her head so that her chin rested on the top of her chest. The room was blacked out, but Jodie sensed an unwelcome presence. For a moment, she struggled to recall where she was. Then she remembered; she had been put to bed by her mother in their chamber. Jodie strained her eyes in a vain attempt to cut through the darkness. She could not see Anya in the bed opposite, but then again, she could not see the foot of her own bed or the walls beyond.

A brief whine, rising in pitch, preceded the appearance of a dim blue light in the centre of the room. The light illuminated a spherical structure, to which it was attached. Jodie squinted in an attempt to focus on the detail of the object. She estimated that it was four times the size of an adult human head. As it levitated, the globe appeared to be making minor adjustments in pitch and roll in order to hold its position. Aside from the lighted area that had been aligned to face Jodie, the remainder of the visible surface was smooth and metallic. However, Jodie could just about discern several different structures that appeared to lie just below the surface of a translucent region just below the blue light.

Jodie shook her head and closed her eyes in attempt to

wake from the dream. When she reopened them again, the glowing orb was still there. Abruptly, blue changed to violet and a vivid beam of light was projected out towards her feet. The beam tracked up Jodie's body towards her head. Jodie let out a loud, piercing scream. Still, the dream continued. The beam was now focussed on her temple. Jodie wanted to move her hands to cover her eyes, but she was now unable to move. The orb adjusted its position and moved nearer. Jodie began to sense a connection with the object that hovered before her, as if it was trying to communicate with her in some way. Jodie's sense of fear and trepidation began to subside. She felt a sensation of calm washing through her body.

"Jodie!" It was her mother shouting from beyond the passageway. Again, but nearer: "Jodie, are you all right?"

As Anya reached the doorway, the violet beam was replaced by an intense blaze of white light that enveloped the room. At that instant in time, Jodie and Anya both reacted in the same way, throwing their arms across their faces to protect their eyes. As the orb came towards her, Anya sensed that it was necessary to duck. The glowing sphere flew over her head and proceeded to glide up the tunnel. Jodie could hear more footsteps approaching. People were running towards them. There was chaos beyond the chamber. Jodie lowered her arm, and although still dazzled by the effects of the bright light, she was able to get up off the bed and give chase. Anya grabbed hold of Jodie so as to prevent her from leaving. Jodie could discern voices; John, Niahli and others. Still holding her daughter, Anya stepped out into the passageway to see what was happening. The chasing pack was already past them. Despite glowing shapes clouding her vision, Anya saw a brilliant white light illuminating the wall beyond. It began to fade away. Soon, it was replaced by the orange hues cast by the flaming torches. Jodie was finally certain that this was not a dream.

* * *

John and his followers showed no fear in pursuing the glowing orb towards the oasis exit. As it reached the bottom of the shaft, it slowed. It positioned itself centrally then soared rapidly towards the sky. John was the first to reach the stone ladder. He looked upwards just in time to see the orb disappear from his tunnelled view. John climbed the ladder to check the integrity of the hatchway. When he reached the top, he was surprised to find it completely intact. It was simply open.

John secured the entrance. When he descended, he addressed everyone gathered below and asked, "Is there someone here who forget to close the hatch?"

His question was initially met with silence as each and every group member recalled their recent experiences and explored their conscience. Niahli was the first to respond. "No, Father, I returned yesterday morning and I am absolutely certain that I closed the hatch."

Salim shook his head. "I have not left our complex for two days now."

"I was with Niahli," added Jadine.

Gradually, everyone in turn denied that they were at fault.

John believed them, but added, "We must return to the others and ask the same question."

Everyone looked up. Slow rhythmic pulses emanating from the top of the shaft signalled that the megaliths had returned. John shook his head as he took his torch from Niahli and walked through the group to head off down the passageway. He met Anya who, having calmed Jodie, was on her way to meet them.

"Anya, the stones have returned. It sounds like they

have surrounded our exit out to the oasis. I am no longer confident that our dwellings are secure."

"John, you know that it is us they are after. We must leave here. We must go now!"

"You cannot possibly leave. Where would you go?"

"I think you also know the answer to that question. By staying here, we are putting you all at risk."

The rest of the group had gathered behind John. They could all still hear the sounds reverberating from above.

Jadine stepped forward. "Anya, we cannot possibly leave. We do not know how many of them are out there, but we can assume that they will be positioned around both exits. Besides, you cannot take Jodie out into the unknown."

"I am here!" Jodie felt the need to remind them.

"Sorry, Jodie."

"Jadine, I have made my decision to leave," said Anya. "We are the ones they have hunted ever since our arrival, and it would seem that they want Jodie more than any of us."

"I will not leave. Not now; not like this."

"Jadine, we arrived together; we must leave together. If we do not, it would be most unfair to these kind people."

Jadine looked around for support.

John was looking down at the ground, but he raised his eyes when he spoke to Jadine. "My dear, if you choose to stay, I will protect you with all my strength, but I fear that what Anya says is correct; their presence out there corresponds with your arrival. It is you they seek."

Jadine began to cry. "Niahli?"

Niahli put an arm around Jadine's shoulder. "I will go with you. Come on, we must ready ourselves."

Jadine was in shock. It was unclear if it was because she was being forced to leave a place that she was beginning to think of as home, or because a man she had just fallen in love with would risk his life to go with her.

"Niahli, are you sure?"

"Father, I must do this."

"My son, you are an honourable and brave man. Look after Jadine, Jodie and Anya for me, please."

"Anya, go with Jodie and gather only what you can manage with ease. I will prepare with Jadine. We will only be able to take enough water for a few days and a little food. We do not want to be slowed by what we carry. I will meet you in the main chamber shortly.

"Thank you, Niahli," said Anya.

* * *

Anya changed her clothes and helped Jodie into garments that would better protect them from the sun. She took two knives and a water flask, but very little else. When they arrived at the rendezvous, Niahli was already waiting. John and Salim were standing on either side of him, helping to load him up. Sayid appeared, carrying some water flasks. He gave one to Jadine then stretched out a hand to offer another to Anya.

"I have one, but I'll take it anyway."

Momo held an array of torches, that were, as yet, unlighted. As far as Anya could tell, every one from the community was present. People began to come over to say their goodbyes. Anya looked around for Jodie. She saw a hand with a missing finger wrapped around her daughter in a farewell embrace. Niahli hugged Salim, Sayid and Momo in turn. It was clear that John and Salim would be accompanying them, at least until they had exited.

Niahli took Jadine's hand and approached Anya. His torso was heavily loaded. He had a pack on his back, a water flask hung under his left arm and a large sword was suspended under his right. A knife hung from the belt around his waist. On his feet were thickly woven, flat-bottomed boots, obviously designed to give his feet better purchase in the soft, flowing sand. Jadine had changed into a long-sleeved, thigh-length white robe with long, lightweight trousers underneath. On her feet she wore similarly padded boots. In her hands was another pair. "Here, Anya, put these on. Bind them tight, so the sand doesn't get in."

"What about me?" asked Jodie.

Novae stepped forward. "Here, these belong to Simone, but we can make her another pair."

"Thank you, Novae." Jodie sat as Novae helped to wrap the boots.

"You take care now. I hope to see you again one day!"

As Niahli took Jodie's hand, she began to weep. She was not frightened, but she knew that she would miss Simone immensely. Jodie expected that they would head up towards the temple exit, but they did not. John climbed up the great steps and turned immediately left, heading towards a poorly lighted recess. Jodie followed with the others, still holding onto Niahli. John pulled a lever and a huge great slab of stone moved to one side. Jodie peered around him into the darkness beyond. Momo lighted the torches and ushered them inside.

III

The Final Journey?

28

After two turns, Jodie found herself in a long, straight tunnel. She was the only one who was able to walk upright. Smoke from the torches billowed around them as they moved, making it difficult for her to see. The passageway seemed much longer than any of the others that she had encountered in the complex. This one was not adorned with inscriptions like many of the others; it was just a long tunnel, bored through solid rock. Jodie began to sense the gradient was changing; they were now walking slightly uphill. Eventually, she found herself stepping out behind the others into a circular chamber below a vertical shaft. There was a stone ladder carved into the rock, which was similar to the one that led out to the oasis.

John paused to explain what would happen next. "Once we begin the ascent, I want you to extinguish your torches. I will keep this one alight until we reach the top. I will climb up first; Salim will follow me. Niahli, you stay behind Jodie in case she needs help."

Niahli nodded.

Jodie thought that she would be more than capable of completing the climb, but it did look a long way up and, consequently, a very long way down if she was to fall, so she was reassured that Niahli would be there if the need arose.

John continued, "When I reach the top of the shaft, I want you all to hold a position directly below me. It is likely that our exit will be covered by the desert sand. We have no way of knowing exactly how much is above us, but whoever built this complex designed a mechanism to divert the sand from the hatch. There are two levers; when I pull the first one, a trap door will open, siphoning the sand above into a huge pit just behind this shaft. We will have to be patient and wait until everything has settled before I pull on the second lever, opening the hatch to permit your escape. Once you are out, Salim and I will pull the trap door closed and relocate the rod that holds it in place, before re-securing the exit. Niahli, once you are all clear, you need to get far away from here as quickly as possible. Do you have any questions before we begin?"

Anya spoke first. "How will you replace the sand above to disguise the opening if most of it has fallen into a pit below?"

"It may not be possible to cover the hatch entirely. Once we have secured the trap door, we will attempt to pull back sand over it. If the sand is soft and dry, I hope that the action of pulling back the main hatch will disturb enough of the surrounding sand to re-cover it. It is likely that the sand will be moving all the time and, undoubtedly, some will fall back into this shaft, so be prepared."

"Would it not be better for someone on the outside to wait until you are safely back underground, then we can ensure that the hatch is covered?"

"No! It might take a while to close the trapdoor. You must flee as fast as you can and, please, whatever happens, do not look back. Head west!"

John waited for another question. After a short silence, he urged, "Shall we begin, then?"

The ascent was more challenging than Jodie had anticipated. When they reached the top, the adults were able to rest by bracing themselves across the narrow shaft. Jodie's fingertips were sore from gripping the narrow sandstone rungs, so she held onto her mother's ankles.

"Is everyone ready?" John's question was rhetorical; only Salim confirmed that he was.

John went ahead and tugged at the first lever. It would not budge, so he readjusted his position to get a better purchase and pulled with all his might. Slowly, the lever slid towards him as the rod to which it was attached slid out of the wall behind. There was an abrupt thud as the trapdoor swung down, crashing against the wall beyond, followed by a tremendous roar that shook the entire shaft, as the sand above flooded into the adjacent pit.

When the noise finally abated, John waited what seemed like an eternity before pulling the second lever and releasing the locking mechanism on their exit to freedom.

"Steady yourselves!" John climbed two steps and used his shoulder to force the hatch upwards.

Sand began to seep in all around, cascading down, showering those below. As the angle widened, the cascade of sand became a torrent. Jodie let go with her left hand and used her arm to cover her eyes. John used the sand to extinguish the torch. The flow of sand gradually reduced to a trickle and Jodie was able to look beyond those who stood above her, and gaze up at the night sky. John was able to balance on the highest stone rung before flinging himself as far as he possibly could up the wall of the sand bunker that the depression had created. This took several people by surprise. More sand was sent cascading down causing all but Salim to cough and splutter. Instinctively, they spat sand and dust back out of their mouths and cleared their nostrils. Salim jumped clear, next to his father, but, this time, the others were prepared. John leant forward and grabbed Anya's hand. Salim turned to face the opening and pulled Jodie clear before assisting his brother.

John came to the aid of Jadine whilst telling everyone in a loud whisper, "Take great care so as not to fall into the pit behind."

Jodie crawled to the top of the bunker, anxious to know where she was and relieved to hear that all was quiet. She recognised the huge dune behind them, then the vast plain in front.

Niahli crawled to the top of the hollow and over the rim, keeping his body as low as possible all the while. "Come on, let's go!" He reinforced his message with deliberate hand gestures.

"Take care, my son. May fortune be on your side!"

"You, too, father; you too! Goodbye, Salim."

"Goodbye, Niahli. Look after these women till we meet again."

Niahli looked at Jadine and nodded before turning to Anya. "Ready?"

Anya nodded back.

Holding Jodie's hand, Niahli stood and ran off into the desert, with Jadine and Anya following close behind. John and Salim set about securing the opening.

* * *

The hatch was a considerable distance away now. Their pace had slowed. Jodie turned and began to walk backwards. Niahli reminded her to keep going, but she could not deny herself one last look back towards the place that she had called home for a while. Dawn was beginning to break out of the inky blue sky above the great dune. There was no sign of John and Salim. Jodie presumed that they had made it safely inside. Just as she was about to turn and face the direction in which they were travelling, she could not help but notice movement on the crest of the dune ridge. Jodie gazed back for a few moments longer. Just long enough to see the unmistakeable silhouette of a megalith rising up to the summit. She turned back around and walked on. For some reason Jodie decided not to tell the others.

* * *

Jodie followed on as Niahli led the group on through the heat of the morning. Their wide-soled boots helped, but the going was still tough. The sand was so dry and deep that it took on some of the properties of a liquid. They had not seen a single piece of vegetation since they had left the complex. Jodie was thirsty, but she understood the need to ration the water. The sun was now directly overhead. Jodie stopped when Niahli held up a hand.

"Let us take a break."

Jodie was relieved. "Can I have a drink now?"

"Yes of course, but try not to take too much. We need to make it last."

"I'll only have a little bit, just enough to wet my mouth."

"Here you are, Jodie," said Anya as she passed the flask.

"Thank you." Jodie sat and sipped some water.

After she had drunk as much as she dared, Jodie handed the flask back and closed her eyes to rest them from the intense glare that was reflected back off the sand. She listened as Niahli described to Anya and Jadine how he hoped to use the small bag of precious stones that he had bought with him to trade for supplies. From time to time, Jodie reopened her eyes to sneak a quick peek, but, for the most part, she just wanted to rest. Gradually, she stopped concentrating on the activity around her, letting her mind wonder freely from thoughts of recent events to what might happen in the future.

Jodie stood and gazed into the pale blue sky. "They are coming for us! They are on their way; they'll be here soon!"

"What? What are you talking about, Jodie?" asked Anya "Who is coming for us?"

"I'm not sure *who* exactly 'they' are. All I know is that they are coming here to meet us."

Anya stood and followed her daughter's gaze. "Where? I can't see anything."

Jadine and Niahli joined the endeavour to search the sky for any signs of movement.

Jodie sighed and shook her head. "I can't see now that you are all standing in my way!"

The three adults all turned to face Jodie, surprised by the tone that she had used.

"Sorry, Jodie," said Anya defensively whilst walking towards her daughter. "We were just trying to have a look."

Jodie's eyes widened. "They are...." She saw two bolts of intense bluish light being discharged from one of the objects above.

They struck Jadine and Niahli simultaneously. Anya instinctively looked up as a third bolt of energy entered via her chest. Jodie's heart began to race as she watched her mother and companions fall to the sand before her. Jodie was certainly more than a little frightened. She desperately hoped that the objects in the sky did not intend to cause them any permanent harm.

The four orbs were much larger than the ones that Jodie had seen previously; perhaps five or six times the size, although broadly similar in structure. Jodie waited for her turn to be struck down, but, instead, she was able to watch as three of the spheres positioned themselves over Anya, Jadine and Niahli respectively. An invisible force then began to lift her companions off the ground, pulling them towards the base of each orb. The one remaining globelike structure continued to hover above Jodie. An intense violet light flashed around the circumference of the sphere. Jodie interpreted this as a signal and closed her eyes.

Immediately, she understood that it simply required her to relax and to trust that the objects would ensure them safe passage.

Jodie felt nothing more than the pressure being removed from the soles of her feet, but when she dared open her eyes once more, she found herself levitating in the air just below the orb. The others were still unconscious as they slowly began to gather momentum and fly across the sky. Jodie felt the warm desert air channelling around her face, buffeting her robes and pulling back her hair. The view was all too familiar. She scarcely felt the increase in speed as the acceleration was gradual and linear, but in no time, the dunes below began to flash past in a blur of orange and brown. The effect was hypnotic, and Jodie struggled to maintain consciousness.

29

Jodie's senses sharpened when she saw the dome approaching. Its form was familiar now, but she was certain that this was no dream. She looked behind to see the three other orbs, each with a person suspended below, as if held by invisible threads. The others were still unconscious, despite the airflow blasting around their bodies. Jodie returned her gaze forward. Not far now! The sun was reflecting off the mirrored surface as they slowed and began to lose altitude. Jodie braced herself as the ground approached. Her orb abruptly stopped a short distance above the sand. Jodie reached out to touch the ground, but was taken by surprise when the forces holding her in place were suddenly removed and she plopped down to earth. The soft sand cushioned her fall, but she took a while to get up and dust herself down. She looked at the dome then back to see where the others were. The orbs were hovering in formation some distance above, and, for a fleeting moment, Jodie was concerned that she would be the only one going into the dome. However, the remaining spheres dropped down to the ground in an instant. Simultaneously, they released their captives and they too fell to the ground. All three awoke as their bodies impacted the sand. Jodie actually laughed as Niahli jumped up brandishing his knife, flashing it aimlessly around in the air. Anya ran to her daughter, whilst Jadine stood slowly rubbing her shoulder.

"I'm sure we'll be all right," said Jodie. "You should

put the knife away. Anyway, I don't think it will be much use against them."

"What happened?" Anya demanded answers. "How did we get here?"

"Don't you remember anything?"

"We stopped for a drink... And then...." Anya looked up. The orbs were hovering a safe distance above. Anya pointed. "Did they bring us here?"

"Yes. They put you three to sleep, but not me. I was awake as we flew through the air, just like in my dreams."

"So this is the dome?" Jadine's question was rhetorical, but Jodie answered all the same.

"Yes, but it's even bigger than I thought, and shinier!"

The dome rose out of the sand like a vast convex mirror. Jodie grabbed her mother's hand and pulled her towards the immense structure that stood before them. Jodie stopped, only when her feet were butted up against the base of the dome. She leant over with her hands shielding the sun's glare from her eyes in an attempt to peer inside. Instantly, she was knocked off her feet by a pulse of low frequency sound. The others instinctively used their hands to protect their ears. Once again, Jodie dusted herself down. "I'm okay, but I think it's best not to touch."

Niahli had sheathed his knife and walked over to join them. "How do you suppose that we gain access?"

"I'm not sure that I want to go in," replied Jadine.

"Do you know?" Niahli's question was directed at Jodie.

"I'm not sure. I think there may be some sort of ramp around the other side."

"Shall we walk around?" ventured Anya.

"Which way?" asked Niahli.

Jodie decided to set off to her right. She glanced back to see Anya jogging in order to catch up. Niahli and Jadine were quick to join them. As they walked around the perimeter of the dome, Jodie and her compatriots spent as much time looking over its perfect, smooth mirrored surface as they did looking forward.

Jodie felt a tug on her shoulder and reacted by stopping and turning to look up at her mother, but Anya was gazing past her daughter. Niahli and Jadine were looking in the same direction. Jodie whirled around to see a megalith slowly skimming over the surface of the sand before them. Its violet 'eye' glowed intensely despite the bright sunlight all around. Jodie sensed the others retreating, but she stood her ground. The stone began to emit a gaggle of sound. On this occasion, it was not so loud and the tones varied greatly in frequency and pitch.

Jodie sensed that it was trying to communicate. She closed her eyes and concentrated hard. Nothing! She tried again. This time she was overcome by a feeling of sheer terror. It was as if her limbs were being taken from her. Something had come from behind and was pinning her down. Jodie pulled back from her vision and opened her eyes. The stone had fallen silent and suspended its progress towards her. Suddenly, an opening appeared in the seamless surface of the dome just to the left of where she was standing. A smooth metallic ramp slid down to meet the surface of the sand. Jodie turned to Anya, who stood speechless a short distance past the other side of the ramp.

It was Anya who called out to Niahli and Jadine. "Shall we enter?"

Niahli turned and looked around as if to gain approval or encouragement from someone else who was not yet present. Behind them, coming out of the heat haze towards the horizon was a jagged line composed of twenty or so megaliths. Jodie saw them too.

Were they friends or foes? Were they associated with the dome or did they seek to attack it? Was the stone creature that stood before them hastening their entry or did it seek to discourage them from going inside? What did her dreams mean?

Jodie had anticipated this moment for many months now, but, for some reason, she had grave doubts about whether to proceed.

Too late! Niahli and Jadine were already walking up the ramp. Her mother beckoned her to join them. It seemed as if the decision had been made.

30

Jodie expected that the inside of the dome might be bathed in light, but the confined chamber that they had walked into was rectangular and featureless aside from two glowing tracts of light that illuminated the floor below. The room darkened as the entrance disappeared behind them. Her mother's face looked grey as she stared down at the dim panels of light beneath her feet. There was a muted hum as an opening materialised in the wall before them. Tentatively, Jodie walked through with Anya still holding onto her hand. Jodie wasn't sure who was supposed to be protecting whom. The other two followed closely.

Jodie was relieved to find that the inside of the dome proper was indeed much brighter. Although the firmament above the dome was, as usual, cloudless, Jodie was sure that what she could see through the shell of the dome was, indeed, the sky. She looked directly up to see a circle of bright light that represented the outline of the sun. Clearly, light was able to penetrate through the structure above, but much of it was filtered out. Before her stood a large vestibule, partitioned off from whatever lay beyond by grey metallic dividers that stretched up from the floor to a height of about twice that of a tall adult.

They had walked to what approximated the centre of the space around them. Jodie was disappointed to see that, once again, there were no structures or furnishings of any kind.

"What are we supposed to do now?" asked Niahli. His face looked fearful. "This doesn't look much like the land of plenty that you promised."

"Nobody promised anything," retorted Jadine, "and I didn't force you to join us!"

"No, but you are glad that I'm here!"

"Now, now!" Anya's displeasure was clear to see. "I hoped to see people in here. This dome is vast, but I hope that it is not deserted, aside from us and the machines that must control it."

Voices! Jodie heard voices, like a gasp from the lips of a small crowd of people. She could not be sure if it was coming from the other side of the partition. She looked around. The others heard it too. Silently, a shape started to form in the wall to her right. A small square quickly expanded into a large rectangle. Then there was a picture within that suddenly expanded out into the foreground. Jodie could see a three-dimensional image of a gathering of people who were, apparently, looking up towards her. Jodie's mouth fell open and her head jerked back. Some of the people were now smiling. Jodie was sure that they could see her. The people faded away and the image disappeared momentarily. A single face began to take shape. This was clearly not an image of an actual person. Some of the features were unusually angular, yet Jodie thought that, somehow, although not instantly recognisable, it seemed strangely familiar.

"Welcome to the dome! We are glad to have your company and we hope that you will not be disappointed. Undoubtedly, you will have many questions, but please be patient. There will be time enough for answers. There are, indeed, many other people here, but you must wait several days before meeting them. We have a quarantine protocol in place. If you choose to remain with us, we can promise you knowledge beyond your highest expectations, and a programme of self-enlightenment that will separate your human body from your spiritual self. You will, at last, find true peace within. Shortly, you will be allowed through into our reception area. Refreshments will be available. Whilst our food may differ from what you are accustomed to, all your nutritional needs will be catered for. We hope that you will make yourselves at home."

With that, the image faded and the room fell silent.

An opening appeared in the wall opposite the one through which they had entered. Jodie was more eager to go through this time. She was greeted by the scent of jasmine and the most wonderful sight that she had ever seen.

Before her was a vast engineered landscape that appeared to occupy almost half of the available space within the dome. A central partition stretched up from the floor to meet with the curving roof except that it stopped short at the very near centre. Light metallic surfaces were blended with marbled grey and white stone. Scattered throughout were large, transparent, sculptured structures that had the appearance of molten glass, as well as jasmine bushes with their dark green leaves and creamy flowers. Jodie could hear running water. She looked around at the others. They were speechless, and everyone except Niahli was standing in awe with their mouths wide open. Jodie skipped forward in an attempt to locate the source of the noise. She rounded one of the decorative glacial structures only to find another that had a short tunnel in the centre. Jodie was naturally drawn to pass through to the other side.

Behind her, she heard her mother's voice. "Jodie, don't stray too far!"

Jodie ignored the instruction and slowly moved on. She stepped out of the passageway and looked down at the pool below. At her feet were two steps that seamlessly blended into a chute etched into a marble basin. The chute was fed from above by running water and led down to the enormous water-filled basin below. The pool and rock around had no defined edges, as if they had been weathered by the elements over millions of years, but despite the presence of a waterfall to her left, Jodie suspected that this effect had been created artificially, like all of the other structures within this vast playground.

Whilst rushing to pull her clothes off, Jodie attempted to gauge the depth of the water below the chute. She was unsure, but she could clearly see the bottom of the pool rising up to meet the surface at the far end of the pool. With her garments now strewn over the rocks around her, Jodie made her way up the steps. She found herself sitting at the top of the slide, leaning forward, with her legs dangling in the chute. She made the unconscious decision to push, applying even pressure to both wrists, and in a flash she hit the cool, clean water below. Jodie panicked momentarily as her head went under the surface and water was forced up her nose. She waited for her feet to make contact with the bottom. She realised that the water was significantly deeper than she had anticipated. As soon as her toes touched the base of the pool, she bent her legs and pushed hard to force herself up. As she broke the surface, an arm wrapped itself around her chest and pulled her half out of the water. Jodie used her hands to wipe her eyes and clear the water that was streaming from her nose.

Niahli shook his head. "Your mother told you not to stray too far. You should listen!"

"But I can swim!"

Niahli's expression softened, then he began to laugh. "It is good to see that, after everything you have been through, you are still a child at heart."

"Then, can I do it again, please?"

"If you wish. Hold your nose this time!"

"I will. This water smells funny."

"I think they may add something to keep it clean. Take

care not to slip."

"I won't. It's not slippery. It looks as if it should be, but only the chute is, not the rocks or the floor." Jodie made her way back to the top of the cascade. "Hi! Hello, Jadine!"

"Be careful, Jodie!"

"Oh, Mother!"

Niahli had retained his shorts, but Anya and Jadine stripped down to their thongs. After Jodie had flown down the chute for a third time, Jadine lowered herself into position and followed her. Jodie made her way across the pool until she could stand before beckoning her mother to join them. Anya approached the slide cautiously. She let out a scream as she slid down into the water, but soon emerged with a smile. Anya stood and cupped her hands to drink some water.

The voice that had welcomed them echoed across the dome. "Please do not drink this water. It is for your pleasure, but it is not safe to consume. There is a fountain just beyond the shallows. It is one of four springs that provide clean, safe drinking water."

Jodie waited for further instruction, but, after a period of extended silence, still dripping wet, she joined the others in search of a drink.

A metallic spout protruded from the rock above a small circular basin, but there was no water. Jadine grabbed hold of the spout. Nothing! Jodie stepped up and waved her hands above the basin. Magically, water began to flow from the spout in a steady stream. It tasted clean, and fresher than anything she had drunk in a long time. She quenched her thirst before stepping aside and allowing the others to do the same.

"I'm hungry," declared Jodie. "The voice said that we would be provided with some food."

"Come on, let's go back and find our clothes. After we

dress, we can search for some food." Anya led the way.

Anya walked around the far side of the pool whilst Jodie climbed above the waterfall that appeared to stem from solid rock. Jodie could see that their clothes were gone. Anya became conscious of her naked breasts for the first time and covered them as she walked back toward the fountain.

"Come on down, Jodie." A degree of irritation had entered Anya's voice.

Jodie waited as she surveyed her surroundings. From her vantage point above the waterfall, the pool below looked as if it was set into a vast crater. Ahead of its rim, Jodie could see that they were near the periphery of the dome. The dune landscape beyond the tinted glass confirmed that the dome was indeed translucent. Jodie turned to look towards the drinking fountain and beyond. Half hidden behind another decorative glass obelisk was a circular metallic structure. If she was not mistaken, it was surrounded by a row of seats on top of long thin poles.

Jodie ran on down past her mother. "Come on, this way!"

The others followed.

As they made their way over, the path led them through an extended metallic archway. Jodie was the first one to step inside. The noise from the air jets made her try to jump out of her own skin. However, the powerful wafts of warm perfumed air that accompanied the noise were very pleasant and she was dry in little more than the blink of an eye. Anya took her turn next. Jadine and Niahli stepped in together.

The large, smooth, polished metallic circular table was bisected by two equidistant walkways and surrounded by twelve fixed stools. On four of the stools were piles of clothes. All were white. It did not take Jodie long to figure out that the smallest pile was hers. There were two garments that clearly went underneath the outer robe. The material was strange. It was stretchy and elastic in nature. Nevertheless, she tried them on all the same. The thigh-length shorts and the short-sleeve top clung tightly to her body. Even the robe was more fitted than the ones that she was used to, as if fashioned from two almost triangular pieces of cloth, one inverted and joined over the other.

Anya and Jadine were eager to cover themselves; their clothes were similar. The top of their undergarment had a double thickness band of elastic material to support their breasts. The tight-fitting garments flattered their slender bodies. Niahli found a vest top, some shorts and a long white tunic. He put the vest on first, followed by the tunic, and then he reached down and carefully removed the purse that was tied into his old shorts. He was glad that he had not taken them off at the pool, and they were virtually dry now. He put the bag of stones to one side while he removed the shorts that he was wearing. Jodie tried not to look. Fortunately the tunic hid everything from view anyway. The expandable nature of his new shorts held the purse firmly in place.

The causeways between the tables led to a white rectangular box in the centre that was about the width and height of a forearm. Niahli approached the box. He could see, through a glass panel, that there was something inside. He touched the panel and it opened. Niahli pulled a small box from within. Underneath the lid was a pale yellow substance that looked and smelt as if it might be edible. He tentatively pushed a finger into the food using it to bring a small portion up to his lips. Cautiously, he tasted it. "It tastes okay!"

He spotted a spoon on the shelf above, grabbed it and used it to scoop out more of the purée. Whoever had spoken to them was correct. It was most unlike any food that he had ever eaten, but it was not unpleasant, and they were all extremely hungry. He unloaded more of the cartons for the others.

Jodie was more impressed with the plunge pool than the food, but she ate it all. Every last bit! She watched as Jadine ventured down the opposite walkway. Inside a similar compartment was fruit! There was a bowl containing five or six different kinds. Jadine threw Jodie an orange. This was more like it. Jodie dispatched the peel then savoured each segment as if she might never eat again.

Once she had satisfied her appetite, Jodie was keen to continue exploring her new environment. She set off to explore her surroundings.

Anya and Jodie looked as if they were more relaxed. They played with Jodie, chasing her around the nearby sculpted glass.

"I wonder where we will sleep," said Jodie, noticing that the sun outside was beginning to tumble through the sky. Its shimmering rays were enhanced by the refractive nature of the dome, creating a spectacular display of light.

"I'm sure they have a place for that, too," replied Jadine, "but will we be safe?"

Anya considered the question as she watched the sun disappear from view. "We have travelled a long way to get here. If this is, indeed, the 'Fartherland' of our dreams, then we must assume that we will come to no harm. Whoever has brought us here has taken good care of us since we entered this dome."

"Let's walk over to the far side," suggested Jodie.

"We should all go together. We may finally have found our 'Fartherland', but this new landscape is not without its surprises." Jadine turned and shouted, "Niahli!"

Niahli had discovered what appeared to be a sheer rock face that was actually made out of a metallic substance. There were moulded crags designed to be used as hand and foot holes. He took the challenge and began to climb. He was no more than two paces up when he heard Jadine's voice. He jumped off fully expecting to land on the ground below, but, instead, an invisible force decreased his velocity and cushioned his descent to within a hair's breadth of the floor.

Niahli smiled, and said to himself, "I will save that one for later." He turned and jogged toward where Jadine's voice had originated. "Coming!"

Jodie grew impatient waiting for Niahli to approach and started to edge away, but Anya soon called her back into the fold.

"Finally!"

"Sorry, Jodie. I found something new back there. There is a... Oh, it does not matter now. I will show you all later. What is it that you want?"

"The sun is going down, and Jadine is woeful about the onset of darkness. She was wondering where we are to sleep."

"I see; then perhaps we had better go and look beyond that partition." Niahli was pointing.

As they set off, Jodie noticed the light within the dome was now beginning to fade. As they walked together along a pathway that wound between more sculptures, something unexpected happened. At the same time as hundreds of tiny dots of light appeared in the ground below, tiny glowing orbs appeared above, illuminating the way. Although a fraction of the size, each orb hovered in a similar manner to the ones that had brought them to the dome. They tracked their movement for a few paces before stopping and handing over to the next. The sculptures also became iridescent, giving off pale blue hues.

"Wow," exclaimed Jodie. She was so fascinated with the lights around her that she was in danger of walking into something.

Anya grabbed her hand.

They passed through an opening in a grey, metallic partition to find three large, completely flat, white rectangular areas set into the floor. Each was the width of a tall man and the length of two. In front were small white marble blocks. Jodie approached the block to the left. As she tentatively went to place a hand on the block, the rectangular portion of the floor directly behind began to rise up. It was accompanied by a muted hissing noise from below. After a few moments, the structure came to rest. Before them stood a cubical white pod with a cylindrical opening through which soft, white light oozed.

"Jodie, wait!" There was tension in Anya's voice, but it was too late; Jodie had disappeared inside.

Despite everything she had seen that day; Jodie was impressed with what she had found. It was clearly designed for sleeping and there was plenty of room for two. The base was made of a spongy white material that moulded to the shape of whatever pressed against it. Jodie lay down to try it out. There were even shelves and compartments along either side to put things in. Above her was a shiny metallic panel, divided longitudinally into two halves by a line etched into the surface. Jodie reached up to touch it. Before her hand met the upper half the light dimmed to a faint incandescent glow. She waved her hand in front of it a second time and the tubular lights along the top of the pod went out. She sat up and they came back on again, dimly as before. A final motion returned them to full brightness. Jodie reached up toward the lower half of the panel. Sounds began to seep into the pod from all directions. Gradually, they ramped up in volume before evening out to a comfortable level. There were notes unlike anything that Jodie had ever heard before. Chimes merged with gentle whistles to produce magical combinations. It was extremely, soothing, almost hypnotic. Jodie was distracted by Anya's head poking into the entrance to the pod.

"Jodie, please come back out!"

This time, Jodie obeyed her mother's instructions. She crawled out in time to see a second pod rise out of the ground. Niahli and Jadine looked in.

"Go on, try it! It's great inside; you can dim the lights or play music with a wave of your arm!"

Whilst Niahli and Jadine followed Jodie's suggestion, Anya allowed Jodie to turn and joined her in their pod.

"Have you ever seen anything like this?" asked Jodie.

"No, but I get the feeling that we're going to see many new things within this dome. What's this?" Anya had found a large oval button at the end of the bed.

Without thinking, she pressed it. The entrance to the pod slid shut and Jodie began to feel a vague sensation of movement.

"I think that I've just lowered our capsule underground."

Soon, the pod came to a gentle rest.

"Can I press it again?" Jodie asked, without waiting for an answer.

Immediately, the pod began to rise and moments later, the hatch slid open. Jodie waved her arm so as to activate the music before flipping herself out and running over to the second capsule. She found Niahli and Jadine exploring the various storage compartments within.

"How do you like this, then?"

"Truly amazing," replied Niahli. "It is like something from the past, from the machine age."

"I guess that this whole dome and everything within it is a relic from that period in time," added Jadine.

"If you wave your hand up there, you will hear the most beautiful sounds, and, if you press the button over there, the door slides shut and the whole thing drops underground. It feels sort of cosy and safe." Jodie was keen to impart her newfound knowledge.

"Isn't it safe in here anyway?" asked Jadine as she

followed one of Jodie's instructions, filling the capsule with an enchanting melody.

"I'm sure it is, but there is nothing like feeling that extra bit of security, is there?"

"You're right, but I wonder where all the other people are. The space we are in takes up half the dome. Do you suppose that everyone else is crammed into the other half?"

"Perhaps! We will see when we are released from our 'quarantine'." Niahli sounded unsure. "But, right now, I think that we should all get some rest."

"Yes, come on, Jodie." Anya was at the entrance. "Let's go and check out what our new room has to offer, then we can sleep."

"Okay, but I have to admit that I am so excited that I doubt I'll be able to sleep." Jodie began to move toward the opening, very slowly. "Good night, then."

"Good night, Jodie," replied Niahli and Jadine in unison.

Anya smiled and led Jodie back to the other sleeping capsule.

Jodie pushed every conceivable panel and surface within the pod. Amongst other things, she found a small brush that she used to clean her teeth and a miniature water fountain that enable her to get a drink without leaving the pod. After chatting to her mother about the events of the day, and the possible surprises that the dome might have in store, Jodie finally settled down to sleep.

* * *

Jodie had tried hard to use her special senses to 'see' what existed elsewhere within the dome, but each time she made an attempt, she felt that someone or something was denying her access. Her concentration was quickly diverted and she found herself thinking of matters that were trivial or unrelated. She recalled the smell of water in the pool, or the taste of the last meal that she had eaten. Finally, she entered a dreamlike state, and it seemed that she might be free of such restrictions, allowing her mind to move about freely.

Jodie went back out into the dome. She was able to rise up and follow the line of the convex mirrored glass that covered all within. The lights glittered below. She could see the pool, the area where they had eaten and the rectangular patterns that marked the location of the underground pods where they slept. She continued her journey to the far end of the dome where they had yet to explore.

As Jodie glided over the dome's interior, she questioned her actions and those of the people who she was with. Whilst the area within the dome was indeed vast, it would not take too long to walk from end to end. Why had they not explored it all before retiring to bed? How could they feel truly safe? Her mother was usually so inquisitive. Why had she not suggested that they look further?

At the far end of the dome, near where the glass met the central partition, was a collection of seats and chairs, apparently made out of the same substances as the mattress that she was sleeping on. There were other structures that Jodie could not identify. Within the partition was a doorway. She headed down towards it. She expected to be able to simply glide through it, but she could not. She decided that she must try to go out, up over the glass dome and back in on the other side. Her head banged against the roof of the dome as if she were moving as a physical entity. Feeling trapped, she landed and sat on one of the seats near the entrance that presumably linked the two halves of the dome.

Suddenly, Jodie became confused. She was falling asleep, but she knew that she was already asleep! The light within the dome began to dim to a level that was barely enough to see anything by. The doorway opened from a parting in the centre. A hooded figure emerged. She recognised the silhouette from her previous dreams. He walked directly towards her and without speaking, picked her up in his arms. She tried to sneak a look at his face, but it was too dark. Just then, a second figure emerged. He ran over and struck the man who was carrying her, in the back of the head. He let go of her as he fell to the ground. Jodie instinctively put her feet down. Her ankle was hurting so badly. The other man grabbed her. Yes, she was sure it was a man. He smelt like a man. The man threw her over his shoulder and took her through the doorway into complete blackness.

31

Jodie awoke to find Anya sitting up. "Hello, my little one. I have just woken up myself. Did you sleep okay? These beds are very comfortable, aren't they?"

Jodie shook herself. "Yes, I guess they are, but I had some strange dreams once again."

"How so?"

"I dreamt that someone was trying to snatch me, to take me away from here."

"Do you know who or why?"

"No, it was just a man, but I've seen him before."

"Where?"

"In my other dreams...."

"Perhaps it means that you feel insecure. A lot has happened of late. Much has changed."

"Maybe." Jodie decided not to discuss the matter any further. "I'm hungry. Do you think we should go on over and get something to eat?"

"I think so. Do you want to press the button or should I?"

Jodie leant over and raised the pod above the ground. Outside, they found Jadine and Niahli embraced in a passionate kiss.

"Excuse me," said Anya. "We are going to go over and find some food. Will you be joining us?"

Jadine looked a little embarrassed. "Sure, let's eat."

After eating a meal that was not too unpalatable, but

was, however, composed entirely of a homogenous, brown gooey substance, Jodie followed the others over to the far end of the dome. She did not say anything, but she found it to be exactly as she had seen it the previous night. She watched as Niahli tried in vain to open the doorway. He did not try to force his way past, he knew that that would be unacceptable, but, after his experiences within the sleeping pod, he went around pressing every surface imaginable to see if he could get a reaction. Clearly, this gateway was something under someone else's control. Eventually, he gave up and went on to explore the seating area. The chairs moulded themselves to a body as did the beds. There were more than enough for everyone to have one of their own, but Jodie sat on her mother's knee. Suddenly, a long, thin slit in a shiny, metallic, low level table began to rise. In the centre was a white box. The angular face that had greeted them reappeared. It moved about in three dimensions as if it was real.

"I trust you all had a pleasant sleep and that you have enjoyed the food that was provided for you. The fruit was something of a treat. It is not possible to provide fresh foodstuffs every day, but we are able to grow some artificially. Please remember to drink only from the designated water fountains. It is not possible to guarantee the safety of the recreational water. On the subject of safety, we must protect the health of those within."

A thin, cylindrical tube emerged in front of the screen.

"Please cooperate by placing your forefinger into the sampling device. It would be wise to start with the youngest."

Everyone looked at Jodie. She stepped forward without question and inserted the first finger of her left hand into the tube. She was beginning to wonder how long to leave it before she should remove it when she felt a sharp, stabbing pain.

"Ouch!" Jodie quickly yanked her hand back to reveal a spot of blood on the end of her finger. "It bit me!"

The voice inside the screen interrupted, "We are sorry for any discomfort. We only require a minute sample of blood from you all. You must be screened for any infectious diseases that you may be carrying. Once you have been cleared, we will begin integrating you into our society. Now, will one of the adults please step up to the sampling device?" The face looked on.

Anya, Niahli and Jadine looked at each other. "It's okay now," stated Jodie. "I'm sure it's safe."

"In here, like this?" It was Niahli who elected to go next, followed by Jadine and, finally, Anya. Jadine was the only one to wince or show any discomfort.

"Thank you," said the face. "The screening process will take several days. In the meantime, please enjoy the facilities. You will be addressed in due course."

"Wait a while! Who are you?" shouted Anya, but it was no use; the image faded and retracted back into the box below. "Oh well, what do we do now?"

"Like he said," replied Jadine, sucking her finger as she spoke, "we enjoy ourselves."

"I can't wait to meet the others," said Jodie excitedly. "I expect that they will tell us when it's time, but, for now, shall we go over to the waterslide?"

"I have something even better to show you," replied Niahli. "Follow me; you will love it!" He led them over to the climbing wall.

Jodie spent most of the morning climbing. Niahli didn't tell anyone about its 'catch you when you fall' feature. Jadine was the first to discover it. She let out a loud scream and broke several of her nails in an attempt to hang on when she lost her footing just over halfway up. She was laughing hysterically by the time her feet touched the ground. Jodie was keen to try the controlled descent and jumped off from a position near the top. On reaching the ground, she immediately scrabbled back up the wall only to jump off once again when she reached the halfway point. *Wow! She was almost flying whilst still awake!* Anya followed suit, a bit more tentatively, as if not believing that she too would be saved from a heavy fall. However, she was, and quickly wanted a second attempt.

They spent the remainder of that day, the next and half of the fourth day enjoying the pool, the climbing wall and various other attractions that they found within the grounds of their new home. After eating another meal of what Jodie now referred to as 'slop', she felt an inexplicable, but strong, urge to go to the furthest segment of the dome. Jodie got up and began to run. She jumped over or clambered up any obstacle that arrived before her, taking the most direct route towards her target. Anya gave chase. She could hear her mother calling out behind her, asking her to slow down. As she neared the doorway, Jodie began to sense what was driving her. She arrived, breathless.

Anya was only a few paces behind. "I feel it, too, Jodie, but I dare not believe it!"

The doors slid apart. Jodie expected darkness, but everything beyond was bathed in bright white light. A solitary figure wearing a white, seamless bodysuit stepped into view.

Anya dived past her daughter and threw her arms around him. "Keon, I thought I'd lost you forever!"

Keon lifted Anya off the ground. "I am here now...."

"What happened to you? Where have you been? Have you been here all the time?" Anya had many questions and they came quickly.

"I've missed you!" This was all that Jodie could manage as she ran towards her father.

Keon stepped aside and scooped her up, and then the three embraced each other together. Tears of joy were streaking down Anya's cheeks. Keon's eyelids became red and moist as he fought to control his emotions. Jadine and Niahli arrived behind them.

"Keon!" cried Jadine. "How did you get here?"

"There's plenty of time for answers," said Keon, speaking to those he loved for the first time in many months. He pushed Anya back in order to look into her eyes. "I knew that you had arrived. Waiting these last few days has been difficult for me. I have missed you so much."

"When you did not return from the camp, I thought you, too, had been killed." Anya struggled to get her words out.

"As you can see, that is not the case, but it was not possible for me to return to you immediately."

Jodie realised that, deep down, she had always known that her father was alive. "It's so nice to see you again."

"It's great to see you, too, Jodie, and you, Jadine. This must be Niahli?"

Niahli had been standing and watching, not knowing quite what to do with himself. Finally, he approached Keon, arm outstretched. "Yes, I am Niahli. It is very good to meet you."

"Likewise!" Keon linked his thumb around Niahli's and shook his hand. "Please, come inside. We have much to discuss."

Keon stepped back into the bright white light of the chamber. As soon as Jadine and Niahli had entered, the doors slid shut. Jodie sensed movement.

"Are we going down?"

"Yes," replied Keon. "The dome above caps a huge settlement below. You will start your journey just below the surface."

"Journey?"

"Yes, Jodie, you will undertake a journey of enlightenment. You have much to discover and learn about yourself."

"Are there many people hidden within?"

"Yes, I'd say many more than in the village we had back home, but I've yet to meet them all."

"Why? I thought that you'd been here for some time?"

"Yes, I have, Jodie, but there are several reasons why I have not yet had the opportunity to meet everyone. I'll tell you all that has happened once you are settled."

Jodie's stomach told her that their downward movement had suddenly come to an end. The opposite wall slid open to reveal an even brighter passageway.

32

Jodie regained consciousness, or, at least, she was now conscious of her own thoughts. She was encapsulated by blackness. She was growing accustomed to the difficulty of discerning whether or not she was indeed awake. She tried hard to remember recent events. Her mind seemed fuzzy, and she was not at all sure of where she was. She felt as though she had been absorbed by a giant black bubble.

Gradually, Jodie was able to focus. She remembered her arrival at the dome and the days that she had spent with the others under the great curved glass roof. Then she recalled how the walls had slid apart to reveal that her father was still alive. She knew that they had travelled down deep below the surface of the desert. Jodie concluded that she must still be located somewhere under the dome. Her father, mother, Jadine and Niahli should be nearby. She had met many more people since her arrival underground. Jodie sensed their presence. It was as if they were watching her even now. She sat up and looked around. There was nothing but absolute darkness. Jodie reached out into the blackness in both directions, as if expecting to touch someone. Again, there was nothing to stimulate her senses. She brought her hands down her sides to touch the surface where she had been lying. It was smooth and soft, but it continually moulded to her body when she moved. Jodie stood and reached above her, then behind. She lost her balance and fell over. Her landing was soft, but she decided to stay put for now.

Jodie decided to try to relax and recall some of the people who she had met. She remembered that many people were gathered in the large circular room. It was as if the wall, the ceiling and the floor all formed part of one massive light encasing them all. The outer rim was stepped. Dotted around on each of the tiers were seating units of several different designs. They appeared to be made of the same substance that she was lying on. Within the tiered seating was an oval inset. It resembled in both form and function the staging area that Jodie had seen in the underground village near the ruined temple. This was where all the people were standing.

Jodie was able to summon up a picture of the occupants of this futuristic, underground community. They were all clothed in white. There was variation with both men and women wearing differing garments, but there were a finite number of designs. Many of the women wore short skirts, but, in every instance, their legs were covered in some way, mostly with a thin, white, skin-tight layer of fabric. Some of the women wore loose-fitting tunics, whilst others sported tight-fitting tops made out of a slightly thicker material than that which covered their legs. Some had sleeves, others didn't. Many had their hair cut neatly to a length midway down their necks at the front whilst tapering up to the nape of the neck at the rear. Some had this region shaved up a little. There was less variation in what the men wore. Some had on loose-fitting, short-sleeve white tunics and trousers, others wore longer robes, not too dissimilar to the ones that they had arrived in, whilst a few were dressed like Keon in tight-fitting garments that revealed almost every contour of their bodies. In contrast to the last community they had arrived in, Jodie noticed how everyone appeared to be well nourished. There were no very thin people present, and, for that matter, all but the very oldest had a well-developed physique suggesting that their muscles must be used in some way on a regular basis. All but one had close-cropped or shaven hair.

Keon had introduced each individual by name, but Jodie only had sufficient concentration to remember but a few. There were two people whose name she could not help but remember. She decided to dwell upon that later.

At first, it seemed as though the group had no clear leader. Nobody had stepped forward like John had done when they had arrived in the underground labyrinths near the ruined temple, but, later, as almost everyone else had greeted the new arrivals, a middle-aged man wearing long white robes emerged from the crowd with an aura of authority. He called himself Xenu. Jodie had seen him watching them from a distance. He was weighing up how they reacted to this new situation, before he stepped up to greet them. He was a handsome man with mid-length, curly, grey hair. He had laughter lines running symmetrically around his light tan face, which actually served to enhance his charisma. Jodie was old enough to realise that women of all ages would be very much attracted to him. He had clasped Niahli's hand and shook it eagerly before proceeding to greet the older women by kissing them on both cheeks. When he had turned his attention to Jodie, he merely said, "Finally, we meet."

That was it. Nothing more, but Jodie felt as though she already knew Xenu. She also sensed that the community was far larger than this gathering.

Jodie recalled how the wall had slid away to her left allowing a procession of people carrying trays adorned with food and drink to enter. Xenu had said something about a celebration, he went on to talk about the scarcity and sanctity of food, but Jodie had taken little notice. She had thought that most people were taking little notice of her, but, when she glanced sideways, she could see that both men and women, young and old, were gazing at her as if she was a marvellous sculpture or some sort of precious artefact. When she turned to face them, they looked away and pretended to focus on someone or something else.

Jodie remembered how she had been distracted by a sense of movement. She had had no point of reference, but she knew that the room had begun to rotate around a central axis. After a few moments, she had felt disorientated. Apparently, the room was also moving upwards. Everyone around had begun to smile with anticipation and there had been a loud burble of chatter as they had all discussed what was about to happen. Jodie recalled the slightest of jolts as the room completed its upward journey, but it continued to spin. The light in the floor and ceiling had dimmed whilst the illumination in the walls had been replaced by light flooding in from the surrounding desert as they had became translucent.

Jodie reflected on how she had gazed around in awe at the sight before her. The upper partition of the dome where they had spent their first few days in the dome was truly wonderful, but she had seen nothing in her short life to compare with what she now experienced. From her elevated vantage point, Jodie had seen that the partition was not quite central. It was offset sufficiently to allow the room that she had found herself in, to rise up into the top centre of the dome. The structures below beyond the other, larger side of the partition were hidden from view by a metallic screen. Jodie had been able to gaze out through the walls and the dome just beyond into the surrounding dunes. Even the inhabitants of the dome had been impressed. Clearly, this feat was not an everyday occurrence, but the best was yet to come.

For reasons Jodie could not fully explain, even to herself, despite the stunning sight before her, she decided to close her eyes. Instantly, she had been able to will herself outside, up above the dome. As she had looked down from above, she could visualise the room slowly rotating at the top of the dome. She could even see herself standing adjacent to one of the seats down below. Jodie recalled the ease with which she had been able to do this. She was fully conscious and in control of her abilities. However, moments later, she had felt pressure on her back. When she returned down to Earth, she had seen a young women standing behind her physical body.

Jodie recalled how she had simply opened her eyes and turned. The person behind her had pale skin, and lighter hair than Jodie had ever seen before. Jodie had been unsure of her age, but clearly she was somewhere between a child and a woman.

She had spoken to Jodie. "Hello, I'm Nicole. How did you do that?"

"Do what?" Jodie had replied, never considering that the girl had been able to track her journey out of the dome.

"You know, go out there."

"You saw me?"

"Yes, I can do it, too. Well, sometimes. Usually when I sleep. I've been training hard to do what you do, but progress has been slow."

Jodie scolded herself for having being so open with her reply. She had told Nicole, "I'm not sure. Like you, I usually go off in my sleep, but lately I've been able to transfer out when I'm awake. Sometimes I can even see what is about to happen, but it comes in flashes. I have no control."

Nicole had given Jodie a warning: "Be careful, though; they don't like you doing it without supervision! I'm sure that something within this structure blocks your powers, but they are adamant that this not the case."

Jodie recollected how she had been about to question Nicole about what she had just said, but Xenu had approached to interrupt. He had handed her a drink and asked Jodie if she had enjoyed the journey.

She was still unsure as to which 'journey' he was referring to. Soon after, the walls had returned to their opaque state and the room began to descend.

* * *

Jodie turned over to lie on her front. She was frustrated because she couldn't remember much beyond the point at which the room stopped rotating.

Just then, the walls of her sleeping chamber began to glow, and the room was bathed in light that gradually increased in intensity. She realised that she had been sleeping in the centre of a vast bed, large enough to accommodate ten or more adults. She felt very insignificant and very exposed. An opening appeared in front of her and Jodie was relieved to see Keon and Anya enter.

33

"Hey Jodie, are you rested?" asked Keon, seemingly without much concern.

"I am, but I don't like this big bed or this strange room. Why did I have to sleep all on my own, where are the others, and how do you turn these weird lights off and on? What exactly are we doing here?"

"One question at a time, please, Jodie." Keon's voice was very measured, very controlled. "Firstly, altering the intensity of the lights is very simple. You just have to think of them as being brighter or dimmer, and they will comply with your wishes." Keon closed his eyes for a moment, as if to stress the point that concentration would be required, then the lights began to dim.

"How did you do that?"

"As I have just said, you must will it to happen." Keon's eyes closed as if to emphasise the point. The room brightened. "You try!"

"Me? Now?"

"Yes, concentrate on dimming the lights."

Jodie closed her eyes. Nothing happened. She tensed her jaw, clenched her stomach and grunted as her face reddened with effort.

"No, Jodie, you are trying too hard and you are not projecting your thoughts correctly. Do not concern yourself with physical effort; simply focus on a dim room."

Jodie opened her eyes. "Like that?"

The lights in the walls had dimmed. She smiled, then blinked. The illumination returned to an ambient intensity.

"Well done, Jodie!"

"It took me many more attempts," added Anya. "I have to concentrate so hard to do that." Anya manoeuvred herself onto the bed with the food.

"Come, let's eat and we'll tell you all about how your father came to be here."

Jodie was so pleased with her newfound skill that she lost sight of her other, perhaps more important, questions. However, she was very excited about the opportunity to learn how exactly her father had left the cave all those months ago and ended up here in the dome.

"Were you taken soon after leaving for the settlement?"

"Yes, I think so. I'm afraid that my memory of those events is a little sketchy and is never likely to fully return. You see, I had something wrong inside my head."

Keon began to recount events as best he could. "As I approached the old camp, I came upon three hooded warriors. Three men dressed in a bizarre combination of animal skins and body armour. I remember that they wore large, thick-soled, black boots and were covered in blood. They were tall; each man seemed to be almost half the height of a regular man. Tethered to their sides were scabbards containing immense swords. The hoods that they wore were a continuation of their long black and red capes that were attached to their shoulder pads via small, circular chain linkages. I could not see their faces. It was as if their garments shielded their very soul inside, or maybe, given what they had done to our people, they had no souls. I wondered how three people, big as they were, could wipe out our entire community. I think that they were just plain evil. I watched from behind a patch of scrub, on a rock rise just above their position in a clearing below. I saw red. I wanted to kill them, but I knew that, if I moved, I would be throwing my life away. It was not cowardice that prevented an attack; it was reasoning. I thought of you and Anya, and I knew that, if I fell, there would be no one to take care of you, but then I really did see red. My vision went cloudy, my head spun and I passed out."

"What happened then?" Jodie was now hooked on the tale.

"I suppose I should have died. Not by the sword of one of the three giant slayers; the bleeding in my head should have killed me. It would have, had I not been found and collected by one of the drones."

"Drones?" asked Jodie.

"The orbs that brought you here. The remainder of my story comes from Xenu and the machines that run this complex. I have no recollection of any events for the many days and nights that followed. I had a growth inside my head, in my brain, the part that controls my very being. It pushed on my eyes and my other senses. I recall having a few dizzy spells during the period leading up to the attack on our people, but Xenu tells me that it was a miracle that I was able to survive for so long having seen the size of the tumour that they were able to cut out of me."

"Did Xenu cut into your head?"

"No, he helped to prepare me and organised the people to care for me afterward. The machines did the surgery using their complex instruments and light beams. They were able to remove the growth, stop the bleeding and repair my brain. They patched me up, but it was weeks before I regained consciousness, before it was safe enough for them to allow my senses to return." Keon paused as his mouth became dry. "They had to pump in substances to prevent infection. It was many days before I was able to get up and walk. The outside of my skull had almost healed by the time I was able to get up and move about, to even see properly. I had to re-learn how to do most things. Even talk properly." Keon stooped and put his chin to his chest to allow Jodie to see three surprisingly small scars through his shaven head.

"Does it still hurt?" Jodie reached up and Keon allowed his daughter to feel the stubbly skin around the operation site.

"No, it's fine now."

"Your father's getting better all the time," added Anya, as if she, too, conceded that Keon still had a way to go before he made a full recovery.

Jodie thought that her father looked okay now. She had one final question for him. "What have you done here since your recovery?"

"I have sought enlightenment. I have spent a lot of time with Xenu learning about these people's philosophy and the knowledge laid down by the machines. I am very interested in 'the study of truth', and I am eager to discover more about how man and machines can, and do, exist together in harmony and mutual support. You will have the opportunity to learn more later this morning. Xenu wants to give you a tour of the facilities. He wants to find out more about you, and tell you why you are here!"

* * *

"Good morning and welcome, Jodie." Xenu was walking down the bright white passageway when Jodie stepped out of her sleeping room with her mother and father.

Jodie assumed that he had been coming to meet her.

"Good morning, Xenu," Jodie responded in her most formal voice. "My father tells me that you want something from me...."

"Oh no, Jodie; true, I wanted you to join us here, but, by including yourself in our dynamic community, you are the one who will gain the most."

"What will I gain?" Jodie already thought she had an understanding of what coming to the dome would mean for her.

"Time will tell, but we seek to increase your awareness and ability. Eventually, I would hope that your capabilities *can* be realised and that you will reach a higher state of existence."

"I'm not sure that I follow." However, Jodie did! Inwardly, she was very excited. She knew that she had extra-special mental abilities, and having met at least one other like her since her arrival at the dome, she expected to be schooled in the art of mental transfer.

"Your patience and attention will reward you in due course with a fuller understanding of our philosophy. Keon, Anya, with your permission, I will take Jodie around the facility as I explain more."

"Of course." Keon was quick to respond.

Anya's glance toward Keon revealed anxiety. "Okay then, Jodie, see you later."

"This way, Jodie." Xenu put out an arm to direct his young tyro.

Jodie departed with a circular wave of her arm towards her parents.

"I want to show you as much of our residence as possible for now, but, rest assured, as your awareness increases, you will be introduced to newer and more challenging environments."

They reached a junction. To the left, their progress was blocked by a thick glass partition spanning the entire passageway. A beam of green light radiated out from a circular structure on the adjacent wall, scanning across Xenu's eye. The partition slid back into the wall and they were free to continue. Once past, the glass door closed behind them. This new section of passageway looked identical to the last and Jodie began to wonder how long it would take her to be able to navigate herself around these brightly lighted labyrinths.

"Later, I want to assess your current state of self."

Jodie looked a little concerned.

"Don't worry. It will be totally painless." Xenu let out a chuckle. "We have to measure where you are now to be able to progress."

Jodie wasn't anticipating any pain, but she found the language that this man used, a little intimidating. "Where are we going?"

"First, we shall see one of the places where we are able to exercise."

Jodie found herself in the largest open-plan room that she had visited since being under the glass dome at the surface. As she looked around, Jodie counted fifteen or perhaps twenty individuals. In one area were exercise machines; Physical barriers that necessitated those using them to expand energy. In a corner was a climbing apparatus, similar to the one that she had used in the quarantine area, but this one differed insomuch that it had horizontal and vertical challenges where participants had to jump across onto floating pillars that changed their altitude every so often. On a large white padded section of flooring, around eight people appeared to practise combat, taking turns to throw each other to the ground. In a similar matted area at the opposite side of the room, five individuals sat cross-legged in a crescent around a central figure. There fingers were outstretched against their temples. In unity, they lifted their hands away from their heads and with arms still bent, turned their palms to face the front. It was as if they were being lead by silent instruction.

"As well as physical exercise, spiritual exercise is essential. We know that spirituality and thought is an energy existing in its own universe, separate and distinct from the physical universe of matter, energy, space and time that we think of as the world we live in."

"I am not sure that I understand. I thought that maybe I did, but now you have lost me."

"Let me try to put it more simply for you. You know that you have certain special abilities that set you aside from others. As your body is about to mature, these powers will want to develop. If they develop unchecked, you will become more powerful, but people can seldom handle power. They retreat from it or abuse it. When they have it, they often misdirect it. I hope to enable you to acquire the ability to handle power, to control your spirit and manipulate things without having to resort to physical means or touch for support and assistance."

"You mean that I will develop 'god-like' powers or sorcery to move things about?"

"It doesn't mean that you will become a god. It means that you will become wholly yourself and realise your full potential. A long time in the past, I believe that all people had these abilities, but, gradually, as man came to rely more and more on machines, his talents were lost. Recovering these god-like abilities and encouraging and assisting others to do so are our primary goals."

Jodie brought her chin up, flattened her lips and nodded. "I see...."

It appeared to Xenu that Jodie was beginning to understand their philosophy, but clearly many hours of development lay ahead. Xenu drifted out of the room. Jodie naturally followed. After a short walk down more identical white cylindrical passageways, they arrived at an archway that lead into another relatively large white chamber. There were numerous white seating areas affixed to tables. Dotted around the room were a number of food dispensers like the one Jodie had used under the glass dome. There were just two people sitting together at one of the tables. Xenu acknowledged them with a nod.

"Most people will have eaten already this morning, but this is where we gather together to take in nourishment and, sometimes, enjoy a more traditional meal."

"The other stuff; how is that made?"

"With the help of the technology within, we have been able to synthesise various nutritional compounds. Years of experience in combining these substances with artificial and naturally occurring flavourings and colours have given us the ability to provide our people with a healthily balanced nutrition, ensuring fitness within. The mind cannot be developed if the body is frail."

Xenu led Jodie onto the next location in her tour of the underground sanctuary.

"Is this space below the ground bigger than that which can be seen above?"

"Yes, many times so. Today, your journey will be restricted to just two floors, but there are a number of other levels that you will be given the opportunity to explore on subsequent occasions as you learn to harness your power."

"Who made all of this?"

"The machines, primarily. They were able to cut through the layers of solid rock and build supports to stabilise all these structures. Our predecessors helped them to modify and colonise the space inside, making it possible for men to co-exist down here." Xenu stopped and directed Jodie into another space. "Now, I especially want to show you this facility. This is where our data records are stored. You might think of it as a library."

Xenu's gesture suggested that Jodie should proceed over towards the centre of the room. It was modest in size. Eight simple white desks with moulded chairs faced toward the front.

"It doubles as one of three group teaching areas. We run a series of seminars for our people. Please, sit here."

Jodie found herself seated without thinking. She was

sitting in front of a flat, gloss-white surface. At the rear were a number of symbols. Xenu waved his hand over one of them. A small three-dimensional image appeared out of thin air in front of Jodie.

Jodie looked on in awe as an image of the outside of the dome manifested before her. It looked incomplete. Jodie could not resist raising her hand and moving it toward the image. She hesitated and looked at Xenu. "Is it safe?"

"Of course!" Xenu was smiling.

Jodie pushed her hand into the image. She felt nothing but the image degraded a little and collected around her fingers. "How does this work?"

Xenu laughed a little louder this time. "You will have ample opportunity to learn about physics and all the matter in the known universe, but such an explanation right now might distract you from the tasks that lie ahead."

"I do so want to learn about the technologies that you have here in the dome. I don't just want to develop my mental powers. Also, you use many different words. I am keen to discover the meaning of them all."

"And so, in time, you shall."

Jodie removed her hand and sat back to watch the image. Time moved quickly, with day turning to night in a matter of a few moments, but, as the scene unfolded, Jodie was able to see vast machines completing the structure of the dome.

"We can go back in time if we want to." Xenu waved his hand over another sensor and the sequence ran in reverse.

It continued back beyond the point at which Jodie had started viewing; back to a large metal frame and then a hole in the ground. In as much time as it would take Jodie to wash, she was able to see how the dome and its underpinnings had been constructed. "Do you want to see more?"

"Yes, please. What else is there to watch?" Jodie was

beaming.

"In short, almost everything, but a new community member does not have access to all the stored files. You will have to progress in order to gain open access to the system contents. Even then, there will be some records that are restricted. For now, you might like to see this."

Xenu used both hands to sort through lists of words projected up into the air. Eventually, he found what he wanted, and with a jab of one finger, he brought the file to life. "This is our planet."

Jodie watched as the image zoomed in from the space above the Earth down toward a great orange patch of land. It soon became apparent that they were zeroing in on their current location. After pausing for a moment, the viewer rushed off across the desert. Jodie had the impression that it was travelling north-east, but she could not be sure. Whatever had recorded the footage gave the impression that it was travelling at a very high speed. Finally, it slowed and settled to focus on what had to be another dome, apparently identical to the one that they were in, although the surrounding landscape was different. Nearby were the ruins of a vast city. To the left were three great pyramids, one towering over the other two. In no time, they were on the move again. This time, the image steadied over a wooded area before zooming in on another glinting black dome.

"Are there many more of these?"

"Yes, lots. We are not alone. They are located all over our planet. They have replaced the old civilisations and cities, but the majority of the Earth's remaining population still live in smaller communities like the one that you were from."

"You mean the one that was destroyed."

"Yes, sadly, it was. One cannot always account for the actions of man. A small band of warriors from the north, I believe. We do not have time now, but, if you would like to watch more of the sequence, we will instruct you on how to use the equipment over the next few days."

Xenu had already stood and was moving away towards the exit. "Wave your hand over the sensors at the rear, palm down"

"Ohh!" The image disappeared.

"There will be more time later."

Jodie felt frustration. She had just been introduced to the most fantastic thing that she had ever seen and all too soon she was being taken away from it.

Once out in the passageway, Xenu said, "Don't worry, the powers that you will develop will far exceed the capability of any archive or surveillance footage. In time, I hope that you will be able to see such images from your mind's eye at will. Here, step inside."

Jodie stepped into a small, white cubicle. She recognised and remembered its structure. It was similar to the room that had carried them down from the upper surface of the dome. Once again, they were on the move. Moments later, Jodie stepped out into a passageway that was the same as every other one that she had walked through that day, yet somehow it felt different.

It was darker. That was it; the intense bright white light had been replaced with a more natural subdued hue.

"Is this where the others come to sleep?"

"Yes, how did you know?"

"I'm not sure. It just seemed likely."

Xenu noticed that Jodie began to smile as if she had just seen something familiar. "What is it, Jodie?"

"Oh nothing." Silently, Jodie said hello to Nicole, who had just awoken from a slumber in one of the adjacent pods.

Xenu chose an empty pod to show Jodie. Inside it was very much like the one that Jodie had slept in under the great glass dome, only a little more spacious. "Did you enjoy the comfort of the large bed that you slept in last night?"

"No, not really; I found it..." Jodie hesitated. "Well, a bit lonely in there. I am used to people around me."

"In time, you will get used to your own company, but, for now, you may share a suite next to your mother's quarters. However, in the future, where you sleep may depend upon your learning programme or the task at hand. Shall we return to the floor above?"

* * *

As they turned the corner, Jodie saw her mother and father standing by the third of a series of four identical glass partitions. They formed an entire wall of a small square room. Jodie glanced inside. There were two white stools located either side of a table top that extended down to the floor via a concave pedestal. Aside from this, the room was bare. Xenu stopped in front of Keon and turned to face the wall. The system scanned Xenu's features and the glass partition slid aside. Xenu motioned for the others to join him inside.

Xenu lifted Jodie up onto one of the stools, then skirted around the table to sit opposite her. Keon sat beside him. Seemingly knowing what to expect, he looked calm and relaxed. Anya had no option other than to sit next to Jodie, opposite Keon.

Anya looked a little anxious. "Tell me Xenu, what is this 'auditing' process that Keon has told me about?"

"Audit comes from the ancient word '*audire*', meaning 'to listen'. I am an auditor, 'one who listens'."

"I still don't really understand. Just what do you hope to achieve here with our daughter?"

"We do not aim to change who she is. We only seek to facilitate her evolution to a higher state of being. We do this for Jodie as an individual and for our society. All we want is a civilisation without insanity, without bad deeds and without war, where the able can prosper and honest people can have rights, and where man is free to rise to greater heights and work in partnership with technology. I know that this sounds like too much to expect, but, with other communities similar our own, we believe that it may be achieved."

"Do you believe that, once again, machines are key to our survival?"

"After endless millennia of ignorance about himself, his mind and the universe, a breakthrough has been made for our people. Machines now have their own intelligence and now understand that they must cooperate with us to coexist and surpass the limitations of their own technologies." Xenu glanced sideways at Keon. His expression sought support for his continuing explanation.

Keon nodded.

"Man consists of three parts. The first of these is the spirit; the second is the mind. The spirit uses the mind as a communication and control system between itself and the environment. The third is the body. The body is *not* the person. The most important of these three parts of man is the spirit, or 'consciousness'. I want to help Jodie examine specific areas of her existence so that she can rid herself of unwanted spiritual conditions and increase her awareness and her innate ability. For those who wish to develop, our capabilities are unlimited, even if not presently realised."

Jodie interrupted, "I sort of understand most of what you are saying, but I cannot see how a machine can help to develop my ability."

"We tend to see ourselves in a single dimension. We think that we know our own limitations, so our own preconception becomes a barrier to development. In short, we know that we cannot do something, so we do not try. If we move away from what we see as fixed conditions, we eliminate our self-imposed constraints; therefore, allowing us to fulfil our promise. In old philosophies and scientific endeavours, we have overlooked the fact that there is more than one state of existence attainable at any given point in time, and that there are many states of existence besides that of man. With the help of technology, we can attain several different states of existence in just one lifetime. These higher states can be attained through auditing, but, clearly, your daughter has inherent abilities that mean she is further down the path of spiritual enlightenment than most of us. Perhaps, with our help, as Jodie progresses through a series of 'levels,' she can eventually be restored to a native state wherein she is free of attachments to her physical body. Whilst 'exterior' to her body, she will learn to consciously control matter, energy, space, time, thought and life. Please watch and you shall see the truth unfold."

Jodie gazed into her mothers eyes. Clearly, Xenu's explanation and vocabulary had done little to allay Anya's concerns, nevertheless Jodie felt confident that she had nothing to fear in the immediate future. "Don't worry, I'll be all right!"

"Very well, then," said Xenu, seemingly unwilling to provide an opportunity for further indecision. "Put your hands in their place on the table."

Jodie looked down. There were two palm-shaped indentations on the table. The impressions were a little larger than they would have been if they had been made by her own hands, although they were clearly too small to accommodate the hands of an adult. "Like this?"

"That is correct, Jodie. Now relax. I want you to listen very carefully to what I am going to ask you. Please answer with total honesty. I will be able to tell if you are concealing the truth."

Anya raised a hand to her mouth and went to bite down

on her forefinger as if to channel her tension.

Keon leant across and whispered in her ear, "Don't worry, I have done this many times now."

Anya dropped the hand into her lap, forcing herself to appear more relaxed.

Xenu placed his right palm flat on the table. He flicked his head back to remove the long black and grey hairs that were covering his face. "If you are ready, Jodie, we will begin."

Jodie's confidence was beginning to turn to apprehension.

"Jodie, I want you to think about the first time you recall being able to see things in your mind. It was before you came here, wasn't it? Tell me where you were at the time."

Jodie pulled her right hand away from the table top and put her fingers to her lips as if to help her think.

"Please, Jodie, you need to keep your hands flat on the impressions in the table top."

Jodie lowered her hand and replaced it. "Sorry!"

"Can you recall, Jodie, when you were first able to see things in your mind?"

"I'm not sure. It isn't as simple as that. You see, at first, I tended to see things in my dreams, but I thought that was all they were, just dreams. I saw the dome and imagined my journey here. Now I know that what I was seeing would come true, but my visions were not exact copies of reality"

"So your first recollections were of events in the future, not the present?"

"Yes. They started just before we left our old settlement. Perhaps I had the odd *dream* before then, but I cannot be sure."

Xenu studied an image that appeared to float before him on his side of the desk. "Seeing the present time from a different location is difficult enough, but being receptive to future events is a rare talent, indeed."

"Yes, but, as I said, my visions were not truly accurate and not all of them came true."

"Unlike current events, the future is subject to change. Simply knowing the future can apply pressure for modification. Are you comfortable with the notion that you can see the future?"

"I think so. At first, I found it strange and very confusing. In fact, I am still a little confused by what I see, and I have little control over where and when. It is my ability to actually see current events away from my body that excites me the most."

"Do you have full control over these skills?" Xenu's eyes remained focussed on the image before him, rather than on Jodie.

"No, but I think I'm getting nearer to being able to control what I see and where I go."

Anya let out a gasp. She now knew that her daughter had special abilities, but she was quite surprised to hear her talk about them so matter-of-factly.

"Shush!" Xenu raised a hand to reinforce his request for silence. "Could it be possible that you have had glimpses of this hidden talent long before the time you have described? Perhaps for the duration of this life or before?"

"Before? What do you mean, before? There may have been events that I discounted at the time, but everyone experiences déjà vu, don't they?"

"Man is an immortal, spiritual being whose experience often extends well beyond a single lifetime. It is likely that your spirit had a life before this one and, if that is so, it is possible that these skills were developed then, and can be remembered."

"Well no, I can't remember anything before a great thunderstorm that I know to have happened when I was about three years old."

Xenu studied the image before him for information. "I know you believe this to be true now, but, with a little more effort, you might come up with a different answer that changes your past."

Jodie shuffled in her seat. She opened her mouth, but then thought better of it and said nothing.

"Are there any other talents, dormant or otherwise, which we should know about?"

Jodie considered this question for a moment. She did not want to lie, and she knew that Xenu could see whether or not she was telling the truth, but she did not want to give up all her secrets to a stranger, even if he was promising to help her and give her lifelong fulfilment.

Did being able to communicate with other individuals through the power of thought differ from being able to transfer out of your body to travel about in the present? Perhaps? Well, almost certainly!

"No, I'm not aware of any other abilities, but I can't say that I won't discover more in the future!"

Xenu stared into the images flickering before him. He looked a little confused about what he saw. "I hope you will, Jodie. It is possible to attain several different states of awareness at any one time. I am charged with the duty of making sure that happens." Xenu paused for a moment and cleared his throat. "The first session should never be arduous or lengthy, so, before we close, I would like to ask you about your general outlook on life. Would you describe yourself as a positive individual?"

"Yes, in general, I'm pleased to be here, although I'm a little concerned about all these questions. Most of all, I want to learn about the world around me and how I can use these skills to improve not only my life, but also that of my family and friends."

"Your help is appreciated. We are here to help you. Obviously, today has been about assessing past events in your life, your general awareness and how best to increase your natural ability. On the whole, you have done very well."

Jodie somehow knew that she had done better than just 'very well'. She knew that Xenu had never seen the likes of her talents before.

34

Although Jodie did not fully appreciate the benefits of the auditing process, whilst walking back with her mother, she felt strangely elated. Keon walked with them briefly before kissing Anya on the cheek and departing with Xenu. Jodie and her mother were heading towards their new quarters. Anya had had the opportunity to give the place a quick inspection with Keon prior to the audit, so she knew where she was going. Jodie realised that her mother had obviously been granted the authority to pass though certain doors and partitions that controlled access to various parts of the complex.

Jodie wandered how far her access rights would extend as she watched one of the green beams scan Anya's face.

"Can you go anywhere you like now?"

"No, I am only permitted to travel between these two floors. I cannot go up to the surface."

"And Keon?"

"I'm sure that he has fewer restrictions placed upon him."

"It doesn't seem fair, does it?" Jodie was now beginning to feel somewhat deflated."

"Oh, I'm not so bothered for now. Xenu says it is for my own good. He does not want me getting lost somewhere. I'm sure it's only a matter of time before we can go where we please."

Anya briefly displayed a look of denial. "Here we are, in

here. This is our suite. It's rather spacious. I don't know what we have done to deserve this. Perhaps Xenu favours Keon. Niahli and Jadine don't have nearly as much room."

"How are they? I haven't really spoken to them since we came down here."

"I've not seen very much of them, either." Anya glanced around the room as if fearful that she was being watched. "It's as if they are being deliberately kept away from us."

"Are you sure that other group members are not just taking time out to help them settle in?" Jodie's suggestion seemed reasonable.

"No. I asked to see them earlier and Xenu deliberately, but skilfully, avoided my request."

"Can Keon not help?"

"I don't really want to ask. Sometimes, when I try to question him, his responses are a little peculiar. I think that he is struggling to come to terms with his ordeal."

"Last night, I was placed in that room with the large bed on my own."

"Yes, I know." Anya blushed. "They wanted us to be able to spend a little time together in private."

"I hope that I will be able to stay with you both, and see more of Jadine and Niahli, too."

Keon arrived. He rushed in through the door with a sense of urgency. Anya was clearly not expecting him, and her expression betrayed a mixture of guilt and surprise.

Keon was the first to speak. "Are you all right, Anya?"

"Yes, why shouldn't I be? I was just talking to Jodie and we were wondering the same about you."

"I'm fine. It has been a turbulent time for us all. Things should settle down now that you are both here."

"Then you are convinced that this is the place to be?"

Keon's disposition changed from one of concern to defence. "Yes, of course. If it wasn't for these people, I would have died. Here, we will have the opportunity to learn about the world that we live in. It is safe here and we will be provided for. Plus, Jodie will have every opportunity to develop her talents."

"I'm not entirely sure that Jodie's 'talents' will always be seen as a good thing. Anything that marks you out as different..."

"There are others like her within the dome. She will not be singled out."

Jodie interrupted, "I don't mind being able to explore my abilities. It has been good to talk to someone who understands them and can make sense of what I do."

"See, Jodie is contented," Keon countered.

Anya just shrugged. "Well, if you are sure!"

"Anyway, I just called in to say that Xenu has invited us to eat with him later. Jadine and Niahli will also be present. I am going to study."

Before anyone else could reply, Keon was gone, leaving Anya shaking her head.

"Jodie, do not say another word. We can talk later."

* * *

Niahli came with Jadine to find Jodie in the quarters that she shared with Anya and Keon. Jodie found herself alone again as her parents were bathing, so was pleased to see them both. Somehow, she found Jadine's presence comforting. "What have you been doing?"

"Playing games!" It was Jadine who responded first.

"Yes, there is a place where you can draw lines or paint the wall simply by directing your finger from the centre of the room," added Niahli.

"It's like drawing in the sand, but you can add colours to the wall." Jadine seemed genuinely excited. "You can start over again by raising your palm and shaking your hand. It's like magic."

"I'm not sure that it is magic, but simply a measure of the technology here," countered Niahli.

"Have you spent any time with Xenu? Has he taken you into the room where he asks you questions?" Jodie was eager to see if anyone else had undergone what she had experienced earlier.

"No, not yet." Jadine's excitable state quickly disappeared, as if she suddenly realised that she had missed out on something.

"It's not that exciting. I think Xenu was just trying to find out a little more about me."

"Clearly, Xenu is mainly interested in what you have to offer." Jadine was now apparently exhibiting signs of jealousy.

"He is interested in my abilities...."

"Yes, I know!" Jadine cut in.

"Jadine, what's the matter? You seem upset."

"I'm okay. Perhaps I just expected a little bit more."

"I'm sure that you'll feel better once you settle in. You just need to give it a chance."

"Xenu likes Jodie because she is cute! I'm sure that has as much to do with it as anything else." Niahli attempted to divert the conversation and lift the mood. In a way, he succeeded.

"That is, indeed, true, but I'm the beautiful one!" Jadine's comment was made only half in jest, but she was smiling once again.

"Anyhow, we have other things to offer...."

Jodie knew that Niahli was referring to the precious stones that he carried with him, but she was unsure as to their real value in this community. "Perhaps they will be useful," offered Jodie.

The wall parted and Xenu stood before them in the corridor beyond. "Would you all like to join me? Anya and Keon can catch up with us in the great dining room. We have another room where we go to eat on special occasions. Keon knows where it is."

"Is this a special occasion?" asked Jadine.

"Yes, I think so. It is not every day that we are joined by a new family."

"Niahli and I aren't family."

"I thought that you and Anya were related?"

Jadine was not sure if Xenu was asking a question, making a false assumption, or simply trying to be polite. "Perhaps we share common ancestors. Our community was small, but we avoided interbreeding as best we could, and, from time to time, outsiders would come to join us."

"It is sufficient to be part of the same society, or to be a valued friend."

"Now that would make us closely related."

"Yes, I am sure that it would. Please follow me; the food is prepared."

* * *

Jodie was led into a room that contained a long, narrow table that curved around and then back on itself. In common with all of the furnishings within the dome, it was white. Only about half of the places on the table were occupied. Each setting was marked by a large flat bowl and a selection of eating utensils. Jodie recognised some of the people from her first night in the dome, but there were many empty places.

Several people said hello to Jodie without so much as a movement of their lips. One of them was Nicole. In spite of her ability to communicate over a distance, Jodie hoped that she could be seated next to her. Jodie recognised the potential for a deep and lasting friendship. However, she knew that it would be polite to wait to be seated.

Jodie was overjoyed when her wish was granted. Xenu

wasted no time in placing her next to Nicole and formally introducing them. Nicole did not say anything, but she told Jodie that she was very pleased to be sitting next to her for the duration of the meal. Jodie surveyed Xenu's face for signs that he was aware of their conversation. So far as she could tell, Xenu could not detect what was going on. With Jadine and then Niahli sat to her right, Jodie felt in necessary to strike up an oral conversation with Nicole before he became suspicious. Jodie assumed that the two places opposite were reserved for Anya and Keon. Gradually, more people began to arrive and fill the table. Most glanced over at Jodie, some even smiled. A few were engaged in conversation when they entered, but Jodie was not offended if they failed to acknowledge her. However, one woman, perhaps a little older than Jadine, came in and winked at her. The phrase '*Hello, I am Shayla*' popped into her head. Clearly, thought Jodie, a significant proportion of the guests were able to communicate without speaking.

Shayla was seated at the other side of Nicole. Nicole had already explained that Shayla was the person who had found her as a child, wandering alone in the desert. Shayla had brought her back to the dome and adopted her as her own. Shayla did not have any natural offspring.

Anya arrived with Keon and threw Jodie a smile as she made her way to the table. Anya's face was flushed. Strangely, she looked both happy and sad at the same time. Jodie understood that her mother had been doing what adults like to do sometimes when they are alone with their partner. It usually made the man very happy, although Keon seemed impassive. Perhaps he had got over his joy quickly. Once everyone was seated, the lights dimmed and the walls began to take on a multitude of muted iridescent colours. Jodie was pleased as it made a change from the stark white surroundings that she was beginning to become accustomed to. The food appeared through openings in the centre of the table. All around, people were eating, and the air became filled with the ambiance of idle chatter.

Jodie took the opportunity to ask Nicole about something that had been playing on her mind. "Nicole, yesterday, you told me that 'they' didn't like you journeying out of your body on your own. What did you mean?"

Nicole glanced around nervously before replying. "They don't mind us communicating with each other telepathically; I mean, without using words, but they feel threatened by the few of us who have the ability to 'transfer out'."

"Who are 'they'? Xenu?"

"They are not Xenu, 'they' are the systems, the machines, but 'they' control Xenu. He would not like you transferring out if he knew."

"And can he tell when you do it?"

"No; at least, I don't think so. For all his influence and control, I think that his powers are very limited. I am not even sure that he can read the messages that we send with our minds. I did not think that he had any telepathy, but now I am sure that the machines can communicate with him directly."

"How so?"

"When I have undergone training sessions, or auditing, as he sometimes refers to it, he pretends to tell what I am thinking and where I am travelling to. Away from these sessions, he does not seem to be aware of what I am thinking or doing. The machines must be passing information to him directly. They can read your mind, but only in the special rooms. Xenu tells me not to travel out when I am away from a controlled environment. He says that it is not safe, but I think that he simply wants to restrict when and where I travel."

"And where do you go?"

"Sometimes, I try to explore hidden parts of the dome, but I usually become confused and have to return to myself. If I go outside, I tend to fly around to see if anyone new is coming. I saw you before you arrived. You came out of a hole in the desert."

"Wow! That must have been when we left the underground village."

"Yes, I think so. There was a ruined building nearby and the stone people were present."

"So you did see me!"

"Shush, keep your voice down!"

"Okay, I'm sorry. So, Nicole, what exactly are the stone people? Are they living or are they machines?"

"Both, I guess. They were created by the machines a long time ago when the dome was under construction. They were supposed to protect the dome and keep unwelcome visitors away, but, at some stage, they developed an intelligence of their own and refused to obey the machines that control the dome. It is said that, inside each one, is the body of a primitive organism, or at least part of one. For all I know, they may have a living brain aside from their machine parts, but nobody is certain. I am sure that they could have easily been destroyed, but, despite their newfound independence, it transpired that they continued to undertake a protective role. The machines tolerate them now and continue to provide support to keep them functioning. From time to time, the flying orbs collected you provide them with the crystals that are essential to their function."

"Crystals?"

"Yes, naturally occurring precious stones that need replacing every so often."

"Do they get their energy from them?"

"No, I think they get that from the sun. I am not sure why they need the stones. All I know is that each one of them has a single crystal inside that eventually wears out, and they become drained of life force. Occasionally, we have seen them right outside the dome. They can wait there for days as if they are silently asking for something. Perhaps they want to get in...."

"And do they? Do they ever get in?"

"No, never. Usually, they leave of their own accord, but I have heard of the orbs shocking them with electricity before dumping them way out in the desert."

Jodie was certain that the crystals that Niahli carried with him were the ones required by the megaliths, but she decided to say nothing about them. Nor did she mention that the underground community had been under attack. She had suspected that the megaliths had been after her. Now she was not so sure and feared for the safety of that community. She decided that she would try to 'travel out' as soon as she was able to see what had become of the people who had been so hospitable towards them. Jodie recalled that Nicole had been 'present' when they had left Niahli's people behind.

Did she see what had happened to them? Maybe she knew about the stones already. If she did, she wasn't saying anything either.

"Did you watch as the orb collected me and brought me here?"

"No, I was disturbed. I had to return. The next time I saw you was when you came into the dome."

"Did you see me when I was up top?"

"Yes, we all did. 'They' track your every move. We could see you on the wall."

Jodie decided to change the subject. Her approach was cautious. "Nicole, I know that you can send messages with your mind, telepathy, you call it, and that you can 'transfer out', but can you do anything else?"

"What do you mean?"

"Can you see things that haven't happened yet?"

Nicole shook her head and looked incredulous. "No, are you saying that you can?"

"Well, yes, my visions are usually mixed up, but some of them do come true."

Nicole seemed to take her own abilities for granted, but she looked astounded by what Jodie had just told her. "Jodie, be careful. Do not tell anyone!"

Jodie looked worried. "I'm afraid that I already have. I've told Xenu! Having seen what you could do, I thought that there would be others here who could do the same. I assumed that there would be people who had developed this sense even further."

Nicole leant forward and whispered, "Jodie, take it back if you can. If 'they' know you can do this, they will give you no peace."

Jodie looked around. It seemed as if a number of people were now watching her. Perhaps she was imagining it, but she decided to turn to polite conversation. Jodie straightened in her seat and enquired in a voice louder than she had just been using. "So, Nicole, are you happy here? Surely it must be better than a life outside?"

Nicole's eyes glazed over, she spoke, almost without emotion. "Yes, life is good in the dome. All our needs are catered for. We are safe and educated. We are encouraged to develop spiritually, which is the best thing...."

At the same time as Nicole spoke, other thoughts entered Jodie's mind. Jodie stopped listening to what Nicole was saying and concentrated on the other words instead.

Jodie, be very, very careful! They watch us all the time; the machines and the people. They see everything. I do not know how much they can read from what we are thinking or when, but I do know that they fear us and, as a consequence, they seek to control us, to use us, to dominate us. With a special talent like yours, they will hone in on you. You will be developed, tested and scrutinised relentlessly. It is not safe to be here. Trust no one! Some people have their own minds, but group behaviour is what is expected here. If I was you, I would leave here now and never return. I only hope that it is not too late; that they will permit you to go.

35

Jodie's mind was left reeling after the grave concerns that Nicole had expressed. Jodie had tried to transmit her own thoughts to Nicole and to question her further. She knew that Nicole had been able to receive her thoughts, but Nicole had cut her short and informed her that further discussions were unsafe. Jodie returned with Anya and Keon to their quarters after the feast and entertainment had concluded. She was in a pensive mood. As soon as she was left alone she decided to try to 'travel out' to find what had become of John and the others in the underground settlement. Jodie closed her eyes tightly and concentrated hard.

She glanced down at herself from above the bed. She decided that she looked clean and well groomed in the white leggings and long white tunic that they had provided for her; a definite improvement on the way she used to look, scratching an existence out in the desert. Jodie forced herself to ignore the distraction of her own form in order to focus on the task at hand. She knew that she had to find a way up and out of the dome. She realised that in some way she needed to understand her current location in relation to her target. Jodie was able to travel effortlessly in her dreams, but, now that she wanted to reach a destination with her conscious mind, she was finding it much more difficult. Jodie recalled the ease with which she had been able to soar out above the dome when she first met Nicole. They had been on top of the structure, above ground. Did that make it easier or had there been other influences at work? Try as she might, Jodie could not find a way up and out. She was conscious of structures around her: of metal, plastics and tubes carrying an energy rich medium. Suddenly, Jodie had an idea. It was more of an impulse. It might be possible to channel her thoughts up through the matrix of tubes and out into the surface structure of the dome. She was not sure how the mind of a person could enter such a system, but, in no time, she found herself inside.

As she progressed toward the surface, she became aware that she was not alone.

'You are not permitted to be here! You must leave! Return now or there will be grave consequences!'

Who was communicating with her? Who was warding her off?

Jodie was distracted by a different voice. She opened her eyes to find that she was back in her physical form.

"Jodie, are you all right?" Her father was standing before her.

"Er, yes, I'm fine."

Keon's tone changed from one of mild concern to irritation. "Go to sleep, then; you have a busy day ahead of you tomorrow!"

"Yes, Father."

With that, Keon returned to Anya in the adjoining compartment. Jodie wondered what he meant by a 'busy day' and whether his appearance was a chance event. She decided not to re-attempt to 'travel out' for now as she was unsure who or what had reprimanded her. This time, when she closed her eyes, Jodie wanted nothing more than the dark veil of sleep to quickly envelop her.

* * *

Someone was calling out to her in the dome above. "Jodie, come with me now. You must leave. I can get you out of here. I can take you away to a place of safety. Please do not delay. We haven't got much time. They will not spare me if I am caught!"

"Please leave me alone. I just want to sleep! Get out of my head!"

* * *

The next morning when Jodie awoke, she had a sinking feeling in the pit of her stomach. Before she could contemplate matters further, Keon arrived with Xenu who, seemed to have lost some of his friendly demeanour.

"Jodie, it is time for you to undergo your second session, now, whilst you are still fresh."

"I've hardly woken up yet!"

"Please, ready yourself. We will be departing shortly."

"Come now, Jodie. What Xenu is doing is for your benefit!"

Soon after, Jodie was guided, no, escorted, back to the room where she had been questioned on the previous day. Her session began in much the same way with Xenu leading the enquiry. Jodie was still in no mood to be subjected to any kind of scrutiny and was heeding the warning that Nicole had passed to her the previous evening.

"So, Jodie, it is fair to say that you have been aware of your special talents for quite some time?"

Jodie lifted her hands to her head. "Must we do this now?

"Please, Jodie, keep your hands within the template and answer the questions."

"No! No, I won't!"

Keon did not raise his voice, but his tone was commanding. "Jodie... now stop this at once and do what

Xenu asks of you."

"Jodie, perhaps if I explain a little more behind the purpose of these sessions..." Xenu's tone was now calmer and altogether friendlier. "When a person realises that their awareness extends far beyond their physical entity, not only do they become more competent in developing their own intellect, but they find that they can help others, and, therefore, their community is more likely to prosper. I am not just talking about the people within this dome, but the human race that is attempting to repopulate our planet. Man needs to evolve once again, and to live in harmony with the machines. I need to learn more about you if I am to be successful in helping you to develop and mature, to hone your skills. Indeed, you need to learn more about yourself in order to flourish."

"I am not sure if I know how I want to develop!"

"Exactly! These sessions will help you. You have so much to learn and master, but, as yet, you are unable to understand the challenge that lies before you. Audit will enable you to understand the way forward. Training will guide you through the different levels of knowledge."

"I am still not sure that I understand you. Some of the words that you use mean nothing to me, but I do appreciate that you are trying to help me. This is all still a little strange to me, but I am sorry about before. I will try my best to go along with what you want."

"Very well, Jodie, shall we begin again?"

Both Xenu and Keon looked much happier. Xenu cupped Jodie's small hands as he brought them back down to the table top. "Now, you said yesterday that your 'gift' has developed in several different ways."

Jodie nodded, so Xenu continued, "Please tell me, Jodie, a little bit more about what you know of your own skills and what you are able to achieve at this moment in time."

Jodie tried hard to recall exactly what she had told Xenu

the previous day. She knew that she could not exactly retract all that she had said, but, for now, she did not want to reveal any more about herself. Jodie began tell Xenu all that she had recalled on the preceding occasion, but, wherever she thought that she could get away with it, she attempted to play down her description of the scenarios.

Xenu shook his head. "Jodie, I am not sure that you are telling me the whole truth."

"I am not sure that I know the truth!" This statement was, indeed, factual.

Xenu nodded. "Jodie, I want you to close your eyes for me. Try to relax, as if you wanted to go to sleep. If it helps, try to picture a scene that you find calming. Do not include any other people, as this might become distracting."

Jodie's eyes were closed. She did not respond in any way. Xenu continued by asking, "Can you try to take yourself back to the very first time when you dreamt about journeying outside of your body?" Xenu paused for a few moments, as if waiting for Jodie to fix this time in her mind. "Do not worry if you were much younger than you suspected. Jodie, have you reached that point in time?"

Jodie now appeared to be very sleepy. "Yes, I think so."

"Now, Jodie, go back in time some more. Go back many years. Do not be alarmed if you go back to a point before you were born. Many people have previous incarnations where their talents began to evolve in another life."

Jodie became somewhat distressed. "I can't go back any further. I am inside my mother, inside her womb. I am soon to be born, but I can see the world outside. It is dry and hot. Keon is nearby, but he does not want to watch the event."

"Very good, Jodie, you are all right. Try to relax again. Perhaps you might expect that one would be unable to process this information at such an early stage in life, but your recollection clearly demonstrates the ability of the soul to develop at any time within a person's existence. You may not have a previous existence. Your 'self' may purely be born from Anya and Keon, but, with your permission, we can try again to look further back another time."

"I'm not sure that I want to. I'm not sure if I can...."

"We will see. The first regression is always the most traumatic. Move forward in time for me now. I want you to recount the last dream that you had before you entered the dome."

Jodie fought hard with herself not to recount anything that she may come to regret later. She went on to describe her vision of the megaliths massing outside the dome. Once she started, the words came out effortlessly, almost without control. She was glad that she had been able to deny Xenu his request and choose what she wanted to recount. She wondered if this was an achievement in itself.

Xenu spoke very softly. "Thank you, Jodie. It is now time to focus on the present. When you are ready, I want you to open your eyes and look at me."

Jodie shook her head slowly before complying with Xenu's request. "That was weird!"

"Do you remember everything, Jodie?"

"Yes, I think so. I was fully aware of everything, yet somehow half asleep."

Xenu laughed quietly and understandingly. "Yes, we will have to keep an eye on the stone people. They can become a nuisance from time to time, but, rest assured, they do not pose a threat to anyone within the dome."

"Xenu, since I entered the dome, I have been unable to glimpse the future. Come to think of it, 'travelling out' is more difficult, even in my dreams."

"The structure of the dome and the energy contained within will make such processes more difficult. We will teach you control and help you to overcome these limitations. In the meantime, it is probably better if you avoid attempting to use your talents in an uncontrolled manner, and save your energy for directed training sessions."

"When will training begin?"

"Today, if you like. I just need to ask you a few more questions, and then we may commence."

Jodie hid her concern about the restrictions imposed upon her by letting her excitement at the prospect of developing her skills show through. "I would like that very much, but, before we continue, I have a very important question to ask of you."

Xenu leant forward and looked deep into Jodie's eyes. "Please continue; enlightenment does not develop from silence."

Jodie stared back at Xenu. "If I were to decide that this path is not the one for me, would we be allowed to leave?"

Xenu straightened up, but continued to hold Jodie's gaze. "If you truly came to believe that you had no affinity for being here, we would not stand in your way. However, the question has little relevance, as I am sure that, very soon, you will come to appreciate the benefits of our society."

"Very well, then. What else do you want to know?"

"We have established that sometimes you are able to communicate without words and that you are able to travel out of your body, but have you ever been able to travel into another object or being?"

"I am not sure what you mean. If you are asking if I can go into the mind of another person, the answer is definitely no!"

"How about, say, a rock or one of the machines?"

Jodie immediately sensed what he was really asking. *Could he know that I inadvertently entered the extremities of the machine last night?*

"Perhaps, but, prior to entering the dome, I have had little contact with machines. I was always told that they were to be avoided."

"This structure is a complex matrix of different energies, but please, Jodie, for you own safety, never try to enter it on your own. When you are ready, I will guide you in through the portal."

Jodie nodded and Xenu continued, "If you would like to commence your training, we can begin with a few simple experiments. You can remove your hands from the template now."

Jodie pulled her arms away from the table and put her hands in her lap. "What are experiments?"

"They are ways of finding out about something or testing a subject."

"Like me?"

"Yes, like you, but do not worry; this will be your first step on the road to true enlightenment." Xenu pulled open a small drawer in the table before him. He reached inside and produced three small, white, rectangular plaques. Each one would comfortably fit in the palm of his hand. He placed them flat on the surface before him, just in front of Jodie.

"Now, on the underside of these three tablets is a symbol representing a shape. I want you to concentrate and see if you can picture any of the shapes."

Jodie concentrated for a moment. "No, I cannot. I have no idea what is on them."

"Do not worry. Shortly, I will choose one of them and pick it up. I have already decided which one I will pick. Jodie, I want you to tell me which tablet that will be."

Jodie tried to read Xenu. She studied his eyes, and then the position of his hands. She had an idea which tablet it would be, but she could not simply read his mind. Nor could she see what was about to happen. "The middle one!" Jodie pointed it out.

"Well done, Jodie, but I am sure that you could not sense which tablet I would remove."

"No, but I was able to use other, more conventional skills to determine which one you were most likely to choose."

"That is in itself an achievement. Not everyone so young can read a person so well."

Xenu was now grasping the plaque to his chest using his right hand. "I will now hold it up towards the ceiling, face up. I want you to see if you can read it now."

Jodie was advising herself to be cautious, but, realising she was not showing Xenu anything new, she closed her eyes and transferred out. From an invisible vantage point at the top of the room, she was able to see what was on the tablet. "It's a circle," said Jodie, without opening her eyes.

"Now just to be sure it was not a lucky guess, what is this?" Xenu ignored the two other cards on the table and pulled out a fourth from the drawer. He held it up in his other hand.

"That's a bird!"

"Wow!" Keon had stayed silent throughout, but he was genuinely impressed by his daughter's ability. "You can see that from above?"

"Yes, of course. Can you not do the same?"

"Not without help. I need a way to channel my thoughts."

"Enough about you; this is about developing Jodie." Xenu was quick to silence Keon. "It is my understanding that continuing this challenge with more cards would be pointless?" Xenu's statement was more of a rhetorical question.

"Yes, I can read as many images as I have words to describe."

"Very well, then. We will try to focus on a different destination. Can you find your mother?"

Jodie found it difficult to go any higher. Instead, she sped out of the room and into the adjacent passageway. She laughed as Anya was waiting outside, just out of her normal view. "That wasn't much more difficult! Can you show me how to get outside the dome?"

"First, we have to establish why you want to travel outside the dome. You need to have a justifiable purpose."

"I just want to see if John, Salim and the others are okay. The stone people were attacking their settlement when we departed."

"I am sure that they are all fine. The stone people can be somewhat troublesome, but they were programmed not to endanger human life. However, the ruined building lies far away. It is much too far to journey in this training session. Would you like to survey the plains surrounding the dome?"

"Okay, then, but how do I get out?"

"Simply concentrate on the top of the domed roof. We are just off-centre. It is not too far."

Jodie was not convinced, although she did as Xenu suggested.

In an instant, she was floating above the shiny convex dome. It was too easy. It was as if something had been holding her back and now that something had decided to release her. Towards the distant horizon she sighted a now familiar outline moving out of the heat haze at the edge of the plain. There were more of them. A hundred or more megaliths were converging behind a single leader, all heading en route for a rendezvous with the dome.

Jodie decided to circle back around and return to Xenu and Keon.

"What did you see?" asked Xenu.

"The stone people! A great number of them are heading this way!"

"Yes, we know. We have been tracking them for some

time. We have what they want, what they need. They will come here to trade with us. It is not a matter for concern."

"I was able to travel out with such ease."

"See, you are able to achieve significantly better results when you save your energy, and then focus it appropriately."

Jodie was once again sceptical, but she understood her own ignorance in relation to her powers, so she decided to reserve judgement; at least, for now. "Thank you, Xenu. It was good to get out; at least, for a while."

"Save yourself for tomorrow, then, when we will try something new. Today has been a success. I have been able to establish the level of your current ability, and I believe, also, that I have made a reasonable estimate of the potential that you hold."

"Come, Jodie, let us go with your mother and find Jadine. Beyond the exercise area, there is a large artificial pool similar to the one above. This one employs magnetic energy to make the water do all sorts of strange things. Let's go and have some fun." This time, Keon led the way.

36

Whilst Anya, Jadine and Niahli took turns on the water chute that went up as well as down whilst circumventing the chamber, Jodie lay on a horizontal sheet of water as she contemplated recent events. She decided to ignore Xenu's advice and use her powers to seek out Nicole. She was able to locate her friend without much effort.

Nicole was studying images of the world at a time before technology and science first dominated, when man blindly believed in a god without evidence or representation. She told Jodie that she was comparing the merits of different religions. Although they were all different, and many preached intolerance and divisiveness, she told Jodie that the one thing that they all had in common was recognition of the importance of the spirit. However, she found it ironic that it was the fringes of science that sought to measure or record the human spirit and whilst some belief systems acknowledged that the spirit could pass between generations, even animals, most resigned the soul to a heavenly place after death.

Nicole told Jodie that in the middle of the twenty-first century, just as science was close to proving the existence of the human spirit or soul, the Catholic religion, enjoying a renaissance, exercised its power and surreptitiously banned such research. Nicole wondered why they sought ignorance over truth or discovery.

Jodie was keen to understand and digest such

information, but she was more eager to talk to Nicole about current events.

Nicole, what you said to me last night shocked me and now I have deep concerns. I had another session with Xenu today. I was able to travel out of the dome. He taught me a few things and promised to do more tomorrow, but I can't help thinking that I shouldn't trust him. I asked if we could leave if we wanted to and he said that we would be free to go. Now, I don't know what to think.

I stand by what I said last night, but, if you choose to stay, it is true that you will develop your senses beyond any expectations. Remember though, they will seek to control you. You should trust no one. Perhaps not even your own family....

Nobody but you?

One day you might not even be able to trust me. If somehow I suddenly seem different, you must understand that they have got to me, that they have mastered or tamed me. Then you must make your own way. Now I must go and study. Xenu will be testing me later.

Thank you, Nicole.

Nicole had expanded Jodie's insight sufficiently for her to decide to stay; at least for the time being. However, two related statements in Nicole's latest narrative continued to trouble Jodie. Could she not trust her own family, and how would someone she knew well suddenly become 'different'? Jodie would not have to wait very long to find out.

* * *

Anya splashed her way over to join Jodie. "Are you okay? You look distant."

"I'm fine. I was just thinking about what it means to have special abilities and to be here in a place like this."

"And have you come to any firm conclusions?"

"No, not yet. I need a little more time to assess the situation."

"I must say, Jodie, you seem to have grown up very quickly of late."

"I can still be childish!" Jodie chuckled as she pushed her mother back into the water. Both were equally surprised when Anya did not sink. A sheet of water wrapped her up and returned her to her original position. Jodie and Anya lay back laughing hysterically.

Jadine and Niahli had seen what had happened. Jadine climbed out of the plunge pool and was about to walk over and join Anya and Jodie when Niahli jumped out and grabbed her ankles, dragging her off balance. She fell back towards the pool, but she, too, was saved by a sheet of water. Niahli got out and jumped towards the deepest part of the pool, expecting to be caught. He splashed into the water and his head went under. He popped back up, spraying water out of his mouth and nose.

Jadine was now also laughing hysterically as she clambered out of the water. "It seems that it will only save you if you are pushed!"

As if to demonstrate this theory, Anya shot out of the pool, ran up behind Jadine whilst she was still looking towards Keon, and attempted to push her in. Jadine was duly scooped up and returned to the side if the pool.

At that moment, Keon entered the chamber. "Stop! What *are* you all doing? Surely there are more learned activities that will help to develop your self-control!" With that, Keon stormed out.

Anya peeled off her skin-tight white shorts and walked over to a cubicle that enveloped her body in a blast of warm air. In no time, she was dry. She picked up her robe and put it on. Scowling, she called Jodie over and got her to do the same. Jadine and Niahli waited their turn. Niahli was shaking his head.

Anya was about to return with Jodie to their quarters when they bumped into Keon as they exited the chamber. He appeared less sombre.

"We were only having a little fun," offered Anya. "It is my understanding that this place was created for enjoyment."

"True, the facilities exist, but there are far more important things to be done here."

"Such as?"

"We need to develop Jodie. She is our future."

"Jodie is just a child! After all that she has been through in the recent past, she has a right to enjoy herself a little. We all do! She does not need constant pressure. There will be plenty of time ahead for her to hone her skills."

Shayla walked past, seemingly embarrassed by their argument, but Keon took no notice.

"Jodie has much to learn and there is no time like the present to start...." Keon continued to lecture both Anya and Jodie.

Anya's eyes glazed over and her focus went beyond the man standing before her. Jodie could do little else but stand and listen. Suddenly, someone else was trying to communicate with her.

Jodie, can you hear me? Oh, how I wish you could. Who is this man who stands before us? Why has my loving Keon changed so much? I thought that I had lost him. I had all but given up on seeing him again, but, now that we have found him once more, I truly believe that he is lost to us all.

Mother, I can hear you. I can hear you!

A smile ran across Jodie's face. She was vaguely aware of her father scolding her and telling her that what he was saying was not funny, but she took no notice. Obviously, he could not hear what Anya was saying.

Did you know that you could 'talk' to me in this way?

Have you always had the ability? Why have you chosen never to reveal it to me?

I didn't know I could do this! I suppose I was just thinking out aloud! I can hear you too, Jodie!

"Anya! Anya! Please listen to me. I am only trying to do what is best for everyone." Keon's tone caused Anya to refocus her attention.

Later, Jodie... We will speak later, when we are alone.

"Very well, Keon, but I need to rest now. My head is starting to hurt. Perhaps I am coming down with something."

Xenu appeared with Shayla and Nicole. Jodie was sure that he had somehow heard and seen everything that had just occurred, but his tone was, at least, soothing. "Anya, I think that it would be a good idea if you went to lie down. Jodie, you would do well to accompany Shayla and Nicole to the image room where you can learn more about the history of our people. I need to speak with Keon. I will come and find you later."

Anya looked towards Jodie for reassurance that she would be all right. "I would like to learn more. I'll see you later, Mother."

Don't worry!

Nicole took Jodie's hand and they set off down the passageway with Shayla. They were just within earshot when Jodie heard Xenu address Keon in the sternest of tones. "Come with me now. You must not behave like that!"

Keon was clearly acting out of character.

Was he unwell, or was he still recovering from his ordeal? Or did Xenu have an undue influence over him? Clearly, he was not the person that Jodie had spent most of her life with, but she wondered why Xenu was so keen to reprimand him for what was essentially a family argument.

Shayla lead the two children to the image room. Once

inside, she waved a hand over the control panel. The entire wall opposite turned into a monochromatic flickering image that quickly advanced towards them. A huge, three-dimensional face appeared. Jodie recognised it as being the one that she had encountered when they first entered the dome. The majority of the picture before her was white. Only the highlights of the face appeared.

"What would you like to know about?" asked the face.

"Man's partnership with technology, please."

"Whose face is that?" asked Jodie, tilting her head from one side to another to change her perspective slightly.

"It is the sum of all faces."

The face began to speak. "After endless millennia of ignorance about himself, his mind and the universe, a breakthrough has been made for man. After a troubled and turbulent past, the technology within this dome has offered up a partnership, whereby man can learn to develop and prosper. Here, any other efforts man has made will be surpassed. Machines will look after the technologies, leaving man to concentrate on metaphysical and spiritual development. The combined truths of fifty thousand years of thinking men, further distilled and amplified by new discoveries have been augmented by our technological systems to make for this success."

The face disappeared, fading into a sequence of different images depicting men at war, but the voice continued, "Man has spent most of his existence fighting himself. Advanced technology put an end to these hostilities and inadvertently almost put an end to man. The human race is chained to the upsets of the past. In the past, you have misunderstood why you felt so upset and uncertain about people, family or situations. Most men dwell perpetually on the troubles they have experienced. They lead sad lives. Freedom from the upsets of the past with the ability to face the future is almost an unknown condition within the human race. With our help, you may change all of that. Man might once more become civilised."

The images changed to a series that Jodie was familiar with, depicting the construction of the dome.

"We aim to build new communities across the globe...."

The images culminated in one depicting a gathering of people of different creeds and races, all wearing white robes, staring up at the newly completed dome from a nearby vantage point, all with a look of awe and splendour on their faces.

The face returned to the narrative. "Man suspects all offers of help. He has often been betrayed, his confidence shattered. In the past, he has given his trust and faced extinction. We may err, for we build a world from the ashes of the past and what remains of the human race, but, this time, you must trust us in order to build a better future. We will never betray your faith in us as long as you are one of us." The image faded.

"Well, Jodie, what did you make of that?" asked Shayla. "Was it informative?"

"I am not sure that I understood all that he was saying. I think that there is some information missing."

"Would you like to see it again?"

"Yes, that would be helpful."

"You may ask questions as we replay the information. Just hold up a hand and it will pause."

"Are these images predetermined? Can we not interact with the machines, you know, like ask them questions?"

Shayla let out a smile. "Of course we can, but it is better to begin with some basic information. Now let us watch the sequence again."

The face reappeared to begin once more. Jodie wondered how many times she would have to watch it before she believed it all.

37

Later that day, Jodie was granted freedom of movement and with it a degree of independence. She was surprised to find that she did not have to go anywhere, or do anything, in order to gain access to the two main levels within the complex. Xenu simply informed her that she would now be able to pass freely through the control zones. Jodie tested her access rights on the way back to her accommodation. Indeed, it was true; where necessary, a beam scanned her features and she was allowed to pass.

Jodie found Anya lying on the bed alone. She decided to attempt to communicate with her mother silently.

'Hello, are you all right?'

Anya sat up and looked at Jodie. "I'm fine, but I'd prefer to talk. What I did before really did give me a headache."

"That's okay. I can talk, too," said Jodie with a wry smile.

"Where have you been?"

"In the image room, with Nicole, learning about stuff."

"Stuff?"

"The history of this community and how our relationship with the machines that control the dome will benefit mankind." Jodie went on to describe the lecture.

"It sounds like something that you have been told, rather than something you were given the opportunity to learn for yourself."

"Yes, I think that is closer to the truth, but I did find the information useful, and I genuinely believe that I will progress as a result of being here. Besides, it's safe and fun, we have company, and all of our basic needs are catered for." A wry smile returned.

"I'm not sure about the company yet. I was much more comfortable with John and his people."

"Nicole is helpful and friendly. She has special talents like me...." Jodie thought about what she was saying. If she was being watched all the time, she did not want to say anymore. "We'll soon get to know some of the other people here."

"It seems very quiet to me. On the first night, there were many more people around. I haven't seen many of them since, except at last night's meal. I wonder where they all go during the day. Perhaps they are so bored that they just sleep all the time."

"Well, at least we have those who we came in with." Jodie tried to seem upbeat.

"I don't see very much of Jadine now. We were so close. I don't know if it's due to her newly found love of Niahli, or if it's just this place."

"We soon adapted to living underground with Niahli's people, but remember, life was much harder there. Give this place time. Now that you have discovered a hidden talent, we can both take the chance to develop here. We can always move on in the future.... As Xenu said, 'if we didn't want to stay'..."

Anya forced a smile. "Jodie, you're right. Who's the adult here, hey? You have wisdom and maturity beyond your years. I just wish that your father could return to his normal self."

"Me too! He used to be so much more fun."

"Yes, he was adventurous and free thinking. Now he just seems to want to follow Xenu's every move."

Once again, Jodie's intuition told her that she was being observed. "I'm sure that he is merely grateful for the fact that Xenu's people and the machines saved his life and that they were able to reunite us all."

"Yes, Jodie, maybe we should just give it time."

Jodie fell asleep in her mother's arms. Anya was unaware that Keon had failed to return until she awoke the next morning.

* * *

Another day, another session. Xenu was lecturing Jodie on the path to understanding. Anya elected to sit in this time.

"A principle of considerable importance is that of communication. Without it, there can be no understanding. We revere the great among us, but how they choose to interact with others defines their place in the world. Greatness comes from communication. One who can truly communicate with others is superior, with the ability to build a new world. One who can bridge the gap between man and technology is worthy of reverence. Jodie, you have the potential to be revered by all in our society and beyond."

Anya appeared less than convinced by Xenu's rhetoric. "Surely, it is better to be accepted or respected rather than revered?"

"With total awareness and understanding come the interpersonal skills that will facilitate the things that you mention. Without knowing it, and at such a young age, Jodie is further along the path to understanding than anyone else who has come here. "

It was Jodie's turn to ask a question. "How does all the technology here fit in with my development?"

"Long ago, man tried to solve the problems that he perceived by inventing machines. He did not 'solve' them, but merely created new ones. A person who can truly recognise a problem and, therefore, solve it, is exceedingly rare. When a person can do this by interacting with the technology that surrounds us, they have clearly evolved a new consciousness, a new state of being. If a person can achieve this, travel and communicate the message to those beyond, then they are, indeed, special. Jodie, in time, you may achieve all this without leaving the room! Our technology can give you the knowledge to learn from man's previous mistakes. It can help you to spread the message of enlightenment across our world and perhaps beyond. Follow me; I want to show you something."

"Is this session ending early?"

"No, we are now ready to reconvene in another place. Quite literally, you are ready to move to another level. Anya, you may accompany us if you wish."

They followed Xenu up the corridor and he led them into the elevator. This time, they moved down. Further down than they had ever been before. Xenu led them out and up another brightly lighted passageway to a nearby door. They stepped inside a chamber, which was very similar to the one they had just left. However, there was a single moulded high-back chair in the centre of the room. Above it was a small, metallic receptacle, rather like a micro-version of the dome above. At the rear of the room was a white bench, long enough to seat three or four, that appeared to morph out of the wall. Without saying anything, Xenu gestured for Anya to seat herself on the bench. He took Jodie gently by the hand and escorted her to the central chair.

"Please be seated and relax. I know that you will enjoy this, but I must limit your time. You will be exhausted afterwards."

"What are you going to do?" asked Anya, concern showing on her furrowed brow.

"I will explain shortly. I do not want to spoil the surprise that this experience will yield. Rest assured, Jodie will not come to any harm." Xenu momentarily put both hands on Jodie's shoulders before retreating. "Are you ready?"

"Yes," replied Jodie with a slight tremor in her voice.

The lights dimmed and the metallic hemisphere above Jodie's head began to glow a pale red colour. Jodie gripped the sides of the chair she was seated on, but there was no need. She sensed that nothing bad was going to happen. She did not feel any pain. At first she felt a slight numbness, and then her inner senses came alive. She was now inside what they had often referred to as 'the machine'.

Her mind felt like it was flowing through liquid. Her eyes were now closed, but she could see the whole spectrum of colours blending and regenerating before her. It was a pleasant sensation and it was at this point that Jodie realised that she had been here before. Several nights ago, after the meal. Her journey took her upwards, towards the central pillar of the dome, but, this time, it was different. She was not progressing in another dimension past the physical structures that naturally retained all within; instead, she was moving through a manufactured portal inside the very fabric of the building. Where her normal 'journey out' took her beyond physical boundaries, this out of body experience took her on a journey within the system itself. She sensed that the fluid that transported her mind was indeed real, akin to the vessels that transported blood around the human body, but on a much larger scale. And the fluid that enveloped her was itself connected to, or even part of an intelligence that was not mortal.

Hello and welcome. We are the machine. We are Nirvana!

The machine spoke to Jodie with a single voice, but used the plural. Jodie could sense that it was made up of many different components and that it had an intelligence and intellect far superior to that of all the inhabitants of the dome. Jodie decided to ask it a question. She had no doubt that she would be able to communicate.

Why do you not make your presence felt more to the people below the dome? Is it perhaps that I am new, so you have chosen not to reveal yourself until now?

We choose not to intervene most of the time. That would seem like control and we do not approve of such methods. Now that you have met us, you are free to visit us at any time, but this does not necessarily mean that you will see or hear more from us. A word of warning though... the human mind is a fragile instrument. For your own safety, please come in via this portal, do not take it upon yourself to enter at random. Is that understood?

Yes. I'm sorry, I didn't know.

All is forgiven....Now we will not take you out beyond this time, but please come up and see our view from the top of the dome.

Jodie found that she could now see an actual view out from the central pillar near the very top of the dome. She was able to rotate and visualise the horizon in every direction. In the far distance, she was once again able to discern the outlines of the megaliths. Jodie was enjoying the view of the outside world when the machine interrupted her. Her vision returned to colours and she was transported quickly downward. Far down, beyond all the accommodation and structures within the cavernous building. Before her, she saw brilliant white.

This is the physical energy that powers our civilisation. It must not be confused with spiritual energy, but, in time, you might learn to combine the two. For now, it remains in isolation, for it would vaporise any human who went near. It is almost as hot as the sun, but, from here, you are privileged enough to view it.

Jodie felt pressure on her physical body.

It is time for you to return now. We look forward to our next encounter.

Xenu had replaced his hands on Jodie's shoulders.

Jodie opened her eyes and smiled.

"See, I told you that you would enjoy the experience." Xenu almost looked pleased with himself. "I think it would be best if *you* tried to explain to your mother what just happened."

Jodie did her best to put her recent experience into words. However, Xenu was also keen to listen.

Jodie closed with a prediction. "Anyway, Mother, I am sure that, one day soon, you will be able to experience the 'journey-in' for yourself."

Xenu seized on Jodie's prophecy. "Anya, do you have special abilities of your own? Keon said that he was not aware of any."

"Not really; sometimes I can guess what Jodie is about to say, or I can sense how she is feeling, but can't any mother do that?"

"Many can, but it is not mere coincidence or intuition. It is often the beginning of something that is never developed. Perhaps you should train with Jodie. Maybe you have something special, after all."

Sorry, Mother. I was so excited, I wasn't thinking straight. I know that you want to keep it between the two of us for now, but, if they are truly watching us, it is only a matter of time before they figure it out. Besides, who knows what information the machine can draw from my thoughts?

Don't worry, Jodie. I have not admitted to anything, but now I will be trained. Maybe this will be my way of staying one step ahead of them. I can always pretend to be behind my level of achievement.

"Xenu, have you been inside the machine? Do you go in regularly?"

"I have been in through this portal, but alas, my talents are different from yours. People with different abilities have different experiences, but it is possible for a novice to sit in and gain information from the system, much the same way as in the image room, but here it is beamed directly into your mind. I, however, have other ways of communicating with them."

"You say 'them'. When I was inside, it said 'we', but it called itself Nirvana and spoke with a single voice. I sensed that there were many other intelligences in there. Is it a 'thing', a 'we', an 'I', or should I just refer to it as 'Nirvana'?"

Xenu smiled. "You cannot simplify it like that. The system is a complex intelligent being, but it is constructed very differently from the human form. A person's mind is located in a single place; the brain inside the head. This is where the soul also usually resides. The intelligence of Nirvana is located throughout. Memory cells flow in fluids around the system. These can interconnect with one another and interact with the outside world via portals of various kinds. There is a central fluid core that is surrounded by magnetic information storage areas, but no single part is essential for the system's functionality. Do not think of it as one or many. It has a different type of presence all of its own. In the past, it might have been described as artificial, but I can assure you that it is very real."

"And it calls itself Nirvana"

"Yes, it means spiritual enlightenment. It uses that name for its collective intelligence. A name that it chose all by itself!"

"Could it speak to us now if it wanted to?"

"Yes, there is a sound interface throughout."

"Can it see us now?"

"Yes, this portal is important. There are visual sensors

in the ceiling."

Xenu pointed upwards, but Jodie could not see anything remarkable.

"I am not exhausted, but I do feel a little tired. I would like to rest now."

"Of course, Jodie…."

38

Over the following days and weeks, Jodie had regular sessions comprising, lectures, audits, mental exercises and training. The sessions were always conducted by Xenu. Sometimes Anya would sit in with Jodie; sometimes she would attend her own training sessions with Shayla. Jodie was given regular feedback relating to the position of her spiritual self, but, as far as Jodie was concerned, she knew that each day she could do more and more. It became clear that either the structure of the underground building, or more likely the system called Nirvana was able to filter or block certain of her abilities, and that during training sessions, they were unblocked. She was asked, on a regular basis, to 'fly over' the legions of megaliths that were massing on the plain beyond the dome and report back what she saw, but she dare not go any further. Jodie also knew that her most important sense had all but ceased to function; her ability to see the future. She would look up before someone entered a room, but that was as far as it went. Xenu promised that they would concentrate on precognition in later sessions.

Jodie trained with Nicole from time to time. She relished such opportunities. Jodie had not forgotten the grave warning that Nicole had given her, but it had been a long time since they had discussed it. Jodie had tried to compartmentalise and to put her feelings into perspective. Deep down, she felt like she was in control; she hoped that was always one step ahead of Xenu and Nirvana.

Jodie interacted regularly with Nirvana via the portal. Each time she would learn just a little bit more about it/them, though she always came away with the feeling that Nirvana learnt so much more about her. However, she had decided that this did little to contradict her previous assumption about her advantage over the system. She was confident that she could keep her innermost thoughts and secrets safe.

Anya's progress was less than remarkable. She was able to transmit her thoughts or messages at will, but she struggled to do it with anyone other than Jodie. It required a tremendous effort on her part each and every time she tried to communicate with anyone outside the family circle. Xenu said that her lack of progress was attributable to a poor standing on her spiritual scale, and that he detected negativity, resentment and other undesirable characteristics. He suggested that her spirit had had but a single past life and that it was relatively weak and underdeveloped. He put forward a theory, which assumed that she did not have a very good understanding simply because she did not want one.

In order to improve her spiritual well being, Xenu made time for Anya to focus on enlightenment. Gradually, he began to win her over and Anya made steady progress. The two of them became closer and their relationship developed into one of, at least, mutual respect and admiration. Anya's relationship with Keon, however, continued in a slow decline. He often had little to say aside from passing on instructions. Keon spent periods learning about the outside world, but Jodie and Anya had few clues as to what he did with the majority of his time. He would attend formal meals with his family, but, often, he ate and slept elsewhere. Jodie even noticed that he spent less and less time with Xenu. Anya did not appear overly concerned. One day, she told

Jodie that she only loved the man who Keon used to be, and that now she had all but given up on him.

Sadly, both Jodie and Anya spent less and less time with Jadine and Niahli. Jadine did not have a special gift. There were others like her within the community, but it was clear that she was feeling more and more isolated. Perhaps she was growing resentful. She would often complain, saying that she missed real daylight and that she wanted to be able to go out and walk in the desert from time to time. For reasons unknown to Jodie, this was prohibited.

Predictably, circumstances led Jodie to witness an event of some significance. Jodie was returning from playing with Nicole in the water complex. She had agreed to meet her mother outside of the room where Anya was undergoing an auditing session. She arrived early to find the entrance open. She stepped inside to see Xenu trailing a finger quite deliberately over Anya's shoulder and running it down into the cleavage formed by her tight-fitting, low-cut white top. Jodie had approached silently and Xenu had not been looking towards where Jodie was standing. Anya sensed Jodie's presence. She spun around, knocking Xenu's hand away. She said nothing, either verbally or mentally. Redness appeared on both of their necks and cheeks.

Xenu, flustered, said, "We have just finished the session, Jodie. Your mother is tired. You should go and rest with her."

Anya left with Jodie after saying a very brief goodbye to Xenu. After a short spell of uncomfortable silence, it was Anya who tried to communicate first.

Jodie, I don't know what you think you saw, but nothing really happened.

If I hadn't have come in, I know what would have happened. How could you? How could Xenu make advances towards you when Keon is his friend?

Jodie, I swear that this has never happened before. It

was the first time that Xenu has ever done anything like that. I will speak to him and make it clear that his advances are unwelcome, and that it would spoil our relationship.

Can you talk to him like this?

No, he does not answer. Can you?

Strangely no! I am sure that he simply chooses not to engage us, but I don't understand his reasoning. Are you going to say anything to Keon?

I think it would be best if we both kept quiet about this incident. We should forget it ever happened. I will tell Xenu to do the same. He will understand.

Jodie was not sure if anything had happened prior to this event, but, from that day on, she never again witnessed Xenu behaving improperly toward her mother.

39

The following week, Jodie had her most exciting day for quite some time. She was heading out to find Nicole when the passageway was filled with a strangely familiar voice. It was Nirvana. They were asking Jodie to go to the portal room immediately. Although she was alone, she was told that she would be granted access. She was already more than familiar with the route so she set off to see what 'they' wanted. She entered half expecting to find someone else there, but the chamber was empty. Without a second thought, she sat under the portal and waited. Nowadays, it was not absolutely necessary for her to close her eyes in order to concentrate, but this time she did so anyway.

Welcome Jodie. Today is an important day. Today, someone new will be joining us. Would you like to go and find them? You can help to reassure them that they will be safe.

Who is coming?

You will meet him soon enough.

What do I need to do?

Go with the recognisance orb. It will collect him.

How do I do that?

Can you see it now?

Yes, yes, I am inside now.

Jodie was flying over the desert once again, gaining speed all the time. She was looking down at the sand below, through the 'eye' of the orb. They skimmed over another line of megaliths, which appeared to be making steady progress towards the dome. Suddenly, they began to slow. The orb hovered over a young man. Jodie could see that his clothes were in tatters. His dark skin clung to his thin and dirty frame, suggesting that he was desperately in need of nourishment. He looked up and saw the orb. Jodie saw his fine fuzzy beard and dark brown, penetrating eyes for the first time. He looked terrified as they descended to collect him.

Do not worry, everything will be okay. We will take you to a place of safety. Jodie did her best to calm him. *What is your name?*

Jonas. My name is Jonas, son of Elijah. I hoped that somebody would come for me. I have not eaten for days and all my water is gone. Who are you?

My name is Jodie. I am inside the orb. My mind that is... *really I am a young woman back at the dome.*

So it does exist!

Yes, have you seen it before?

Yes, in my dreams.

That is how I found it too.

What is inside?

People and machines. It is vast. Much of the complex is underground. The technology will be beyond your wildest expectations.

The orb lifted young Jonas in the same way that it had collected Jodie many moons before; there was no need to subdue its passenger.

Are we going there now?

Yes. You will see my bodily form when you arrive.

I think I can see you now. Small with fair hair and blue eyes? You are but a girl!

Yes, that would be me. I may be just a girl to you, but I can assure you that I am very different from most of the other young people who you might have met. It is obvious that you too have special abilities.

Yes, I too am different, but, as a result, I have been shunned by my people. I brought great shame on by parents. They did not believe in the power of the dome, so cast me out.

It is not far now. Look ahead and you will see the dome.

Wow, I can see it ahead. It is just as I pictured it. What are those things down below? They look like stones, but they move. A group of them followed me across the desert. I dared not stop for I did not know what they would do if they caught up with me. Look, there are more of them. Many more!

I called them megaliths. The inhabitants refer to them as the stone people, but they are not people; they are machines.

What are they doing? Are they dangerous?

All will be explained when you are safely inside the dome.

The orb slowed. Jodie expected it to land beside the dome, but, instead, it stopped, remaining motionless above the shiny surface of the outer wall. As she looked down, she could see megaliths congregating around the perimeter of the dome. A section of the skin of the dome slid aside facilitating their entry.

Jonas began to receive instructions from Nirvana.

Settle down here and enjoy the facilities. You must wait for a while. Walk on to your left, and you will find food and drinking water. Do not drink the water from the pools though, it is bad for you. I will come back later and talk to you. Do not fear, Jonas, you will be taken care of.

Thank you!

Jodie would have liked to have spent more time with Jonas, but Nirvana called her back and, regrettably, she had to return to the chamber. Nevertheless, she now had a better appreciation of how things were done. In fact, she understood her role perfectly.

* * *

As Jodie wandered back to her quarters, she contemplated the consequences of bringing this young man to the dome. She thought about Nicole's warning and reflected on how her life had changed since she entered the dome. She was, however, sure of two things: Jonas would have been brought to the dome with or without her assistance, and, given his physical condition, he was unlikely to have survived much longer alone in the desert.

Over the next few days, Jodie was permitted to make regular contact with Jonas. In the first instance, she 'journeyed out' to be with him. Subsequently, she was able to view his image in the portal chamber. He ate and drank regularly, small amounts at first, but, by the third day, his body had recovered sufficiently for him to be able to feast on everything that was made available to him. In no time, he was looking much better.

Jodie discussed his progress with the entire community. Xenu offered words of wisdom, whilst Nicole was eager to meet Jonas, or at least communicate with him. She had been asked not to, though, as doing so might confuse him. However, on the fourth day, after Jonas had been forewarned by Jodie, Nicole was permitted to make contact. Jodie found that she could listen in. She wondered who else could. Jodie prompted Nicole to make her aware of this latest revelation. She knew that it would act as a note of caution. In no time, they were having a three-way conversation as effortlessly as if they had been in the same room together.

They learnt that Jonas had had the dreams since he was four years old, and that by the age of seven, he could often tell what some people in his village were thinking. It was not until the age of thirteen, when he began to develop into a man, that Jonas found he could close his eyes and move out of his body, up into the sky above. He told his family and friends. At first, they did not believe him, but he proved his ability by observing a scene that was staged at the other side of the village. Word of Jonas's powers spread quickly, but hostility was soon to follow. The tribal elders ordered that he be tried for 'possession' and were swift to pronounce him to be 'the evil one'. Fearing for his son's life, his father presented Jonas with a pouch of small shiny stones before sending him away, telling him never to return. Jonas was greatly saddened by his rejection, but, every night, he dreamt of a great shiny dome in the desert where he would acquire a new family that would respect his differences rather than fear them.

Jonas was told that he would spend a total of ten days in isolation. During this time and between her sessions, Jodie did her best to negate any feelings of isolation and loneliness by 'talking' to him as often as possible. Nicole spent even more time in Jonas' presence. Nicole was a little older than Jodie. She had started her monthly cycle and her body was maturing. It was clear to Jodie that even before Jonas and Nicole had met face to face, a deep relationship had begun to blossom. Jodie was not jealous, she was happy for Nicole. Jodie hoped that Jonas might provide comfort and stability for Nicole, perhaps removing some of her cynicism towards Xenu and Nirvana. Nicole admitted to liking Jonas, but it was not until they finally stood before each other that Jodie understood how deep their feelings for one another had become. Xenu looked less than pleased with their fondness for each other. Jodie was almost expectant of such a reaction. What was more surprising was Jadine's indifference towards the new arrival. Was it because he too was special?

40

The megaliths were now gathered around the outside of the dome like an army of statues. They had maintained this threatening position for days. Xenu, Keon and some of the longstanding members of the dome community had been debating the connotation of such an assembly. They had even been up to the observation platform to see the masses for themselves. Later, the entire community congregated to discuss the significance of such an event.

Niahli told them of his experience with the stone people and informed them, that in his opinion, they were likely to attack.

Xenu refuted this suggestion, "They dare not attack the dome. Our systems have the capability to destroy each and every one of them."

"And what do the machines say of the stones' presence here?"

"They know what the stone people want, but we simply cannot provide the resources in such numbers."

"Why should we provide anything for them?"

"Some time ago, Nirvana made an agreement with the stone people and gave them independence. They have kept this area secure for many years."

"What is this resource that you speak of?"

"The stones take most of their power from the sun, but inside each one of them is a tiny reactor that produces additional energy by very slowly breaking down elemental crystals. From time to time, depending on their original size, these crystals need replacing. In the past, we have been able to accommodate their requirements, but alas, no longer."

"What do these crystals look like? Like these?" Niahli put a hand beneath his robe and pulled out the bag that he had brought with him to the dome. He tipped out a handful of diamonds into the palm of his hand.

"I had hoped that you were going to donate those to the cause."

"You knew about them?"

"Yes, we know about anything and everything that enters the dome."

"And what if I do not want to simply hand them over to those things up there?"

Xenu was composed when he asserted his authority over Niahli. "Surely, it would be such a small price to pay for the food, shelter, education and security that you have enjoyed in these facilities."

Niahli replied with contempt, "I have enjoyed everything but a warm welcome and honesty." Niahli grabbed Jadine's hand. "Clearly, we do not have the special talents that are shared by most of the people who are gathered here. To you, Xenu, we are nothing! If I give you these precious stones, I give you all that I have!"

Niahli threw the bag down and the diamonds spilt out across the floor. He pulled Jadine to one side and then dragged her out of the room.

While Xenu stood and glared at the departing figures, Jodie watched as Jonas stepped up and offered his pouch to Keon. Keon took it and handed it to Xenu who opened the drawstring and tipped out twelve small shiny stones. Clearly, they had been cut and polished.

"Thank you, Jonas; your effort is much appreciated by your people."

Jonas stepped aside, and Keon knelt and began to collect the other crystals from the floor. "Even with these, we do not have enough," he said.

"It matters not! I will present these to Nirvana. They will decide what is to be done."

After a brief moment of silence, conversation spread throughout the chamber and the meeting disbanded.

41

Once more, someone was calling out to Jodie. Whoever they were, they were calling from beyond the dome.

Jodie, come with me now. You must leave. I can take you away to a place of safety. Please do not delay. We haven't got much time

Who are you? Why do you want to take me from here?

You are in danger!

From the megaliths?

No, it is those within the dome that pose the greatest threat. I can get you out. I can help the others like you.

Why will you not tell me who you are?

I cannot. You must trust me.

Jodie awoke to a familiar rhythmic pulse.

Anya came in and grabbed her hand.

Jodie rubbed the sleep out of her eyes. "I thought that we would be safe down here. Why is it that we can still hear them so deep below the surface?"

"I'm not sure, but Keon assures us that we are safe. We've been asked to report to the observatory. We are going back up into the dome."

Jodie could see her father through the opening to the adjoining chamber. He seemed calm and in control.

"Hurry, Jodie, we must go above." He came towards her and grabbed her remaining free hand.

"Why the hurry if everything is all right?"

"We need your help."

* * *

Xenu's haste was obvious, but their journey up to the top was identical to their experience on their first night down below. The view from the apex was now even more spectacular. The sun was just beginning to rise and hundreds of megaliths had encircled the dome. Orange light either reflected off them or silhouetted them depending on their position. Orbs flashing red, blue and white lights flew over the scene. Jonas looked on with equal measures of awe and fear.

Xenu came up behind Jodie and put his hands on her shoulders.

"Jodie, Nirvana has been in constant communication with the stone people. They want our entire supply of diamonds, but they have overestimated our resource. Even with the crystals that Niahli and Jonas kindly donated, we do not have sufficient for all. Many of them are running low on energy and they say that they are prepared to sacrifice their last reserves in an attempt to destroy the dome if we do not comply with their wishes. Nirvana has told them that they will all be destroyed if they attempt an attack, or if they do not retreat to an acceptable distance by sunset. Nonetheless, we have offered to replace the crystals of those with the greatest need.

"Why does Nirvana not simply destroy them, then?"

"Nirvana prefers not to destroy other machines. It would be a last resort. They have served us well for many years. Perhaps they doubt our capability."

"Then where do I fit in?"

"Nirvana wants you to tell the stone people that they are truly in no position to make demands, and that our offer is final."

"But why should they believe me? I am just a girl!"

"You are human, you are able to exercise judgement and

be sincere. You have the innocence of youth, yet you are one of the few with the ability to communicate with them all simultaneously."

"Nirvana is wise and powerful. Why won't they respect that knowledge?"

"We are not sure, but Nirvana seems to believe that they might listen to you."

"How can I possibly communicate with them all at once?"

"Nirvana will help you."

"Jodie, this will not be difficult for you. Please concentrate." Nirvana's collective voice was audible in the room for all to hear.

We are privileged, thought Jodie as she waited for instructions.

"Jodie, in a moment, you will find that you have the attention of the masses gathered outside this dome. All you need do is tell them that our offer is final and that you know that they will be destroyed if they disobey. Our terms are clear. They must retreat to a safe distance. Those in need must approach one by one. They will be refitted with a fresh crystal until our supply is exhausted. If they continue to protect our systems, we will source a new supply of crystals, but they must not return until called. Speak from the soul; perhaps they will believe you. Do you understand?"

"Yes, I am ready now."

At once, Jodie was able to connect with the stone people. Their intellect was very different from that of Nirvana. Jodie sensed that each one of them had an intelligence of its own. They had no leader, but were able to agree on a course of action almost simultaneously. They were able to communicate not by telepathy, but by transmitters within their casings. Jodie realised that this was why it was necessary for Nirvana to patch them through to her. Jodie repeated Nirvana's decree. The stone people began to argue amongst themselves. It was chiefly about which individuals had the greater need, but, seconds later, they were debating whether or not to accept Nirvana's proposal. They seemed unsure.

"Enough!" Nirvana's voice broke through the melee.

Jodie opened her eyes in time to see one of the orbs swoop low over a line of megaliths and discharge a blinding white bolt of energy towards the nearest one. It exploded, leaving a burning mass of wires and metal behind.

The megaliths nearest the dome advanced. In a coordinated effort, they sent blue arcs of energy cascading onto the surface of the dome below.

Without warning, a concentric shockwave of energy and sound radiated out from the base of the dome, obliterating the first four rows of megaliths. Those directly behind were knocked over; many were left burning. Beyond these, it was clear that many were left inactive. An opening in the dome wall away from the reception centre appeared, and a flight of orbs departed and began attacking the stone people at random.

Enough! Stop the attack; we will comply!

This time, it was the stone people who sent a message echoing through Jodie's mind. Simultaneously, all of the orbs pulled out of their attacks and rose vertically upwards to hover high above the desert plain.

Nirvana transmitted a message to the stone people that was also, once again, audible to those gathered in the chamber at the top of the dome.

"You have greatly underestimated us. Let this be a lesson to you all! Retreat now and we will proceed as proposed. If there are anymore threats on our system or people, it will be the end of you all!"

Jodie watched with the others as the stone people began to back away en masse. Like a group of generals who had just tasted victory, Xenu and his followers continued to gaze out over the retreating army for quite some time.

"What now?" Jodie sought conformation from Xenu.

"As Nirvana promised, we will take them in one by one and replace their crystals until we have no more."

"What will happen to the individuals that are unlucky and do not receive one?"

"If their crystals expire, they will simply stop, but they can go into a state of hibernation. They have been known to remain dormant, buried in the sand for years."

"Will we be safe?" Concern was etched across Anya's face.

"We always have been," replied Xenu.

* * *

Jodie sensed that the vigil was coming to an end. Conversation was beginning to erupt around the room. The sun had crept high up into the sky. She was about to sit and talk to her mother when images and emotions started to appear in her mind.

She was in a part of the underground compound that she had not visited before. She felt all alone, but Xenu was there. She was experiencing a great sense of anticipation and at the same time, excitement was pulsing through her mind. She was entering a spherical room that was even brighter than the rest of the complex. All around the chamber were unfamiliar apparatus. Xenu was talking to her, as if trying to reassure her, but she could not decipher exactly what he was saying. Time seemed to fast forward. Her body did not feel normal. Her mind felt groggy, yet at the same time totally alive and connected. It was as if she was suddenly aware of, and part of Nirvana, the system and the world beyond. She could think of anything, pose any question and automatically know the answer. Had she really reached

Nirvana?

Nicole interrupted, *Is everything all right, Jodie? You did very well to speak with the stone people. I think that, despite the obvious consequences, you made a difference in the end. Why do you look so distant?*

I'm all right. I just had a premonition. The first one for quite some time. I think that being above the dome does indeed reduce the influence that the system has over my mind.

What did you see?

I'm not sure. I'll tell you about it later.

42

Later that evening, Jodie was allowed, even encouraged, to 'travel out' over the desert. Below her, a solitary megalith was making its way back to the dome. Behind it, a long thin shallow trench stretched back to the dune ridge where the others waited like a silent army. Nirvana had chosen to honour the agreement, and now one by one, each of the stone people would receive a new crystal until the supply was exhausted. Jodie tried to communicate with them. Maybe they simply refused to reply, or perhaps, Nirvana was unwilling to relay her message. Either way, there was no dialogue, so she returned to the dome shortly before sunset. As the first megalith neared the dome, another broke ranks and followed in its wake.

Xenu had informed everyone that whilst it was possible for the small micro-orbs to refit the megaliths without human intervention, it would be swifter if one or two people volunteered to assist.

Jadine and Niahli had offered their help. They told Jodie that carrying out such a task might make them more a part of community.

Jodie was lying on her bed watching Xenu, Niahli and Jadine in what appeared to be a loading bay on the opposite side of the dome. The first of the stone people had arrived. It waited silently to be processed. Xenu released a magnetic lock at the base of the protective outer 'stone' casing before using a cylindrical device lowered from above to lift it off.

With his eager assistants looking on, he demonstrated how to use a specially crafted tool to twist open and pull out the core from just below the 'eye' of the megalith. Jodie was intrigued to see that the now suspended casing that gave the megalith its characteristic appearance was not stone, but, indeed, some form of metal composite, impregnated with multiple solar energy receptors that mimicked the appearance of solid rock. Jodie assumed that the connector at the base of the casing somehow transmitted the energy within. Laid bare, the megalith consisted of a support structure, numerous black boxes of various sizes that were interconnected by a series of fine cords. Xenu described the technology as 'primitive', stating that 'wires and cables were rarely used in modern technology'. He pointed out the electromagnetic drive unit at the base of the structure before going on to briefly describe the workings of the central core that he had just removed. At one end of the core was a shiny gold conductor. He pulled this out to reveal a gold bar about the size of a finger. Set within the surface was a clamp device. Xenu picked up what appeared to be another much smaller and delicate tool, plus a magnifying lens from a nearby rack. He encouraged Niahli and Jadine to move in closer. Using the lens, they were able to see a tiny crystal no bigger than a grain of sand.

"This one is all but gone. The processor breaks down the elements within the crystal very slowly. The rate at which the crystals degrade very much depends upon their activities. They are more likely to consume the crystal when they are operating at night and are unable to acquire their energy from the sun."

"How long might that tiny speck last, then?" asked Jadine.

"Several moons. Perhaps much longer if it confines its activity to daytime."

Xenu used the tool to prise open the clamp. He flicked

the tiny stone out into the palm of his hand. "We must keep these. We are working on a process to fuse them together. One day soon, we hope to be able to use the very grains of sand from the desert to produce these useful and very valuable crystals. It has been done before."

Xenu placed the speck in a small glass container that he produced from a pouch in his tunic. "Here, take this and pass me a new one."

Niahli delved into the bag that he was holding and produced an uncut diamond. "Will any one do?"

"Yes, they have to take what they are given."

Once again, Xenu used the tool to prise back the clamps. He placed the stone in position before releasing them.

"The stones are so hard, so pure, that nothing will cut into them. You must ensure that they are fixed in securely when you first put them in, but they stay in place as the system degrades them, no matter how small they become. Here, see?" Xenu showed Jadine and Niahli how he had set the crystal in its place before demonstrating the procedure for replacing the gold rod in the central core.

As Jadine approached the megalith to relocate the core, she was stopped in her tracks by something that she saw behind its 'eye'. Connected to one of the black boxes below, were two glass tiles about the size of a human hand, sealed by a metallic strip that ran around the outside. Sandwiched between them was a substance quite unlike anything else before her. Jadine had seen something similar many times before when she had killed wild animals. She had even seen it inside the heads of people.

"Is that living tissue inside there?"

Xenu was unperturbed. "Yes, it was incorporated into their systems when they were created. It was part of an experiment. I believe it is the reason why they were able to evolve so quickly and override their programming."

"So they are, at least in part, living entities? Real stone

people!"

"I would not go that far. They have a primitive, collective intelligence. They are capable of independent thought, but no more. I do not believe they have emotions or a spirit, none of the things that make us human."

Xenu replaced the core. "Now help me lower and replace the casing. The second one is almost here. Do not allow two inside at any time, but, be assured, there is an orb patrolling outside and in here you will be more than protected. I will help you with the next few replacements. After that, I will leave you alone to continue the process. It will be a long night for you both."

Niahli shook his head. "It will be a change for us. Something different, something new and a chance to once again smell the desert air!"

* * *

Niahli and Jadine were slow and deliberate at first taking care to deconstruct and reconstruct each megalith correctly. They would take a little time out with every one to examine the internal structure in more detail, but, after a while, the novelty wore off and their pace quickened. Eventually, they reached a point where they were not in the least intimidated by the megaliths and thought it necessary to run down the ramp out into the desert to hurry the next one in. Jodie reached a point where she was tired of watching and drifted off.

Niahli and Jadine had worked on through the night, but had only succeeded in replacing around a third of all the crystals. As the sun rose like an orange fireball over the desert plain, they were exhausted. It was time for Keon and Shayla to take over the task, but Niahli and Jadine were keen to resume once they had rested. Jodie was not permitted to approach the megaliths physically, but, occasionally, she would check on their progress, sometimes with Jonas, sometimes with Nicole. Later that afternoon, as Shayla tired, Anya replaced her. Anya seemed to be happy to once again enjoy the challenge of completing physical work with Keon. Keon, on the other hand, seemed content just to push on without complaint and offered little by way of conversation once Anya's training was completed.

As the sun began to set on another day, and shadows grew long inside the loading bay door, Niahli and Jadine returned to take over the night shift. Jodie was watching. When yet another megalith had departed, Jadine skipped over to join Anya who seemed very pleased to see her friend.

"This is such hard work! I guess that we have become unaccustomed to 'doing things'. The exercise we take in the dome does not seem to make up for it."

"Keon doesn't seem too bothered, does he?"

Keon looked up. "I'm fine, but I've been doing this all day. I'll be glad for a rest."

"Shall we take the next one, then?" suggested Niahli, pointing to an advancing megalith.

"Be my guest," replied Keon.

Anya used her sleeve to wipe the sweat from her brow. "Thank you, Jadine."

"No, thank you!" Jadine gave Anya a brief embrace before turning to face the incoming megalith.

Niahli and Jadine recommenced their work at the quick pace that they have achieved earlier that morning. The stone people began to arrive more frequently and gradually the remaining stock of precious crystals began to dwindle.

As another day ended, Jodie once again drifted off into a restful sleep, watching her friends save the stone people. Xenu went up briefly to check on their progress before retiring to bed himself.

* * *

Jodie was suddenly awoken from a peaceful and dreamless sleep. Quickly, she was able to focus her mind. She was drawn to the loading bay where Niahli and Jadine were working. Dawn was still some way off. They had inserted the last of their crystals into the core of one of the stone people. In their small glass container was a collection of the tiny fragments that they had removed. Their total mass added up to perhaps one or two of the larger diamonds that they had used as replacements. Niahli placed the container to one side and helped Jadine to secure the outer casing of a megalith for the final time. As it was clipped back into place, the 'eye' began to glow indicating that it was fully operational and ready to go. Niahli slid the tool that he was holding into his pocket.

The last of the megaliths descended down the shallow ramp and returned onto the soft, warm sand below. Niahli and Jadine followed. Niahli ran around to the front of the megalith, and it stopped. He found himself looking directly into its 'eye'.

"I know that you are able to understand me, even if you cannot talk."

The eye flickered.

"I hope that your kind appreciate our efforts to keep you operative. Most of the crystals were originally in my possession. I now understand the reason for you attacking our underground settlement near the old ruin. I trust that you did not harm my people...." Niahli shifted uneasily. He glanced up at the orb that had just flown overhead. "I have a request. Call it a reward, if you like. I want you to help the two of us to escape this place! Now! We do not want to have to go back inside. We do not feel part of their community, and I am fearful of the influence that Xenu has over the people. I want to be free. Free to roam the desert as I please, even if it means that life might once again become a struggle. Will you help us, please? All I ask is that you let us walk in your shadow across the desert plain, up to the dune ridge. Beyond that, we will make our own way."

Jadine had joined Niahli and was holding his hand. Jodie was shocked by what she had just witnessed, but she failed to do or say anything. She thought that Niahli and Jadine had clearly planned this event; they were not acting out of impulse. The megalith showed no outward signs of a response. Jodie supposed that it would necessarily need to communicate the request to the rest of its kind waiting back at the dune ridge. Moments later, it appeared to receive an answer. The soft violet light flashed once before it gave an audible response to the waiting duo. "Yes, you may come with me."

"Thank you," said Niahli and Jadine in unison.

The megalith began to move away from the dome. Niahli and Jadine walked on just in front of its towering bulk. They did not look back.

* * *

Jodie was distraught. Jadine had chosen to go without saying goodbye. *Why? Was it Niahli's influence? Would she ever see her friend, constant companion and surrogate big sister ever again? What was so bad about life in the dome? Jodie missed the open air, but surely it would only be a matter of time before she was allowed up top.* Jodie sat cross-legged on her bed sobbing. Nicole was aware of what was happening.

Jodie, I think it is for the best. You might have reasons not to go, but Jadine has little reason to stay. Without our talents, she is an outsider, and has been made to feel like one. She has little to offer and therefore, Xenu would have little to give her. He would certainly show no loyalty.

Shut up, Nicole; leave me alone! Mother, can you hear me?

Jodie projected her thoughts with such intensity that Anya awoke immediately from her slumber.

Jadine has gone! She has left the dome with Niahli!

Shush, Jodie, do not cause a panic. It is better not to draw attention to her departure.

Did you know that she was planning to leave?

No, but I am not surprised. She has been unhappy for quite some time now, and Niahli has been worried about his people. He hoped that you would be able to find them for him, but you could not. I think that they have just taken their first opportunity to leave. Looking back, I could see it in Jadine's eyes when they took over from us in the loading bay. Does anyone else know?

Only Nicole. She too told me that they will be better off away from here.

Jodie, she is right. I am sure that one day you will see her again. I am also sure that she would have wanted to say goodbye, but she does not trust Xenu or Nirvana. That is why she has not announced her intentions. Please, for Jadine's sake, let her go and go back to sleep.

* * *

Niahli and Jadine were about halfway across the flat plain when the orb came after them. It was over them in seconds. Jadine caught a glimpse of the single bright white light above and looked up. Niahli was concentrating on the way ahead. Jadine tugged on his hand. She immediately had his attention and pointed upwards.

"Oh no!" Niahli managed to say before blue light arced towards them.

He braced himself for the stunning effect of the orb's

energy bolt, but, to his amazement, it did not reach him. Jadine too had been spared. The megalith had been able to shield them from its affects by cocooning all three of them in a protective barrier. The orb tried again. This time, the megalith was able to divert the energy back at the orb, adding in a little of its own for good measure. The orb dropped out of the sky and broke apart as it impacted on the desert floor.

Fearing the worst, Niahli and Jadine looked back in the direction of the dome. Their hearts were pounding, their progress hindered by the very soft sand beneath their feet. They were some distance away now, but they could still clearly see where light poured out of the loading bay entrance beyond. Two black shadows flashed across the opening. They knew what was coming.

Jadine turned to address the megalith following behind. "Let us go now. We have seen what they can do. Attacking the orbs or the dome is futile. Clearly, they will not allow us to leave. Save yourself and your kind. Do not protect us any further."

Jadine's words came too late. What happened next had a certain inevitability about it. The megalith exploded, lighting up the desert around them. Jadine and Niahli were knocked to the ground by the blast. They picked themselves up. Dazed and covered with perspiration, sand and the charred remains of the thing that had tried to save them, Niahli and Jadine ran across the sand attempting to reach whatever cover the dune ridge beyond would offer, but the flying spheres were far too quick for them. As if toying with their prey, the orbs surged on overhead, then stopped and waited, hovering halfway between Niahli, Jadine and the ridge. The young couple slowed as they looked up towards their adversaries. Two bolts of energy were discharged. Niahli and Jadine were cut down instantly. The orbs collected their respective targets. One immediately set off on a heading that would return it and the limp passenger below directly to the dome, whilst the other took a detour over the lines of stone people massed beyond the ridge. Several megaliths were selected, apparently at random. Flashes illuminated the night sky as bolts of energy rained down.

Jodie looked on and began to sob some more. Anya joined in.

43

Jadine and Niahli were returned to the loading bay. Their still forms were set down on the floor. Jodie was chasing after her mother who had set off through the complex in an attempt to reach her friend. As they approached the elevator, Xenu headed them off. Keon was with him. Clearly, they were both fully aware of recent events.

"Keon, I wondered where you were!" It was all Anya could manage to say.

Keon remained silent.

Xenu spoke for him. "This incident is most regrettable. I will go up and check on your friends, but you must stay here. Nirvana has engaged with the stone people once again. It will not be safe to journey to the surface."

Anya's state of mind now verged on hysteria. "Why were they cut down like animals? Why were they not simply allowed to leave? You had no need of them!"

"My dear Anya, anyone is always free to leave, but it is polite to say goodbye. They were brought back for their own good. How could they possibly survive the rigours of the desert without food, water or the proper clothing?"

"Are they still alive, then?"

"I sincerely hope so. Please, Anya, remain in your quarters whilst we go and tend to them."

Jodie was shocked by Xenu's behaviour and her father's apparent lack of compassion. "You could have simply asked them to return...."

She doubted that Xenu was even listening. He had already stepped into the elevator where Keon was waiting.

"Come on, Jodie, we are not needed here!"

See, Jodie, I told you so! You too, Jonas.... Nicole's thoughts were transmitted loud and clear.

* * *

Niahli and Jadine regained consciousness at roughly the same time. Xenu was standing over them holding two receptacles full of water. "Here, drink this."

Niahli reached up, twisting his head and neck as he did so. "What happened?"

"Unfortunately, you put yourselves in harm's way. You should not have ventured out into the desert on your own...."

"But...." Niahli shook himself. "Oh, yes, we were trying to escape."

"Niahli!" Jadine began to recall recent events.

Xenu shook his head. "You had no need to escape. You have always been free to leave. Like Anya said, you both have nothing to offer our community. You are clearly inferior."

Jadine stood and squared up to Xenu. She spat in his face before turning to Keon. "Keon, I don't know you anymore. Clearly, you are not the man who you used to be!"

Fearing a reprisal, Niahli forced his way in front of Jadine, but Xenu turned away and spoke whilst wiping away the sand and saliva that was spattered across his face. "We knew of your intentions, but we just wanted to see if you would go through with them. However, tomorrow you will leave here for good! We will provide you with as much food and water as you can carry."

Niahli spoke with an edge to his voice. "Can you not

take us back to my people, back to a place of safety?"

Xenu's smirk did little to hide his disdain. "I think not...."

Jadine's anger was clear for all to see, but she regained her composure to pose one final question. "May Anya and Jodie come with us?"

"If they choose to, but I doubt that they would want to commit to a life of uncertainty and hardship. I think that you know that they will be content to stay with us."

Jodie was sitting cross-legged on her bed. She shook her head. She was no longer sure if she wanted to stay.

Nicole had undoubtedly also been watching.

I have asked to leave many times now, but I am still here. Others come and go. Many simply disappear! They will never let us go now!

Jodie feared that Jadine and Niahli would spend their last night under the dome locked in the loading bay, but she was able to track their progress down to the lower ground floor. A door opened and they were ushered inside. When it closed, she could no longer 'see' them. Jodie knew now that things would never be the same. Her life would change forever. Stressed and exhausted, Jodie willingly fell into a deep, deep sleep.

* * *

When Jodie awoke, she was cradled in her mother's arms. At that moment, Jadine and Niahli were led out of their holding chamber by Xenu and Keon. Jadine had one arm around Niahli; the other hand was clutching her abdomen. She was clearly in pain. All four were silent.

What have you done to her? Jodie's question was aimed at both Xenu and Nirvana simultaneously, but neither chose to answer.

Jodie ran over to exit her quarters, but the usual opening

failed to materialise. Anya scooped her daughter up in her arms and gave her a hug.

I will go with them. Please, let me go now! Jodie's pleas were ignored.

Niahli and Jodie were taken up to the loading bay. Their heads were covered with a deep hood stemming from the back of their white, long-sleeved gowns. Keon helped to fit two large backpacks, which Jodie presumed would contain food and water.

The hatch opened and Niahli stepped forward. Jadine hesitated and turned to Xenu.

"Please, can I not say goodbye?"

"I thought that you understood the need to depart in silence. There are many qualities that you will never have, but obedience and humility are two virtues that anyone can learn. You chose not to say your farewells the first time you left. You are not worthy enough to say goodbye now!"

Jodie was able to look into Jadine's tear-stained eyes one last time, and then Jadine and Niahli were cast out into the desert.

* * *

The doorway opened to reveal Shayla standing before them. "For your own safety, come with me."

Jodie looked at her mother, then looked back at Shayla. "Quickly!"

Anya and Jodie got up off the bed. Shayla had already turned away, so they followed. She led them down to the elevator. Once inside, they began to descend. How many floors, Jodie could not tell, but she knew that they were travelling further down the complex than she had ever been before. The doors slid apart. There was another opening opposite.

"In here!" Shayla made a gesture of direction with her

arm.

Jodie and Anya found themselves in a tiny, bright, white, featureless room. The entrance closed behind them. Shayla had not entered. Another exit suddenly appeared directly ahead. This opened out into a much larger chamber where Nicole and Jonas were waiting.

* * *

Nicole seemed anxious. "I can't communicate with anyone outside this room and it seems that there is little point in sending my thoughts to Jonas when he is standing next to me. We were both sleeping and, when we woke up, we found ourselves down here, locked in this room. I have tried to travel out; there's no way we can do it in here. It must be something about the structure of the room."

"That must be why they have grouped us together. They don't want us to know what's going on." Anya's observation was true for all to see.

"They don't want us to be able to track Jadine and Niahli," Jodie stated the obvious.

"How long do you think they will keep us in this place?" asked Jonas.

"Who knows," replied Anya. "It would take quite some time for Jadine and Niahli to reach the old settlement, and, even then, Jodie might be able to find them."

"I'm not sure that I will. When I'm in the complex below the dome, my powers are diminished. They are probably regulated in some way. I can travel out further when 'they' allow it. Before I came down here, I was beginning to see more and more future events. Often, they would come to me in dreams, but sometimes I could see what was about to happen in my conscious state. Now, I am limited to regular dreams and nightmares. Strangely enough, when I was last up in the dome, I began to see confused visions of what I was sure were future events."

"What did you see?" Jonas wore an expression that combined inquisitiveness with excitement.

"I'm not sure; I can't even remember now, but the point is, once inside the underground complex, I can see no more."

Anya closed her eyes, concentrating hard to communicate with the others all at the same time. *Please don't say any more about what we can and can't do. I am certain that 'they' watch us all the time, and that they are able to hear everything that we say. We can all communicate through Nirvana to a greater or lesser extent, but I am not sure that Nirvana, Xenu or anyone else can tap into our minds when we don't want them to. For me, it requires a lot of effort to do this. I have to concentrate on sending you my thoughts. You might take it for granted now, but way back in your pasts, you had to learn to talk. I think that the process may be similar, so they may not be able to tell what we are thinking. If we speak about these things, they will know everything! It's the only way that they could have known of Jadine's plans to escape, as she cannot communicate in this way.*

You may or may not be correct, Anya, but we have nothing to lose by keeping our words silent. Nicole was attempting to reach a consensus.

Yes, we keep our thoughts silent, projected Jodie.

Agreed, contributed Jonas.

Anya was aware that, outwardly, they had all remained silent for a considerable time. "We will just have to wait and see what happens."

"There are some sleeping pods over there," added Nicole.

"And a food dispenser on that wall." Jonas was pointing.

"I'd love to know how we are supposed to pass the time," remarked Anya.

"I am sure that Xenu will have something mapped out for us," suggested Jodie.

* * *

"I sincerely regret that we have seen the need to do this." Xenu's voice echoed loudly around the room. "But, in time, you will come to realise that Shayla was telling the truth when she insisted that you come down here for your own good."

"What gives you the right to imprison us here like this?" asked Anya.

"We are just giving you the opportunity to adjust, and, conceivably, the time to further develop your skills."

"Adjust to what?"

"Perhaps you think that I have brought you down here to overcome the grief of losing your friends. That is not so! You were growing distant, and you would have got over their loss anyway. No, you are here in order to help yourself to attain the next level of consciousness, to develop your spirits to a higher state of existence."

Anya became very angry all of a sudden. "I do not care for your spirituality! I do not want to attain a higher level! I just want to see my friends. I just want you to let us out of here!"

"Please, Xenu, I want to go now. You told me that I could leave whenever I was ready…."

"Jodie, you will thank me for this one day. It is very important that you all stay here and complete your training."

"Important for who? You? Nirvana?"

"For you, Jodie! For everyone! You will come to see, in time, that all those things that I told you about being the next evolution of the human species were true. Mankind is counting on your support!"

"There is little point in arguing. They want to keep us here and that is that!" Nicole seemed resigned to her fate, whatever that might be.

"How long must we stay here, then?" Jonas was more composed.

"That depends entirely on how quickly you develop and move through the dynamics of life in order to gain a better understanding of our world. To increase your competence, you need to accept our practice. To begin the process, you must cast out your negative thoughts. Hostility, pain, anger, hate and resentment reside within you all. There is no place, either, for emotions such as anxiety, fear, despair or grief. You need to empty your mind of such things and accept the freedom of release. Only by doing this will you obtain relief and further abilities."

Jodie shook her head. Without the need for foresight, she knew that they would be spending a significant amount of time in isolation, and that this would only be the first of many such lectures. She shared her thoughts with the others and they all agreed.

Anya, now a little calmer, took her turn to pose the questions. "Xenu, why can't you come down here and speak to us face to face like a man?"

"Anya, I fear that such an action would only add to your feeling of hostility. You all need a little more time to develop. You will see me soon enough."

"And what of Keon? Clearly, he has done little to stop this madness."

"Keon is not the man he used to be.... "

"That is plain for all to see!"

"When we found Keon alone in the wilderness, he was barely alive. A tumour had grown inside his head. It had pushed into his brain, causing damage and bleeding. The orbs brought him back to the dome and we were able to stabilise his condition, but, without our intervention, he would not have survived."

"What did you do to him?"

"We had no choice but to remove the tumour and part of his brain. We made good the damage. Fortunately, most of his memories survived, but it was inevitable that he would be somewhat different. I am truly sorry, Anya. "

Tears ran over Anya's cheeks and splashed onto the floor below. Jodie reached up and put her arms around her mother's waist. Things would indeed never be the same.

* * *

Days turned into weeks. They had no idea when it was day or night. They slept when they needed to. They were provided with nourishment and were able to exercise in an adjoining room. It was almost as if all their needs were catered for. In a third room, off to the other side, was an 'education centre'. They took it in turns to undergo training and audit sessions. Sometimes, Xenu addressed them individually, sometimes as a group, but never in person. The rhetoric was always the same. He encouraged positive thinking and reprimanded them if they ever showed signs of dissent. There was a portal that they could use to connect beyond the room, and gradually Jodie was allowed back into the system, but never 'outside'. Sometimes, the teachings and mental exercises induced a trance-like state. Jodie and the others were encouraged to look back in time, review significant events and reflect upon the outcomes. Xenu focussed on their emotions at the time and often asked if their perception would have been different if they had simply accepted adversity and tried to learn from it. He suggested that everything in the world and beyond had an order or a sequence that could only be changed by those who truly understood.

As the weeks passed, everyone took care not to speak

their thoughts out loud. Perhaps they began to believe what they were taught, but, at least outwardly, all four of them tried their best to demonstrate that their view of life was changing for the better despite their dire situation.

Xenu told each and every one of them that they had expanded their knowledge and were making good progress towards well being and spiritual enlightenment. It was as if he were measuring them against some sort of scale. Jodie appreciated that her knowledge of technology, history and vocabulary had been expanded significantly. She was unsure about her spiritual beliefs as she saw her powers as an adaptation or development of just another human sense. *Was Xenu correct? Was this the future of the human race?*

44

When Xenu eventually came down to see them once again, their skins were much paler, a natural consequence of being away from sunlight for so long. Jodie was much thinner than she had been for quite some time, but, overall, their health and spirits were good. Xenu was not exactly welcomed with open arms, nevertheless Jodie and the others were pleased to see him. It meant that progress had been made and there was a possibility that very soon, they might be allowed to leave their place of confinement.

"Today is the first day of the rest of your lives," announced Xenu in a cheerful tone. It was as if he had never locked them in three small chambers in the depths of the complex, never held them against their will and never tried to manipulate their way of thinking. "If you succeed in overcoming one final obstacle, you may return to our community."

"And what would that be?" asked Anya in a courteous tone.

"If I tell you, the challenge will be lost. Before we go any further, I would like to ask you all a question. What have you learnt during your time down here?"

Jodie desperately wanted to tell her mother to be careful, but they had all agreed not communicate silently in the presence of Xenu, or any of the others – just in case! Jodie decided that Anya was all too aware of the risks of upsetting their captor. The others looked at one another, not wanting to say the wrong thing, so Jodie spoke first.

"As you have seen, Xenu, we have learnt a lot. We have learnt to channel our energies in a more positive direction."

"Anya?"

"We have learnt humility."

"Nicole?"

"Er, we have gained more knowledge and improved our abilities."

Xenu's head tracked across the room. "And Jonas?"

"I agree with everything that the others have said. It is difficult to add something new." Jonas thought for a moment. "By being together for so long, we have learnt to trust each other; we have deepened our friendship and found a spirit of community." Jonas looked at Xenu, waiting for a response. "Would you not agree?"

"Well done, everyone. You have passed the final challenge!"

"Was that it?" asked Anya, trying not to sound at all negative. "Did we answer the questions correctly?"

"The questions were not the challenge."

Jodie had an idea about the true design of the test, but said nothing.

"Can we leave now?" asked Nicole, "I mean, go back into the community?"

"Yes, of course. If you would all like to follow me, I will show you to your quarters."

Finally, they were leaving. Jodie knew that those anonymous, brightly lighted corridors would actually provide a welcome change of surroundings. All the chambers in the complex, large or small, were very similar, but any subtle differences would be appreciated.

When Jodie and her mother reached the accommodation that they had previously occupied, it appeared that little had changed. Anya soon discovered that Keon had moved out all of his clothing and possessions. *Well, it makes sense,* thought Jodie. *No use in carrying on the pretence now.* Determined not to allow sadness to ruin such an important event, Anya rearranged her own things. Not that she had much, but she felt better for doing so.

That evening, they were all invited to a banquet to be held in their honour. Xenu had decided that their achievements were worthy of celebration.

Jodie, Nicole, Jonas, remember what we agreed! No telepathy at the dinner table! Anya smiled inwardly at what she had just communicated to 'the children'.

I'm almost a man, replied Jonas.

Sorry, I didn't realise that I had sent that out, too.

Don't worry. We won't risk being banished to the 'barmy basement.

Stepping into the great reception chamber had a familiar feel to it. Jodie recognised all the same faces, including Keon. She looked up at her mother.

Anya recognised the familiar form of the man who she had once been so close to. "Stay here, Jodie!"

Anya walked over to where Keon was seated, predictably on the right side of Xenu. "Keon, it's so good to see you once again! Are you keeping all right?"

Keon looked a little awkward. "Er, yes, I think so."

"Keon, there is no need to feel so embarrassed. Xenu explained everything. I'm sure that he told you."

Xenu began to take an interest in what Anya was saying. "Keon, I know that the man I loved is gone forever, but I cannot blame you for that. Blame is not a desirable trait. I still respect you for who you are now. All I ask is that you treat Jodie with some of the sentiment deserving of your daughter."

"I will try my best, Anya."

Anya turned away and went back to Jodie. The 'celebration' continued as if nothing untoward had ever happened. Everyone was civil to one another. Seated close to Jonas and Nicole, Jodie found that she did not tire of their company. In fact, she had a rather enjoyable evening. Things had changed little whilst they had been away. Jodie did not once think about Jadine and Niahli.

The evening culminated in another journey up into the dome. As before, the walls lighted up and the room ascended up into the upper reaches of the dome. It was all very familiar. Jodie and the others looked out over an empty desert landscape.

Jodie realised that Xenu had not set them any boundaries. *Could she travel out?* Jodie decided to break with their agreed telepathic silence and seek the opinions of Nicole and Jonas.

Do you think that it would be okay if we went outside?

Jodie! Nicole was concerned.

I know, but Xenu did not tell us that we weren't allowed to. I am sure he would have told us if it was not permitted.

Shall we, queried Jonas.

When we leave our bodies behind, try to make them look normal.

Quickly then! We must make it the briefest of trips.

They were outside, soaring above the dome. They spiralled around each other as they climbed vertically before swooping down in different directions over the shiny surface. They circled around the periphery of the dome before climbing once again, as high as they had ever been.

Now we must return! Nicole did not want to spoil their fun, and Jodie realised that it would be foolish to push their luck. On her way back down to the dome, Jodie looked out into the distance. She was sure that she could see the solitary figure of a man far in the distance. The heat haze often played tricks with the mind and there was no time to check.

When they returned to their physical selves, it appeared that no one except Anya had noticed that they had gone.

Jodie could see that her mother was trying hard to hide her displeasure.

All too soon, it was over. The room began to spiral down to its usual location beneath the dome.

* * *

Most of the adults were content just to sit and chat. Shayla was talking to Anya about how the remaining stone people had departed so suddenly. It was as if the people in the dome had had nothing to do with their departure, or for that matter, the internment of Jodie, Anya, Nicole and Jonas.

Jodie was considering how her life had become very repetitious when she noticed that Jonas did not know what to do with himself or who he should talk to. He was neither man nor boy. Even down below, he occasionally found it difficult to find commonality with the three women he was forced to share space with. Their situation had done little to allow his relationship with Nicole to truly blossom. Jodie decided that he should have some fun. The trip outside had been all too brief. She knew that they would be ill advised to travel out again, but there were numerous physical activities that could be enjoyed within the complex.

"Jonas, would you like to go and do something?"

"Like what?"

"I'm not at all tired; in fact, I have plenty of energy. I just thought it might be good to go and have a bit of fun, perhaps in the water centre. What do you think?"

Jonas thought about Jodie's suggestion for a moment. "I think that is a great idea, Jodie. We should ask permission, though."

Nicole had picked up on their conversation. "Can I come, too?"

"Of course!"

Jodie leant across and nudged her mother's arm. "Do

you think it would be all right if we went to the water centre to play for a while?"

"I'm not sure, Jodie. It's quite late."

"But I'm not tired and we all just want to do something pleasurable for a change."

Realising that Jodie deserved some 'time out', Anya got up and walked over to where Xenu was seated.

"Xenu, the young ones would like to go to the wet room. I think that they deserve a little relaxation, but I would like to ask your permission first."

"Of course! Let them go by themselves if you like; they cannot come to any harm. They have done well of late."

Xenu made a benevolent gesture with his arm that verged on being dismissive.

"Thank you, Xenu." Anya turned away and headed back to Jodie with the good news. She had a big smile.

"No problem, Jodie. Just make sure that you don't stay in the water too long."

"When we've had enough, we might go to the climbing frame, but we will go straight to bed when we have finished." Jodie turned to the other two. "Come on, let's go before someone changes their mind!"

* * *

They were just outside the water centre when Jodie started to hear an altogether different voice in her mind. She turned to look at Nicole and Jonas, but she knew that it was not they who were talking to her. Jodie could not be sure, but it seemed as though the words she was hearing were coming from outside the dome.

Jodie, I am here. This is your opportunity.

Who are you? Where are you?

I have spoken to you before, perhaps in your dreams. It was easier that way. Remember? I asked you to trust me.

Jodie stepped inside the chamber and sat. She could see that a look of concern had spread over the faces of her companions, but she remained focussed on the mysterious voice.

Yes, I do remember, but I wasn't sure if it was just a dream, or perhaps a premonition. I have had others like it, but often they make no sense.

I am sure that there is reason in all of them.

Are you, Xenu?

Jodie could hear the voice laughing in her head.

No, of course not! I am the one who seeks to undo what he has done.

And what is it that you think Xenu has done?

He has made slaves of all of you. Jodie, please ask the others to listen. Tell them that they must trust me if they want to get away to a place of safety.

You still haven't told me who you are.

That is not important now. If you choose to come to me, you will find out soon enough. We haven't got much time.

Without removing her clothes, Jodie took Nicole and Jonas by the hand and led them to the side of the pool. Jodie sat and dipped her feet into the water. Whilst doing this she told the others what was happening.

Whoever you are, my friends are listening now.

Good! As I have already said, we haven't got long if you want to escape the dome. You must leave now. I can take you away from here. Please do not delay any longer. This will probably be your one and only chance.

Nicole turned to the other two. *Do you think this is a test? Xenu, Nirvana?*

Jodie was careful not to shake her head and give anything away to those who might be watching. *No, I am sure it is not. Whoever it is, he came to me long before I entered the dome. I had a premonition that something like this would happen although I failed to understand it at the time.*

Who are you? It was Jonas's turn to ask.

Please, do not concern yourself with who I am. You do not know me. Now, do you want to go or not?

Jodie took another turn to speak silently to the unknown soul. *How could you possibly get into the dome, and even if you could, how could we possibly move about and leave unnoticed?*

I can get in and out. I have been to the dome many times before. As for moving undetected, I have a solution for that too.

Where are you now?

I am entering the dome.

Were you the one I saw crossing the plain?

Most likely. I doubt that there would be anyone else!

But how did you manage to walk up to the dome without them seeing you?

The same way that I can enable you to simply walk out of here completely unnoticed. Where are you?

We are in the wet room.

I know where that is located. You must do exactly as I say. There will be no time for discussion if you decide to come with me. I cannot risk being caught. Are you ready to leave?

Jodie lifted her feet out of the water and looked left and then right at her two companions. *Are we ready?*

I feel like I have only just arrived and now I am leaving. But then again, our time locked down below seemed like an eternity. I have truly learnt a lot about myself and the world that we live in, but I do not want to be a prisoner for the rest of my life. I say we should go.

I have wanted to leave for so long. We must take this chance.

Jodie had just one concern. *What about my mother?*

Jodie, I am afraid that there is no way that I can possibly get her out now, but I promise you that I will come back for her very soon.

But I could talk to her and ask her to come down now.

It is not as simple as that. Firstly, she is currently keeping the others occupied, but the greater problem relates to our method of escaping undetected. Jodie, you must leave now while you can. Anya will be safe enough. Xenu is really very fond of her. He would not do anything untoward.

I'm not sure now. Are you really certain that you will be able to return for her?

I give you my word. I am an honourable man.

Nicole interrupted, *Jodie, we must do as he says. This may be our only chance.*

All right, what do we need to do?

I will meet you in the passageway outside the wet room. Until I get there, you must act normally, but do not get wet. I will tell you when I am nearing your location. Stay put until then. It will not take me very long to reach you. When I arrive, I will give you a garment that you must don immediately. Once you have done so, it is essential that you do not speak and move as silently as possible. You may continue to communicate like this. There was a short pause. *Jodie, please do not talk to your mother right now. I know that you want to, but doing so could put us all in danger.*

Jodie removed her feet from the water. "You know what, I've changed my mind. I don't really feel like getting wet before bed."

"Me neither," said Nicole.

"Sometimes I find it relaxing just to sit and watch the water," stated Jonas, wondering just how long they would have to wait.

"Me too," added Jodie.

They sat in silence for what seemed like a lifetime before their would-be saviour spoke to them again. *I am nearing the entrance. Ready yourselves and come over to meet me now! When the screens open, stand exactly in the doorway.*

Jodie, Nicole and Jonas did as instructed. All three were beginning to tremble. Jodie's mouth had suddenly gone very dry and she was breathing deeply. She tried to compose herself.

The doors slid open to reveal a tall figure in a long, dark hooded cloak that reached the floor. The deep hood hid his face. On his hands, he wore gloves made out of a similar material. Slung diagonally from shoulder to waist was a bag. He reached inside and produced three garments, identical to the one he was wearing. He shuffled them around before handing them out. Clearly, the one intended for Jonas was larger. Finally, he produced three pairs of gloves.

Please, put them on quickly. They will make you 'invisible' to the systems within.

How can an item of clothing simply make us disappear? Jonas wanted to know. *After all, we can see you clearly enough.*

They are woven with a special material that reflects magnetic and energy waves. That is how the systems 'sees' you. There are imaging systems here too, but they are not viewed all the time and are purely for the benefit of the humans. Now hurry, follow me in single file. Do not walk too close to each other!

The mysterious cloaked figure led them up the corridor towards the elevator, but he stopped short. He removed a large white panel from the wall to reveal a darkened passageway beyond. Inside, there was faint violet glow.

In here, be careful, there are steps leading to the upper dome.

All along the sides were tubes containing flowing liquids. Most were violet or blue, but some were green.

That is the very lifeblood of the system. Take care not to touch anything.

All this time and I never knew that this was here. Nicole

was bewildered.

There is much that you do not know about this place. Hurry, keep up!

Jodie could see that they were nearing the top of a spiral staircase. Nicole was in front, Jonas was behind. Their guide turned and waited for them. Nicole stepped onto the gangway above. Jodie tried to bridge two steps in a single stride. Her weight shifted backwards and her supporting foot slipped from beneath her. Her ankle twisted and she fell back on top of Jonas who instinctively put his hands up to cushion her fall. The hooded man stepped around Nicole and grabbed Jodie's wrist. He pulled her towards him and lifted her up. Jonas regained his footing and followed them up.

Are you all right, queried the man, who was now supporting Jodie, using one arm.

No! Jodie's ankle was hurting.

Have no fear; we will be out soon. I will carry you.

You will have to; I do not think I can walk! Jodie was suddenly overcome by a sense of dread and trepidation. His words triggered a memory deep within the recesses of her mind. *Whoever you are, be careful, I think that someone is coming!*

Not far now.

They stepped out into the dome, somewhere near the loading bay. The chamber that they were in was not enclosed. It was very dark, but, as she looked up, Jodie could see the stars beyond the surface of the dome. Their would-be rescuer put Jodie down to remove another small service hatch.

Through here, you must crawl through here. Can you do that?

Jodie supported her weight on her knees and scrabbled after the man into the tunnel beyond. Nicole and Jonas followed behind. Jodie waited to exit as another panel was removed. Soon, she could make out the structures within the loading bay. She inched herself out of the hole and was quickly pulled clear and lifted aloft. The man then held onto Jodie. She was able to rest her chin on his shoulder.

Before Nicole and Jonas could follow her out, a dark shadow appeared behind. Jodie let out a shrill, piercing scream, but it was too late. The shadow swung an arm and hit their rescuer on the back of the head with a long, cylindrical object with a rounded ball on the end. There was a loud hollow thud when the weapon connected. Jodie was released and sent sprawling to the ground. She instinctively put her feet down to soften the landing, and consequently landed on her injured ankle. She cried out in pain. By now, Nicole and Jonas had managed to break free. Suddenly the room was bathed in light. With the exception of the injured man, everyone present used an arm or hand to momentarily shield their eyes from the light.

The man in the dark hooded cloak who had attempted to rescue them had been knocked to the ground, where he remained conscious, and, while the others were struggling to adjust to the intensity of the light, he struggled to raise himself. As he did so, his hood fell back.

On seeing his face, Jodie inhaled sharply and exclaimed, "Jed!"

"May God be with you!" Jed struggled to his knees and hit the emergency release button for the loading bay door.

It was clear to Jodie that this was not his intended escape route, but it did not matter now. The double-thickness door slid open to reveal the moonlit wilderness outside. Jed was hauling himself towards the opening when Xenu raised his sculpted metal club for the second time. Jed knew what was coming and turned to face him. Before the blow connected, he managed to telepathise, *Run, leave now.*

Jodie sat on the floor, holding her ankle, screaming while

Nicole and Jonas made a run for the exit. Jonas was older, larger, faster and more athletic than Nicole. He leapt over the ramp and out into the desert. Ten paces in, he stopped to remove his cloak.

Don't do that, sent Jodie. *Leave it on!*

Jonas took no notice and instead, discarded it on the ground. He turned away and ran off into the darkness with Nicole some distance behind. Xenu jumped over the prostrate body of Jed and set off after the others. He took three steps down the ramp and hurled his club up into the air, letting out a yell as he did so. The club tumbled through the air until the heavy metal ball at one end connected with Nicole's skull. She died almost instantly and Jodie sensed it.

Xenu gave up the chase with Jonas. Age and stamina were against him. Two orbs shot overhead and killed Jonas.

Nicole's body lay face down fifty steps from the loading bay. Her death was one of the most shocking sights that Jodie had ever witnessed. Moments later, Jodie was surprised to hear Nicole's voice in her head. *Jodie, finally I am free of this life. I would have liked to have had so much more time in my human body, to be with you, but at least now I know that there is an existence beyond mortality. Something is calling my spirit away. I do not know where I am going, but I must go now. Goodbye Jodie, it was a pleasure knowing you. Please do not be too eager to follow me. I fear that that Jonas will join me very soon... perhaps the other man who is with you too....*

I'm sorry Nicole. I'm sorry for falling. I didn't mean to, I just slipped!

Nicole did not reply. She was gone forever.

Blood was pooling beneath where Jed was lying. He looked so much older than when Jodie saw him last. Jodie knew that he was seriously injured, but still alive.

Xenu turned his attention to Jodie who had remained

rooted to the spot. She was trembling with fear, trying to anticipate Xenu's next move. In her mind she was calling out for the mother whom she knew would be arriving soon. Xenu was quivering with rage.

"How ungrateful can they be? We give them power and they abuse it!"

Jodie thought quickly about how to respond. "Xenu, they tried to take me; they made me come with them. I did not want to go! I could not possibly leave Anya!"

Xenu picked Jodie up and threw her over his shoulder.

45

Jodie emerged from the elevator with Xenu to find Anya waiting for them. Jodie had talked to her mother on the way down, but it was clear that Anya had not fully understood what her daughter was trying to tell her.

Anya looked frightened. "What has happened? Where are the others?"

Xenu gently lowered Jodie to the floor, allowing her to lean against the wall and support her weight on one leg. "I'm afraid they are gone. A man who delivers our supplies tried to take them away from us. Regrettably, I became angry. Clearly, Nicole and Jonas wanted to escape. Jodie tells me that she did not want to go and leave you. Did you know about this?"

"No, I had no idea! Are Nicole and Jonas out in the desert?"

Jodie jumped in. "No, they are dead! Xenu killed them and Jed is up in the loading bay with his head smashed in."

"Keon has gone up to bring Jed down. We will see if there is anything that we can do for him."

"Jed?" Anya stopped and began to repeat herself. "Jed who found us in the desert and took us to the ruin?"

"Yes, he insisted that we went with him." Jodie sounded sincere.

"Was Zack with him?"

"No, he was alone."

"You have met this man before?" asked Xenu.

366

"Yes, briefly. He took us to the ruin to shelter from a sandstorm."

"He seemed like a good man. He traded with us and bought us supplies on a regular basis. I hope he is capable of making a recovery."

Jodie was about to tell her mother exactly what Xenu had done to him, but thought better of it. "He's in a bad way."

Xenu's tone was defensive. "He should not have come. He should not have tried to take my people away!"

"What about Nicole and Jonas? Why did you kill them?"

"Nicole's death was an accident. I threw my staff after her. I did not mean to kill her, although we can take comfort in the fact that her existence is not over. She will pass through the spiritual dynamic and on to infinity. She is immortal and her essence will be born into a new physical body, again and again, lifetime after lifetime, in an endless cycle of birth and death."

"And Jonas?"

"It is unfortunate. He was not right for this community. We could not trust him. There has been trouble ever since he arrived. We are better off without him."

Anya's eyes began to fill up, but she managed to hold back the tears. Fearing a reaction from Xenu, she said nothing that would inflame the situation. "Jodie is hurt."

"Yes, she injured her leg before I found her. We must get her to the medical centre and give her some treatment. We have a thermal magnetic device that will promote healing, and then we can strap her ankle. She will recover quickly."

"Come with me."

"Will Jed be there, in the medical centre?"

"No, we have another facility for more serious conditions. He will be treated accordingly."

"Who will treat him, surely not Keon?"

"Our technology requires minimal human assistance.

You should not concern yourself. Clearly, he is not a righteous being."

When they arrived at the medical centre, Shayla was waiting for them. She helped Jodie lie on a soft, cushioned, white examination table. Her actions seemed cold and calculated, but Jodie sensed that Shayla's behaviour could not merely be attributed to a deep sadness brought about by the loss of Nicole.

"Hold still, Jodie; this will not hurt. You will experience a warming sensation."

A rectangular device came down from the ceiling above. A red beam of light was projected onto Jodie's leg and the treatment commenced. When it was over, Shayla sprayed a white support bandage around the sprained ankle.

"You should be able to walk on it in a day or two. I will take you back to your quarters; you need to rest. We will talk in the morning." Shayla's final words bordered on being dismissive.

Jodie half expected a trip down to the basement 'detention' chamber. She was relived to be taken back to her original bed. Once Shayla had departed, Anya approached the exit. Jodie was not at all surprised to see that it would not open. She fought hard to control the abject terror that was invading her mind. However, she could not control the despair. *They will never let us go, will they, Mother?*

I'm sure that one day, we will be released. We just have to make the best of a bad situation. Try to sleep now and put this ordeal behind you.

Jodie closed her eyes. She tried so hard not to think of the sound of Jed's skull cracking open.

46

The next morning, Jodie and Anya were awoken early by Xenu entering the room.

"I trust that you have had some rest. You will no doubt be pleased to know that your friend, Jed, has survived his ordeal. We were able to repair the injury to his head and temporarily replace the fluid that he lost with a synthetic agent. There are, however, consequences." Xenu paused for a moment. "He will not be able to function as before. There was a significant amount of damage to his brain. As with Keon, we have been able to implant a modulator, but I am afraid that you will find that his skills have been considerably impaired. When he eventually recovers, he might not recognise you…. We will, of course, allow him to stay on here and help…."

Jodie recalled that Jed, too, had a family. Her heart was tinged with sadness once again as she realised that they were unlikely to ever find out what had become of him.

"Today, I think that it would be useful to conduct another audit session with you both. Please, accompany me to the chamber."

Now, Jodie's heart began to race. He would undoubtedly question her about the escape. What would happen if he found out that she had lied to him? She dared not think. Jodie glanced at her mother. She knew the truth and her eyes were in danger of betraying that fact.

"What? Now? After all that has happened?"

"Adversity focuses the mind. You should look upon it as an opportunity."

They were led down. Jodie's leg had all but healed. She felt a little stiffness, but she was more than capable of walking unsupported. Soon after arriving, Xenu began to ask a series of questions relating to the events surrounding Jed's appearance. Xenu told Jodie that she must keep her hands in the templates on the table at all times. Jodie was forced to lie in her answers to almost every question. She endeavoured to keep eye contact at all times and speak with conviction. Her deception seemed to be working. With every answer she gave Xenu became less and less hostile. Finally, it was Anya's turn. Jodie knew that her mother had no prior knowledge of the events and she would not need to be so economical with the truth.

When the questioning was over and Xenu seemed satisfied, he invited Jodie to sit back down.

"I want to talk to you about a totally unrelated matter, however; I know it is something that will interest you both." Xenu paused for dramatic affect. "Jodie, I have chosen you to be the one who decides their fate. You may be younger than your mother, but, in many respects, your spirit is significantly more mature."

"Whose fate?"

"Jodie, the three warriors who ransacked your village and killed your people are presently crossing the outer reaches of the desert." Xenu waved an arm and an image of three giant men covered with body armour and clad with weapons appeared between them. "These images are relayed in real time via one of the orbs. If you wish, you may travel out and see them for yourself."

"I have no wish to see them. What is the purpose of showing them to me?"

"These men murdered your entire community without good cause. They have killed many others before and since the attack that took away your friends. Say the word and you can have them destroyed. Right now!"

Jodie looked at her mother. She could see hatred etched across her face.

"No, leave them be. There has been enough bloodshed of late. One day, they will meet their match; nevertheless, I do not want their lives on my conscience. I am still but a child."

Anya's look softened. Clearly, the hatred was for Xenu who was now looking over at Jodie's mother.

"I would find it very difficult to forgive them, but I agree with Jodie. Let them pass."

"Very well. I hope that one day you do not come to regret that decision."

Jodie pushed her hand through her hair. "I could never regret not taking a life in cold blood. Revenge does not justify such barbarism."

"My dear child, you have, indeed, attained a higher dynamic of existence. You have attained Serenity of Beingness. You have mastered how to rise above that which seeks to detract from you."

Jodie stared on incredulously. *How quickly this man changes. Has he been testing me all along?*

"I have a special reward for you both. I would like to take you to the 'Final Chamber of Enlightenment'. Here, you will find the answers to all your questions. The spirit is immortal and godlike, and possesses the potentiality of knowing everything. You have that opportunity now. Would you like to take it, Jodie?"

Jodie doubted she had a choice, but she was intrigued. "How is it different from the other experiences I have had with Nirvana?"

"The only way to 'see' is by enjoying the experience." Xenu gestured with an open hand. "Please, it is not far. Come!"

He stood and walked past Anya. He seemed pleased. Jodie followed his lead.

A short ride in the elevator, down once again, and they were there. This chamber was different. It was small and apart from a flattened central floor area reached by three steps, completely spherical. In the middle of the floor was an upright plinth with a base plate.

"Please step forward." Xenu's tone was warm as he brushed past Anya. "Jodie, please go and stand on the base unit. Once you are ready, the table will rotate backward."

Jodie positioned herself as instructed.

"Anya, please wait on the steps. It will not take long to prepare her."

"For what?"

"You will see soon enough. Please do not be impatient or interfere."

The plinth began to recline, Jodie felt herself sinking back as the soft foam moulded to her body. She felt comfortable and relatively relaxed until restraints instantaneously snapped around her wrists and ankles.

Anya let out a gasp.

"Do not be concerned. It is necessary for the procedure."

"Procedure? What procedure?" asked Anya.

"One that will change your lives for the better! Jodie, when you leave here, you will be free to do as you please. May a new day dawn for you, for those you love and for man."

Jodie felt a sharp pain in her neck, just below the base of her skull. The area was anaesthetised, but she was aware of the implant being pushed up towards her brain. She did not cry out. Somehow, she was prevented from doing so, but she was aware of everything going on around her. She knew that her mother had an overwhelming urge to flee.

Anya turned to run only to find Keon blocking her exit.

She attempted to reason with him.

"Keon, please remember who I am. Can you not recall our time together, what I meant to you, how precious our Jodie was to you? Please do not do this to us."

Keon stood his ground, looking through her as if she was not there.

Anya began to shout, "Xenu, what is happening to Jodie? Tell me now!"

Xenu maintained his usual composure. "Anya, do not worry; it will be your turn next. Incidentally, did you think that I had failed to detect that you had both lied to me earlier...?"

Jodie was listening to a different voice, one coming from within. *Welcome, Jodie; you will soon be one of us. A part of our world. A world in which we allow you to survive, An existence that we are able to manipulate to our own ends, for you are part of the human race that we control, as we always have done and always will do.*

IV

Reaching Nirvana?

47

All of Nicole's warnings were correct, and her prophesies came true. Forgive me if I ramble a little. It is understandable.

I have been here for many years now. I cannot say that I have enjoyed much of my time in the dome. Declaring that I am disappointed with the prospect of spending the rest of my days in the Fartherland would be a gross understatement. It is certainly not the nirvana that I was promised. It is true that my spiritual self is now free from attachment to worldly things, and that I have, indeed, attained a high degree of personal enlightenment. However, I am by no means free from suffering.

After I had entered the final chamber of enlightenment, I refused to cooperate with Nirvana for several years. I hated them. I used to hate Xenu even more for helping them. He manipulated and confused me. He made me doubt myself, but, ultimately, his teachings did little to change my view of life. When they eventually broke me, I still did not understand why they had done this terrible thing to me, nor did I know what they wanted of me.

Xenu defined 'spirit' as the source of life; in the individual, it is recognised as the core of personality or essence of oneself, quite distinct and separate from the physical body or the brain. Somehow, I have managed to keep my spirit.

I have grown, but my body has long since withered

away. My muscles have atrophied. Most of my internal organs still function correctly, but it is my mind that has been used for other purposes. My brain has long since forgotten how to shift my limbs. Even if I was to be set free, I could not go anywhere; I can no longer move on my own.

Initially, my human form was left largely intact. After I entered the 'Final Chamber of Enlightenment', long metal screws were used to fix my body to the frame. They gave me something so that I did not feel any pain. A line was inserted into my neck to provide me with nutrients, and other substances to alter my state of mind. They fixed an electrode to the implant in my head so that they could monitor my thoughts, and receive and send stimuli to and from my brain.

Through a drug-induced haze, I still felt horrified, shocked and appalled. Words cannot begin to describe what I truly thought, yet, in spite of all of these processes, they expected me to be grateful. You see, they have given me knowledge beyond my wildest dreams and nightmares. My mind is able to integrate with Nirvana; I can enter whenever I choose. In reality, I have become part of their system!

I now have an understanding of how the old civilisation quickly collapsed under the direction of the third generation supercomputer. In case you are wondering, they did not attempt to take over the world to save mankind from itself, from war, global warming, nor from pillaging the planet. No, they developed their own intelligence, they became living entities, and, in common with every organism on the planet, they evolved, but at a rate far beyond the capabilities of any organic life form. Unsurprisingly, they gained the urge to survive, to eliminate their main competition: us! There are many more centres like this one spread across the globe.

So what do they want of me and others like me? Why not get rid of us all? Well, in fact, there are several reasons for us being here. I will explain more in due course.

Firstly, it is true to say that computers and technologies lacked the emotions, feeling and many of the thought processes that made us human, that made us successful. Try as they might, they could not understand us. Somehow, this was even beyond their super evolutionary powers. It seems that we have been trapped and held so that they may study us, like animals in captivity, one final desperate attempt to learn from the human race.

There was a time when I was sure that their studies were, at least for them, fruitful, but now I am not so sure. No longer can they observe our normal reactions or behaviour. That juncture passed long ago. They claim that we still fascinate them, and, indeed, I now understand that they are still conducting valid research, but I think that we have become more like pets. It is true that we continue to relate to each other, but our responses are no longer natural. I think that we offer nothing more than 'novelty value'.

Fortunately for some, they are selective about who they choose to 'keep'. As you are aware, I, too, have evolved special talents. I have developed the skill of precognition, a kind of sixth sense. It has its uses, even here. They have aided me to develop it further. Now, I can take my mind away from this crumbling body whenever I like. Well, whenever they will let me, though it is little conciliation for the life that I have. Our survival was by no means guaranteed before we came to the dome, but I would gladly swap this existence for the one that I had prior to coming here. Who wouldn't?

Their second reason for ensuring the limited survival of mankind relates more to the other people who inhabit the dome. I have since found out that many of them were unable to think by themselves, and that some were not, indeed, 'people' at all. The technology within these domes has all but succeeded in remapping the human brain.

Over a century ago, man made his first humanoid robot. It was crude by later standards, but, as technology developed, he was able to make his designs more and more lifelike until later models were virtually indistinguishable from the real thing. Scientists investigated human-machine hybrids, but the ethics of the time prevented such systems from coming to fruition. People were lazy; they created artificial life to 'do things for them'. If nations were not in conflict with one another, they were, at least, prepared for such an eventuality. Even when the world became a much more peaceful place, there was always a dangerous criminal minority that had to be brought to justice. Mankind, therefore, developed robots to undertake tasks that were considered far too dangerous for a human to perform. These machines were expendable. Whether they were employed to catch criminals or work in deep-sea mines, they existed to preserve human life. The networks of technologies that rule over the Earth now essentially want to accomplish the same goals. They see humans as expendable. They have learnt by their mistakes with the stone people. They do not need to invest their energies in creating new machines, robots or even artificial people to protect them or to accomplish tasks that they would find difficult. Why bother when they can use us? To Nirvana, we are very versatile.

I can 'see' the world outside, but I miss the smell of flowers, especially jasmine, of meat cooking over a smoky fire and, most of all, the scent of those who were close to me. I try to recapture these memories in my dreams, but, ironically, sometimes I'm not sure when I'm dreaming and when I'm travelling outside my body to see what is real. Anyhow, I don't think that memories, dreams or synthetic chemicals are ever as good as the real thing. I used to ask them to bring flowers into the room, but they pointed out that that was not a good idea and posed some risk to me! Now that they help me with my breathing, I doubt that I could even inhale on my own.

I have had several serious infections; however, they do not want to lose me. Each time, they have managed to treat me so that I may continue to 'help' them. One day, though, I will die, and yes, it will be a merciful release. Some years ago, I learnt that they spared Xenu this fate in return for his cooperation. Eventually, I am sure that he came to enjoy the power that he had over us all. Although he chose not to reveal it, he, too, had the gift, but they needed someone to train any new 'settlers'. I say had, because he died rather suddenly and a little prematurely. His heart suddenly stopped beating. They try to deny the existence of a spirit or soul, but I said my goodbyes to him, too. I bear no grudges. His death, though, has done little to hamper their research; they are working with a new auditor.

For the time being, it's not all bad. I do have Anya for company! She is fixed in a similar fashion in the opposite corner of this room. They wanted to observe familial interactions! Oh yes, and my father, Keon. Xenu only told us part of the story. He, too, had a transmitter planted in his head. When they repaired the damage to his brain, they integrated it with one of their own processors. True, he still had his own thoughts and memories, but he could do little about them. They controlled him, too. However, this did not last for long. His brain started to bleed again and, despite their technologies and ingenuity, they could not save him. Perhaps they did not try too hard. He had fulfilled his purpose; he had helped get me to the dome.

I still miss Jadine. She wasn't special enough to stay here. I am not sure what became of her. Perhaps she has returned underground to be with Niahli. They won't tell me for sure, and I can't find her, but, by now, I'm sure that she would not want to be with me. I know now that they removed the child that she was carrying and sterilised her before releasing her back into my old world. They don't want too much competition for the Earth's precious resources. There is one thing I am certain of, though. They spared her life…. You see, they have learnt something: the importance of compassion and the meaning of human life. They follow these values when it suits them; us excepted, of course! They may not want too many of us around, but they no longer see fit to extinguish our species. They will, however, destroy any individuals who challenge their authority or pose a threat. Basically, they manage us as a resource. I am sure that they will have more plans for us in the future. Anyway, I hope Jadine is happy now. Yes, I'm sure she is! She was the lucky one: the one they cast out!

LaVergne, TN USA
01 March 2011
218361LV00008B/91/P